Trucanini's Stare

A central concept in international human rights law and many national constitutions is human dignity. Departing from established approaches to dignity in philosophy and legal theory, Susan Marks takes dignity in everyday life ('dignified care', 'dignity in the workplace', etc.) as a starting-point for reconsidering the concept's history and significance. The result is a highly original work which gives particular attention to colonial and postcolonial engagements with dignity, and emphasises the character of human dignity as not just an idea or abstract value but also a lived experience that cannot be understood without reference to social structures and the inequalities and hierarchies they reproduce. If dignity is an attribute which all human beings possess purely by virtue of being human, Marks shows that it is also an element within the systemic operations of privilege and power.

SUSAN MARKS is a Professor in the School of Law at the London School of Economics and Political Science, focusing on international law and human rights. She is the author of publications that include *The Riddle of All Constitutions*, *International Human Rights Lexicon* (co-written with Andrew Clapham) and *A False Tree of Liberty*, and editor of *International Law on the Left*.

Recent Books in the Hersch Lauterpacht Memorial Lecture Series

Felice Morgenstern and Jan Klabbers *Legal Problems of International Organizations: Reissue with New Foreword by Jan Klabbers*

Michael Wood and Eran Sthoeger *The UN Security Council and International Law*

Tom Ginsburg *Democracies and International Law*

Christine Chinkin *Women, Peace and Security and International Law*

Stephen M. Schwebel, Luke Sobota and Ryan Manton *International Arbitration: Three Salient Problems*

Mary Ellen O'Connell *The Art of Law in the International Community*

Yuval Shany *Questions of Jurisdiction and Admissibility before International Courts*

W. Michael Reisman and Christina Skinner *Fraudulent Evidence before Public International Tribunals: The Dirty Stories of International Law*

Andrés Rigo Sureda *Investment Treaty Arbitration: Judging Under Uncertainty*

Ralph Zacklin *The United Nations Secretariat and the Use of Force in a Unipolar World: Power v. Principle*

John H. Jackson *Sovereignty, the WTO, and Changing Fundamentals of International Law*

Jan Paulsson *Denial of Justice in International Law*

Francisco Orrego Vicuña *International Dispute Settlement in an Evolving Global Society: Constitutionalization, Accessibility, Privatization*

Martti Koskenniemi *The Gentle Civilizer of Nations: The Rise and Fall of International Law 1870–1960*

Thomas M. Franck *Recourse to Force: State Action against Threats and Armed Attacks*

Mohamed Shahabuddeen *Precedent in the World Court*

Antonio Cassese *Self-Determination of Peoples: A Legal Reappraisal*

Trucanini's Stare
Reconsidering Dignity in Theory and Practice

SUSAN MARKS
London School of Economics and Political Science

CAMBRIDGE
UNIVERSITY PRESS

CAMBRIDGE
UNIVERSITY PRESS

Shaftesbury Road, Cambridge CB2 8EA, United Kingdom

One Liberty Plaza, 20th Floor, New York, NY 10006, USA

477 Williamstown Road, Port Melbourne, VIC 3207, Australia

314–321, 3rd Floor, Plot 3, Splendor Forum, Jasola District Centre, New Delhi – 110025, India

103 Penang Road, #05–06/07, Visioncrest Commercial, Singapore 238467

Cambridge University Press is part of Cambridge University Press & Assessment, a department of the University of Cambridge.

We share the University's mission to contribute to society through the pursuit of education, learning and research at the highest international levels of excellence.

www.cambridge.org
Information on this title: www.cambridge.org/9781009543231

DOI: 10.1017/9781009543262

When citing this work, please include a reference to the DOI 10.1017/9781009543262

First published 2024

A catalogue record for this publication is available from the British Library.

Library of Congress Cataloging-in-Publication Data
Names: Marks, Susan (Susan R.), author.
Title: Trucanini's stare : reconsidering dignity in theory and practice / Professor Susan Marks, London School of Economics and Political Science.
Description: Cambridge, United Kingdom ; New York, NY : Cambridge University Press, 2024. | Includes bibliographical references and index.
Identifiers: LCCN 2024029112 (print) | LCCN 2024029113 (ebook) | ISBN 9781009543231 (hardback) | ISBN 9781009543248 (paperback) | ISBN 9781009543262 (epub)
Subjects: LCSH: Respect for persons–Law and legislation. | International law and human rights. | Dignity. | Human rights.
Classification: LCC K3249 .M365 2024 (print) | LCC K3249 (ebook)

LC record available at https://lccn.loc.gov/2024029112
LC ebook record available at https://lccn.loc.gov/2024029113

ISBN 978-1-009-54323-1 Hardback

For Karen
1960–2022

Contents

Figures

Preface

This book is based on the Hersch Lauterpacht Memorial Lectures, which I delivered for the University of Cambridge in March 2021. I am grateful for the invitation to deliver those lectures, and take this opportunity to pay tribute to the founders, organisers and publishers of the Hersch Lauterpacht Memorial Lecture Series, from which I and countless others have learned so much.

The subject of my lectures, and now this book, is dignity. It hardly needs stating that there already exists a vast literature on that concept. As a lecturer on the topic, I was very conscious of following others who had made dignity the focus of their lecture series, including Michael Rosen, who spoke about it in the Benedict Lectures at Boston University in 2007, and Jeremy Waldron, who addressed the same issue in his Tanner Lectures at UC Berkeley in 2009.

I take from the evident popularity of this topic a sense that dignity is important. And, of course, it is important not just to a narrow band of specialists in a limited range of places, but to people in general, especially those whose life-experience is of systematic disesteem. If, despite all the attention, I jump in too, that is because I believe we have yet to get to grips with the concept of dignity as well as we might. For reasons which will emerge, I believe there is more that needs to be said on this frequently rehearsed theme.

Alongside the opportunity to deliver the Hersch Lauterpacht Memorial Lectures, I have benefitted from the chance to present my research at the Law School of the University of Kent (Centre for Critical International Law Annual Lecture), the Max Planck Institute for Human Development (Berlin), and the Wissenschaftskolleg zu Berlin. I was fortunate to be invited to join the cohort of fellows at the Wissenschaftskolleg in 2022–23, and am immensely grateful to the Rector, and to the librarians and other staff there, for their hospitality, interest and support.

In getting started on this project, I was helped by conversations with Elizabeth Edwards and Priyamvada Gopal. I want to thank them for their generosity and advice. At a later stage, Ian Anderson and Gregory Lehman gave me invaluable guidance regarding the material I discuss, the terminology I use, and the images I reproduce in Chapter 3, for which I am greatly indebted. I wish to record special thanks to Clinton Naina for permission to reproduce his wonderful artwork (now in the possession of Jenny Ouliaris), a detail of which appears on the cover of this book.

Nicola Silbert provided excellent research assistance, as well as insightful comments on my drafts. I also received valuable assistance from Tanmay Misra in relation to Chapter 4, and from Lauren Bursey in the preparation of the book's Index. My deep gratitude goes to all three of them. Rosemary Bloom and Guy Marks followed the ups and downs of my writing, and encouraged me along the way. Likewise, and on a daily basis, Philip Green accompanied me as my discussant and facilitator, first reader, critical interlocutor, and ally in all things. No thanks could ever be commensurate with those gifts.

Until her untimely death in September 2022, Karen Knop was Cecil A. Wright Professor in the Faculty of Law at the University of Toronto. She was a pivotal member of my professional circle and a much-loved friend. Karen had agreed to deliver the Hersch Lauterpacht Memorial Lectures in 2025. I so wish I could have heard her lectures and read the luminous book which would have been their sequel. Deprived of that possibility, as of the joyful experience it always was to be in her company, I dedicate this book to her memory.

1

Introduction

Have You Seen Dignity?

One of Bob Dylan's songs from the 1980s is entitled 'Dignity'.[1] 'Have you seen dignity?', goes the refrain. 'Searchin' high, searchin' low / Searchin' everywhere I know / Askin' the cops wherever I go / Have you seen dignity?' I thought of that song when, one day, I was in a car on a motorway near Canberra in Australia, and indeed dignity hove into my line of sight (Figure 1.1).

Of course, Dylan's seeker is not looking for, and failing to find, a *word*. But if his song carries a message about the elusiveness of dignity (or perhaps about its obscurity or mystery), I take that Ford Territory as a vivid reminder that, from another perspective, dignity is all around us – a highly conspicuous word which is not just a word, but also a perceptible occurrence in the world.

The subject of this book is dignity and its worldliness. A few observations will provide an initial sense of the general direction in which my enquiry will go. To focus on dignity is to pick out a term from a conceptual cluster that includes respect, esteem, honour, decorum, propriety, decency, respectability, reputation, regard, pride, prestige, confidence, consideration, worthiness and civility. Dignity is held to be special on diverse grounds, but one feature about which there is widespread consensus is that dignity belongs innately to all human beings. Whether we consult constitutions and human rights instruments or philosophical writings and school

[1] 'Dignity' was originally recorded in 1989, though only released as part of Dylan's *Greatest Hits Volume 3* in 1994.

Figure 1.1 'Dignity'. Ford Territory, seen from behind on a motorway near Canberra.

teaching materials, we will be informed that dignity is inherent. It is something that everyone just has.

Yet if dignity is inherent, we know that, in actuality, the experience of it is far from universal. However solemn, firm and loud our proclamations that dignity belongs to everyone, there can be no mistaking that it is very unevenly distributed. Part of life's comfortable furniture for some, it arrives only hard-won for others – those latter all too aware of the systems of privilege and power that structure access also to this. At the same time, what is striking is how little of that unevenness registers in our most celebrated and influential writing about dignity. In these predominantly abstract studies, the concept is lifted out of history and shaken free of circumstance. It is unfastened from frameworks of privilege and power, so that deficits of dignity come to appear discrete discrepancies between rhetoric and reality, as opposed to signs of a wider and deeper problem to do with the reality itself.

Abstraction, of course, has its place, but I seek, rather, to capture the embeddedness of dignity in historically specific conditions of existence. The present investigation proceeds from the premise that dignity both has social effects and is itself an effect of social processes. The idea that it has social effects raises the question not only of what dignity is, what it means, but also of what it does – how it works as part of the phenomena that configure the world and our relationships within it. The idea that it is an effect of social processes raises the question of how, in turn, the world configures dignity. Studies of dignity in the abstract mode make it seem as though we confront an object that has reached society and the mind fully formed. I am interested in the ways in which dignity is instead produced, defined, shaped and contested in and through collective human activity.

The concept of dignity has had a high-profile, if controversial, role in approaches to bioethical policy and evaluation. In a widely cited editorial contribution to the *British Medical Journal*, Ruth Macklin argued in 2003 that dignity was, in fact, 'useless' in this context because it was 'hopelessly vague', and added nothing to more precise bioethical concepts with well-established implications, such as respect for persons. By her account, dignity was a 'mere slogan' that could 'be eliminated without any loss of content'.[2] Steven Pinker later renewed the charge, characterising dignity as 'a squishy, subjective notion hardly up to the heavyweight moral demands' which bioethicists were assigning it. And that was not yet to broach the ignoble history of 'repressions … rationalized as a defense of the dignity of a state, leader, or creed' which came with it.[3]

My own wish better to understand the concept of dignity arises from its prominence in the sphere of human rights, where I mostly

[2] Ruth Macklin, 'Dignity is a Useless Concept', *British Medical Journal* 327 (2003) 1419, 1419–20.

[3] Steven Pinker, 'The Stupidity of Dignity', *New Republic*, 28 May 2008 (expressing concern about religious, and especially Catholic, influence on biomedical science policy). For a related perspective on legislative developments in Switzerland that protect both human and nonhuman dignity, see also, for example, Alison Abbott, 'Swiss "Dignity" Law is Threat to Plant Biology', *Nature* 452 (2008) 919 and James Toomey, 'Constitutionalizing Nature's Law: Dignity and the Regulation of Biotechnology in Switzerland', *Journal of Law and the Biosciences* 7 (1) (2020) 1.

work, and where its utility and role have been questioned in similar terms. In an essay about 'rights talk' published in 2006, Mirko Bagaric and James Allan criticised dignity as a 'vacuous concept' that had 'little function [in relation to human rights] beyond the polemical'.[4] Less damningly, but still on the theme of unhelpfulness, Samuel Moyn wrote some years later of how 'it's not possible to derive from [the] idea of human dignity all that human rights law might protect. For example, the Universal Declaration [of Human Rights] makes room for economic and social protections, but how can the notion of human dignity justify the declaration's more specific protection of unionization rights or paid vacations?'[5]

While the matter of what can and cannot be derived from the idea of human dignity, or justified with reference to it, is perhaps less clearcut than Moyn suggests here, the main thing to be clarified now is that this book too takes up its topic in a critical spirit, but not out of concern with vacuousness or inefficacy.[6] Squishy subjectivity and hollow sloganeering will not be the problems that preoccupy us here. Rather, our focus will be on dignity's (meaningful, observable, consequential) relation with oppression and exploitation, and with the forms of social hierarchy and modes of popular resistance that have respectively supported and challenged them. I do not postulate the concept's essential or necessary usefulness to emancipatory endeavours, but I do note that it is employed in ways that are replete with significance and distinctly concrete in their implications.

How is one to grasp those ways? *The Promise of Happiness* is a study by Sara Ahmed of what she terms 'the happiness turn' in public policy and culture.[7] The book discusses the emergence of 'happiness indices' and the rise of a 'happiness industry', linked to the pursuit of 'wellness', the practice of 'positive' thinking, and the unremitting search for more and better 'feelgood' factors. In introducing her subject, Ahmed writes of how the 'face of

[4] Mirko Bagaric and James Allan, 'The Vacuous Concept of Dignity', *Journal of Human Rights* 5 (2006) 257, 269, 268.

[5] Samuel Moyn, *Human Rights and the Uses of History* (London: Verso, 2014), 24. (Like Pinker, Moyn highlights the influence of Catholic theologians in promoting dignity as a pivotal or overriding ethical concept.)

[6] See Chapter 6.

[7] Sara Ahmed, *The Promise of Happiness* (Durham, NC: Duke University Press, 2010).

happiness . . . [often] looks rather like the face of privilege'. 'Rather than assuming that happiness is simply found in "happy persons"', she proposes that we should consider 'how claims to happiness make certain forms of personhood valuable'.[8] What is needed – what she will relate – is a history of happiness that challenges the history of which the happiness turn is presented as a culmination by bringing back in 'those who are banished from it, or who enter [it] only as troublemakers, dissenters, killers of joy'.[9]

It is my wager that one might study dignity in something like that manner. Just as Ahmed invites us not simply to assume that happiness is to be found in 'happy persons', but rather to consider how claims to happiness make certain forms of personhood valuable, so we might ask how claims to dignity and ideas about what is dignified confirm privileged people as deserving of their status and power. And just as she brings back into the history of happiness those who have been banished from it or who enter it only as troublemakers, dissenters and killers of joy, so we might attend to dignity's outsiders – those who are denied dignity, those who refuse dignity, those of whom intellectual histories of dignity fail to take adequate account – and thereby be led to interrogate that which, ordinarily, we only ever defend. We might learn from the presumptively undignified – not because they can teach us what it is to be undignified, but because they are instructive guides to the dignity we may think we know.[10]

The outsiders of dignity are many, and they are to be found everywhere. The heart of this book comprises a series of chapters which bring back outsiders from parts of the colonised world, itself also mostly absent from the intellectual histories of dignity. To enable close consideration, we zero in on specific people, events and indeed objects. The first of these chapters examines the issue of dignity in relation to some photographs that were taken in mid-nineteenth century Australia of Trucanini, the Indigenous Tasmanian woman of the Nuennone people to whom my title makes reference.[11] The second of the chapters turns to early

[8] Ibid., 11. [9] Ibid., 17.

[10] Ibid.: 'The sorrow of the stranger might give us a different angle on happiness not because it teaches us what it is like or must be like to be a stranger, but because it might estrange us from the very happiness of the familiar.'

[11] See Chapter 3.

twentieth-century India; we look at the discourse of dignity which was an important element in the campaign for homespun cloth, or *khadi,* waged by M. K. Gandhi and his allies.[12] In the third and final of the chapters, we move forward in time again to twenty-first century South Africa, and probe the place of dignity in the so-called 'toilet wars' waged by black South Africans contesting their country's racialised sanitation arrangements.[13]

Of course, outsiders are not necessarily complete outsiders. In particular, Gandhi is often mentioned in the literature on dignity. Highlighting that he carried himself in a manner that was neither 'haughty' nor 'submissive', and was not 'at all disinclined to press [his] rights' or 'dishonoured by the fact' of doing so,[14] many scholars consider him to have exemplified a modern kind of dignity that contrasts with the 'form of dignity . . . built on a practice requiring the belittling of fellow human beings'.[15] On the subject of Gandhi's own discourse of dignity and its background and reception, however, scholarly discussion is much less common. Enquiry into those matters, and into the other matters just adumbrated, bears on the question of whose history is narrated by a history of dignity and how such a history should be narrated – what is significant for it? who belongs in it? where and in which processes might it be seen to unfold? Through our contextualised snapshots, a concept that can sometimes appear insubstantial will be disclosed as instead rich, complex and contentious, with many usages and a great deal put at stake.

I want to flag up something else which will not form part of this study. Is dignity a quality or property possessed only by humans? At a time of ongoing environmental destruction and catastrophic global warming, the argument is widely made that we need to reconsider ideas which predicate the separation of human beings from the rest of planetary life, and which foster ambitions for ever-expanding mastery or dominion over nature. Dignity is sometimes part of that argument. Thus, one reads in a range of literatures – posthuman studies, animal studies, posthumanist ecology, anti-

[12] See Chapter 4. [13] See Chapter 5.

[14] Michael Meyer, 'Dignity as a (Modern) Virtue', in David Kretzmer and Eckart Klein (eds.), *The Concept of Human Dignity in Human Rights Discourse* (The Hague: Kluwer Law International, 2002), 195, 198.

[15] Ibid., 200.

speciesism, vitalist materialism, post-anthropocentrism, justice for nonhumans, the 'ontological turn' – of the dignity of nonhuman animals and the necessity of respect for it.[16] One also reads of the dignity of, for example, rivers[17] and forests.[18] In the Romantic tradition of European painting, virtues including dignity were conventionally projected onto animals, though that appears to have been less an assertion of nonhuman dignity than a sentimental or parodic artistic genre grounded in anthropomorphism.[19]

Conversely, figurative language involving animality has often been used, at least in English, to denounce, or indeed justify, the ill-treatment of human beings. To be treated 'like an animal' is to be treated in the most undignified possible manner, and it is observed that the force of such figurative language depends on taking for granted the ontological distinction and ethical hierarchy which underpins the violent exploitation of nonhuman animals by humans.[20] To be sure, the force of such figurative language may also depend, as in the case of a pork processing plant in North Carolina on which one study reports, on the actual and even uncannily exact replication of that ethical hierarchy in relations between racialised human groups.[21] Yet, again, it is observed that the worst abuses fall on the nonhuman animals.[22] These seem to me important issues, with which scholars and activists are rightly engaged. However, they are not my issues in this book. My interest here is in the dignity of human beings, and I make no claims either

[16] See, for example, Reed Elizabeth Loder, 'Animal Dignity', *Animal Law* 23(1) (2016) 1.

[17] See, for example, Colin Thorne, 'Restoring the Dignity of Rivers' (7 August 2017), available at: https://blogs.nottingham.ac.uk/blue-greencities/2017/08/07/dignityofrivers/.

[18] See, for example, Arundhati Roy, *Broken Republic* (London: Hamish Hamilton, 2011), 155 (evoking 'the great dignity of the forest I had so recently walked in').

[19] See, for example, Edwin Henry Landseer, *Dignity and Impudence* (London: Tate, 1839), available at: www.tate.org.uk/art/artworks/landseer-dignity-and-impudence-n00604 (depicting two dogs in a parody of the Dutch portrait tradition, one a 'dignified' bloodhound and the other an 'impudent' terrier).

[20] On this point, see, for example, Mary Midgley, *Animals and Why They Matter* (Athens, GA: University of Georgia Press, 1984), 83, and Cary Wolfe, 'Introduction', in Cary Wolfe (ed.), *Zoontologies: The Question of the Animal* (Minneapolis, MN: University of Minnesota Press, 2003), ix, xx.

[21] See Charlie LeDuff, 'At the Slaughterhouse, Some Things Never Die', in Cary Wolfe (ed.), *Zoontologies: The Question of the Animal* (Minneapolis, MN: University of Minnesota Press, 2003), 183.

[22] See Wolfe, 'Introduction', ix, xx–xxi.

for the uniqueness of human dignity or for the critique of a unique human dignity as false dualism.[23] It is time now to begin getting a handle on our subject.

He Just Wanted to Live

Why would someone drive a car with a registration plate bearing the word 'dignity'? This might be strange to hear, but I wondered when I saw it whether perhaps the owner of the car owned a funeral business which he or she was trying to advertise. Clearly, the explanation may have been nothing of the sort, but in the United Kingdom where I live, the market for funerals is, in fact, dominated by a company called Dignity. Dignity is the UK's only publicly listed provider of funeral services, and apparently has 800 funeral locations and operates 46 crematoria. Searching further online, and returning momentarily to the topic of nonhuman dignity, I learned that there is also a pet cremator called Dignity, along with an equine cremator of the same name, which is said to provide a 'dignified send-off for horses, ponies and donkeys of all sizes'.[24]

The Latin root-word of dignity is known to many people as the name of a place in Switzerland where you can go to end your life. The world's first centre for assisted dying, Dignitas, is run as a non-profit members' society, dedicated to 'self-determination, autonomy and dignity'. Its website carries the strapline 'To live with dignity, to die with dignity'.[25] The concept of 'death with dignity' is one that we hear about a lot in debates about euthanasia, assisted suicide, non-resuscitation, and the right to die. A number of states of the United States have Death with Dignity Acts which establish legal frameworks for the voluntary self-administration of lethal doses of drugs prescribed for the purpose by a doctor. Dignity in Dying is a campaigning organisation which advocates for change in the law to allow assisted dying in the United Kingdom.

Apart from that association with death and dying, dignity has a strong association with health care, social care and matters of

[23] On 'the dualistic fantasy of a unique human dignity', see Deborah Anker, *Fictions of Dignity: Embodying Human Rights in World Literature* (Ithaca: Cornell University Press, 2012), 151 (discussing the concept of dignity and its relation to animal being in J. M. Coetzee's novel, *Disgrace*).

[24] See www.dignityequinecremations.co.uk/.

[25] See www.dignitas.ch/?lang=en.

personal hygiene. The concept of 'period dignity', implying the right of access to products and information relating to menstruation, has gained currency in recent years. Equally, 'toilet dignity' is an ongoing issue, as our subsequent discussion of the South African toilet wars will illustrate.[26] In 2018, an organisation was set up in Scotland to distribute what it calls 'Dignity Boxes'. The boxes contain basic toiletries, and the system is that people donate toiletry items, which are then put into small boxes that are left openly in places with high levels of deprivation, to be taken and used by people in need. By making available daily necessities of this kind 'without [the recipients'] having to ask or thank anyone', the organisation hopes, in its words, 'to promote in a small way self-worth and dignity'.[27]

The National Dignity Council of the United Kingdom is a network of health and social care professionals and others, dedicated to promoting what it calls 'Dignity in Care'.[28] Dignity in Care is the basis of a '10 Point Dignity Challenge' – the 'Dignity Do's' – which the Council has elaborated, comprising ten values and actions designed to ensure respect for people's dignity in hospitals, community health services, and care facilities. The Council has designated 1 February an annual Dignity Action Day, with themes such as, on one recent occasion, 'Putting Undignified Care to Bed'.[29] To help in carrying forward its work, the Council appoints a high-profile 'Dignity Ambassador', along with on-the-ground 'Dignity Champions', and distributes 'Dignity in Care' badges and wristbands. Posters prepared or inspired by the National Dignity Council can be seen in doctor's surgeries and hospitals throughout the country.

This emphasis on dignity extends to the field of medical and disability technologies. Dignity Medical Supplies offers for sale mobility aids, dressing aids, shower chairs, grab bars and diagnostic equipment. It also sells a range of incontinence products branded 'Dignity' – one of many product ranges of that kind with that name. Wade Ceramics is a manufacturer of porcelain that produces assistive tableware for use by people with cognitive, motor or visual impairments, which it likewise calls 'Dignity'. Among the items

[26] See Chapter 5. [27] See www.dignityboxes.co.uk/.
[28] See www.dignityincare.org.uk/About/The_10_Point_Dignity_Challenge/.
[29] Dignity Action Day 2023.

available are a two-handed cup and a plate with wide rims designed for people with dementia. Underscoring the fact that these pieces are made out of vitrified earthenware, the company quotes an expert in dementia services: 'If it's not a picnic, there should be no plastic.'[30] Yet another company makes a series of waterless shampoos and body washes to cope with difficulties affecting bathroom access that again carry the brand name 'Dignity'.[31]

As will be already evident from some of the issues on which I have just touched, aged care is a sphere in which dignity has particular prominence. *The Observer* once ran a campaign for 'Dignity at Home', posing the question 'Is dignity at home too much to ask for our elderly?'.[32] It was reported that 'hundreds of thousands of Britain's elderly rely on home care visits to live a dignified life … But as local authorities reduce funding, an increasing number of our most vulnerable citizens are being neglected.' The example given was of a 72-year-old woman from Essex who was housebound due to severe arthritis, and suffered from incontinence. After reducing the number of baths to which she was entitled every week from two to one, the authorities had told her that even that was to end, and she would have to make do with a daily sponge-down. One reads of the reduction of all kinds of visits by care staff, so that '[m]ore and more of us are seeing this indignity … inflicted on our elderly relatives'.[33]

Also germane to our theme is the sphere of workplace relations. At the university where I work, as in many other workplaces in the United Kingdom and elsewhere, there is a 'Dignity at Work Statement' which employees can consult if they wish.[34] The Statement proclaims the goal of promoting an 'enabling and inclusive environment where all staff are treated with dignity and respect', and assigns to managers responsibility for taking the lead in promoting a 'culture of dignity and respect'. In more detailed

[30] See www.wade.co.uk/general/benefits-of-our-assistive-dignity-tableware-for-alzheimers-and-dementia-sufferers/.

[31] The company's name is Dignity LC Services. See www.dignitylcservices.co.uk/.

[32] Jo Revill et al., 'Is Dignity at Home Too Much to Ask for Our Elderly?', *The Guardian*, 17 June 2008. See www.theguardian.com/society/2007/jun/17/longtermcare.politics.

[33] Ibid.

[34] London School of Economics and Political Science, *Dignity at Work Statement* (on file with the author).

sections, the Statement sets out 'expectations regarding appropriate behaviour', along with the means by which complaints of inappropriate behaviour can be addressed and resolved. Inappropriate behaviour is defined as 'any behaviour which is unwanted, unwelcome and undermines an individual's dignity at work', and is further clarified through a series of examples.

Given the phenomenon of statements such as this, we should not be surprised that dignity has high visibility in management consulting, executive coaching, conflict resolution, and related spheres. Donna Hicks is the author of *Dignity: Its Essential Role in Resolving Conflict* and *Leading with Dignity: How to Create a Culture that Brings Out the Best in People.*[35] Hicks writes in these books of her belief in the 'power of dignity' and its primordial significance in human relationships.[36] In her first book, she characterises dignity as the 'missing link' in our understanding of conflict resolution, and sets out a 'Dignity Model' that explains what dignity is, how our evolutionary programming leads us persistently to violate it, and what can be done to overcome that programming and honour the dignity which is everyone's birthright. In her second book, she shows how this model can be used by business leaders and others to build a team and develop an organisational culture oriented towards 'dignity consciousness'.[37]

Let me mention one final association of dignity, which takes us from the English word and its Latin root to the Arabic word conventionally translated as dignity: *karama.* A central concept in the Arab uprisings of the early 2010s, the word featured on protest banners and painted walls, as well as in videos, songs and writing. Asmaa Mahfouz is often held to have played a decisive role in mobilising the Egyptian protests with a video-blog that urged her compatriots: '[i]f we still . . . want to live in dignity on this land, we have to go down [to Tahrir Square] on January 25th'.[38] As Abdelwahab El-Affendi explained, the point was not just to demand jobs and bread. These uprisings were needed 'so that the people would deserve bread'; the uprisings were needed to

[35] Donna Hicks, *Dignity* (New Haven: Yale University Press, 2011) and Donna Hicks, *Leading with Dignity* (New Haven: Yale University Press, 2018).

[36] Hicks, *Dignity*, xxi. [37] Hicks, *Leading with Dignity*, xi.

[38] The video-blog can be watched at www.youtube.com/watch?v=1JW3m8uwcL4. On dignity in the Egyptian protests, see further Zaynab El Bernoussi, *Dignity in the Egyptian Revolution* (Cambridge: Cambridge University Press, 2021).

'[restore] the dignity of the people'.[39] It is notable that the Tunisian revolution is referred to as the 'Dignity Revolution' (*Thawrat al-Karama*), and that the tribunal of transitional justice later set up in that country was named the Truth and Dignity Commission (*Instance Vérité et Dignité*).

In February 2020, an event occurred in Jordan which brought back memories of the self-immolation of Tunisian street vendor Mohamed Bouazizi, to which the Arab uprisings are often traced.[40] It involved a Jordanian street vendor, Anas al-Jamra, driven to take his own life in similar circumstances. Like Bouazizi, al-Jamra was being harassed by city officials seeking to exact unpayable 'licence fees', and as in the case of Bouazizi too, the officials were repeatedly confiscating al-Jamra's stock, leaving him without the means to support himself and his family. It was reported that the death of Anas al-Jamra 'highlights the struggle people face to earn a dignified living in Jordan . . . where many feel that wealth and opportunities are restricted to a privileged few'. A quotation from his great-uncle tells of how the dead man 'was very hardworking and responsible. He worked every day; sometimes he left the house at six in the morning and only came back at night after 10 . . . He just wanted to live with dignity.'

Three Facts about Dignity

That set of references and associations plainly reflects my own particular field of view. I attach no weight to it except insofar as it brings to notice three salient facts about dignity, which I would like us now to review and go into a bit more deeply. In the *first* place, dignity is not just an idea; it's not just in our heads, but is also performative, embodied and ineliminably relational – a social practice and a lived experience. The embodied aspect of dignity becomes immediately apparent if we inflect from the noun 'dignity' to the adjective 'dignified', variously defined in dictionaries as 'marked by dignity of manner, style or appearance', 'stately, noble,

39 Quoted in Marc Lynch, 'The Big Think Behind the Arab Spring', *Foreign Policy blog*, 28 November 2011.

40 Marta Vidal, '"He Just Wanted Dignity": The Tragedy That Captured the Mood of a Nation', *The Guardian*, 27 February 2020, available at: www.theguardian.com/global-development/2020/feb/27/he-just-wanted-dignity-the-tragedy-that-captured-the-mood-of-a-nation.

majestic', 'decorous, controlled, and calm' and 'having or showing a serious manner that is worthy of respect'. Giorgio Agamben advises that even the Latin and medieval concept of *dignitas*, which (as I will discuss further in the next chapter) was primarily a matter of elevated status or personage, also denoted the 'physical appearance' appropriate to that status or personage.[41]

When it comes to contemporary English, Andrew Sayer recalls that dignity is rendered in the language of posture, comportment, expression, orientation and cohesion. We speak of 'holding one's head up high' and 'meeting the other's gaze', of 'standing tall' and not 'stooping low', of 'saving face', 'keeping a level head', and 'maintaining composure'. Yet we also speak of people believing themselves to be 'above' certain things, which they consider 'beneath their dignity'.[42] To the extent that what may be communicated is an attitude of arrogance, haughtiness or snobbery, Sayer remarks that '[d]ignity can easily be confused with rank and dominance'.[43] Instead, the modern idea of dignity is supposed to signal an intrinsic attribute or quality which 'individuals have whatever their situation ... and regardless of whether others recognize it'.[44] If that puts one in mind of an empirical fact, the reality that dignity cannot be taken for granted applies more to some of us than to others, and more to all of us at some times of our lives than at other times. We speak of difficulties faced, and successes achieved, in keeping dignity 'intact'.

Sayer writes of a 'dance of dignity among people in the way they comport themselves in relation to one another'.[45] Beyond the question of how people behave, there is, then, the question of how others treat them. The practice of dignified treatment has received particular attention in fields such as medicine, nursing and social work, where interactions take place with people whose dignity is seen as especially fragile or precarious. I mentioned earlier the UK National Dignity Council's decalogue of Dignity Do's. This is an attempt to distil ideas in circulation about what it is for a doctor, nurse, social worker or other health or social care professional to treat someone they are looking after with dignity.

[41] Giorgio Agamben, *Remnants of Auschwitz* (New York: Zone Books, 2002), 67.
[42] See Andrew Sayer, *Why Things Matter to People* (Cambridge: Cambridge University Press, 2011), 205.
[43] Ibid., 211. [44] Ibid., 192. [45] Ibid., 192.

'Enable people to maintain the maximum possible level of independence, choice and control', is one Dignity Do. Among the rest are: 'treat each person as an individual'; 'listen and support people to express their needs and wants'; 'respect people's privacy'; 'ensure people feel able to complain without fear of retribution'; and 'assist people to maintain confidence and positive self-esteem'.

Harvey Chochinov has put these ideas at the centre of end-of-life care, outlining an influential model of palliative care which he terms 'dignity-conserving care'.[46] The model breaks down the issues affecting dignity into several categories, and identifies therapeutic interventions specific to each that can be made to conserve the patient's dignity. Finding ways to help the patient to live in the moment and maintaining normality to the maximum extent possible are examples of these. Jeannette Pols has studied dignity in a variety of health and social care systems and settings. In one paper, she presents the results of an investigation into care practices at two different institutional sites in the Netherlands: an innovative psychiatric hospital and a more traditional geriatric residential home.[47] In particular, Pols looked at how the nurses/carers in these respective settings handled patients/residents who did not want to wash or be washed. Did they force the patients/residents to wash or be washed, and on what basis did they decide this?

It transpired that the nurses at the psychiatric hospital did not force patients to wash. They said things like: 'I let her keep her dignity in the sense that I take it she will look after herself'. For them, '[w]ashing or not washing was ... a private matter to be decided upon by the patient'.[48] By contrast, the carers at the geriatric residential home did force reluctant residents to be washed. They saw washing as part of the 'clean and well-kept appearance' which staff should help in maintaining, and said things like: 'It's out of bed in the morning, washing [so] that [the residents] look nice, and [so] that they [can] at least feel good about

[46] Harvey Chochinov, 'Dignity-Conserving Care – A New Model for Palliative Care', *Journal of the American Medical Association* 287(17) (2002) 2253. See further Harvey Chochinov, *Dignity Therapy* (Oxford: Oxford University Press, 2012) and, with a frame of reference extending beyond palliative care, Harvey Chochinov, *Dignity in Care* (Oxford: Oxford University Press, 2023).

[47] Jeannette Pols, 'Washing the Patient: Dignity and Aesthetic Values in Nursing Care', *Nursing Philosophy* 14(3) (2013) 186.

[48] Ibid., 192.

that. I find that really important, it's their sense of dignity'.[49] To be sure, there were limits to both approaches. The psychiatric nurses admitted that, at a certain point, they 'could no longer stand it', and would insist that a patient take a shower.[50] Equally, the geriatric care workers accepted that some residents were not accustomed to frequent bathing, and there was no need to 'get into a fight' every day.[51]

The general insight which Pols wants us to take from this research is that dignity has two aspects which together account for its meaning in these contexts. On the one hand, there is privacy in the sense of autonomy – the dignity that comes from self-command and from making decisions about your life for yourself. As she explains, the psychiatric nurses framed the subjects of their care 'as free individuals with equal rights such as the right to privacy. They actively helped their patients to develop and materially shape this individuality and protected [their patients] from interference that eroded their dignity.'[52] On the other hand, there is 'looking nice' – the dignity that comes from fitting in with social norms to do with what is pleasant and seemly and expressive of self-respect. It was of cardinal importance to the geriatric carers to '[create] sociality in the residential home', and in no relevant version of sociality was 'being dirty . . . a binding value'.[53] 'Cleanliness here is about relating to others, within the residential home and within the society at large, in which older people with psychiatric problems or dementia need to get a dignified place.'[54]

Talk of getting a dignified place points to a *second* fact about dignity. It is emergent, rather than predetermined or resolved. In many common usages, dignity denotes a quality, attribute or state of being, but we should not forget that it also denotes a process. There is always a question as to how, in particular circumstances, dignity is (or is not) produced. Illustrations of this abound in the substantial literature on dignity in the fields of anthropology, sociology, applied ethics and related disciplines. Interested in interactions between citizens and state officials, Alex Nading spent time with food-safety inspectors and the owners of food businesses they inspected in a district of Managua, Nicaragua. Anthropological studies of such bureaucratic interactions had tended to stress their

[49] Ibid., 193. [50] Ibid., 196. [51] Ibid., 195. [52] Ibid., 193.
[53] Ibid., 194, 197. [54] Ibid., 194.

character as threats to dignity. However, Nading witnessed encounters that could become dignified insofar as the parties joked with one another, and insofar as the owners of food businesses presented the inspectors with gifts that were graciously received. Whereas making light of things and accepting gifts might betoken incompetence or corruption on the part of an official, here they were means of 'building dignity into … governmental surveillance' by turning inspection into an activity that felt less like law enforcement, and more like participation in a shared effort to make 'cooking, selling, and bureaucratically accounting for food commensurable as forms of dignified work'.[55]

Ernesto Noronha and colleagues investigated dignity in the working lives of security guards in an Indian city.[56] Two groups of guards were encompassed: those employed at pavement kiosks with automated teller machines, and those who guarded the premises of large-scale commercial or industrial enterprises. How did experience at these different sites compare? While the ATM security guards told of poor working conditions and persistent vituperation from passers-by, the commercial and industrial guards described a dignity that came from being required to wear an ironed uniform, keep careful records of their patrols, not chat on the phone when on duty, and remain calm and polite in the case of an altercation. As Noronha and colleagues gloss it, 'dignity and discipline coalesced' in the lives of these guards.[57] This was reinforced by the 'recognition and respect' of others.[58] Unlike the ATM guards, the guards at the commercial and industrial premises were mostly treated courteously and with consideration in their daily interactions. They received training, saw their working conditions improve, and were invited to festive occasions at the premises they guarded. 'Disciplined soldiers' these security guards may in some sense have been, but it was also important that they were 'respected persons'.[59]

An occupation that is often seen as presumptively 'dignity-wounding', because it involves 'dirty work', is garbage collection.

[55] Alex Nading, 'Orientation and Crafted Bureaucracy: Finding Dignity in Nicaraguan Food Safety', *American Anthropologist* 119(3) (2017) 478, 480.

[56] Ernesto Noronha, Saikat Chakraborty and Premilla D'Cruz, '"Doing Dignity Work": Indian Security Guards' Interface with Precariousness', *Journal of Business Ethics* 162 (2020) 553.

[57] Ibid., 569. [58] Ibid. [59] Ibid.

Peter Hamilton and colleagues conducted field research among refuse collectors and street cleaners employed by a local authority in the north-east of England.[60] It emerged that the refuse collectors and street cleaners indeed had experience of offence. Members of the public would walk past them holding their noses or castigate them when they declined to pick up contaminated waste. Yet Hamilton and colleagues observed that the garbage workers did not consider themselves to be engaged in undignified work thanks to a series of self-representational narratives: the men – for they were all men – re-coded their negatively coded dirty work as positive by pointing up its social and environmental usefulness; they developed self-esteem through favourable comparison with alternative work, such as 'robotic' factory work; and they emphasised a form of 'heroic masculinity' that consisted of 'looking out for' vulnerable members of the community while doing their rounds, and always being willing to 'go the extra mile'.[61] Through these interlinked narratives, it is reported that the refuse collectors and street cleaners successfully imbued themselves and their work with dignity.

A more mixed account of dignity-production in the sphere of 'dirty work' is given by Jana Costas. Costas descended for a while into the 'corporate underworld' inhabited by cleaners at an upmarket mall in Berlin.[62] Highlighting invisibility as a key feature of this context, she explains how the cleaners worked at night and in the early morning, and how the zone designated for them was the building's basement, which could not be accessed by others working in the mall or the general public. Pertinent also to the cleaners' invisibility was that they reported to a contract cleaning company, rather than to the mall owner. Costas comments that when work is invisible, it is often valued less, and may come to seem undignified. The cleaners had ways of counteracting that – smiling confidently when they passed people in the mall, standing up for themselves in response to an unfair complaint, outwitting the surveillance measures by which their work was monitored – but lacking

60 Peter Hamilton et al., '"Lower than a Snake's Belly": Discursive Constructions of Dignity and Heroism in Low-Status Garbage Work', *Journal of Business Ethics* 156 (4) (2019) 889.

61 Ibid., 896, 890, 898.

62 Jana Costas, *Dramas of Dignity: Cleaners in the Corporate Underworld of Berlin* (Cambridge: Cambridge University Press, 2022).

an 'institutional anchor', their dignity was 'difficult' to maintain.[63] The basement zone often became a 'refuge from a landscape of indignities',[64] though there too the indignities could continue, especially for cleaners who faced racist and misogynistic slurs from co-workers, with little protection from managers.

In outlining the arrangements for cleaning at the mall, Costas notes that they followed the pattern that began to be established towards the end of the twentieth century, whereby companies and organisations turned to outsourcing as a strategy for reducing costs and increasing flexibility. Such information signals a *third* fact about dignity. It adverts to occurrences that are at once proper to themselves and enmeshed with the wider conditions affecting economy, society and culture. To reckon with dignity is necessarily also to reckon with the historical conjuncture of a particular time and place. Hence, in his study of Nicaraguan food-safety inspectors, Nading sets the bureaucratic routines he finds against the backdrop of received approaches to good governance and the legacy of 'structural violence inherent in a fractured state'.[65] Noronha and colleagues connect their discussion of the work of Indian security guards with literature detailing a decline in the country of high-quality manufacturing jobs and the advent of new forms of precarious employment.[66] And the *Observer*'s campaign for dignity at home in the United Kingdom references an austerity programme that involved sustained cuts to health and welfare spending, diminished financial support for local authorities, and the privatisation of procedures for assessing eligibility for benefits.[67]

When broader systemic conditions and trends are brought into the frame, challenges and achievements involving dignity no longer appear as purely personal or local concerns, and still less can they appear as the outcome of problems thrown up by evolutionary biology, as proposed by Hicks. Rather, we apprehend them as events within a conflictual social order. Attention is directed to the politics of dignity, its relation to developments in the organisation of capitalism, and to the whole range of issues, domains and analytical scales that bear on prevailing processes of social

[63] Ibid., 8, 117. [64] Ibid., 126.
[65] Nading, 'Orientation and Crafted Bureaucracy', 487.
[66] See Noronha, Chakraborty and D'Cruz, '"Doing Dignity Work"', 553.
[67] Jo Revill et al., 'Is Dignity at Home Too Much to Ask for Our Elderly?'.

production and reproduction. The Scottish charity Dignity Boxes implicitly evokes the politics of dignity when it distributes toiletries in areas with high levels of deprivation. So too does Anas al-Jamra's great-uncle when he laments the death of his young relative who 'just wanted to live with dignity'. The observation that life without dignity is hard and sometimes even intolerable reminds us that dignity has beneficial effects; it is an advantage – and some people have all, or almost all, the advantages. Thus, as succeeding sections of this book will discuss, dignity is a right, but also a privilege that maps with grim clarity the contours of our unequal world.

Thinking about dignity as political prompts the reflection, furthermore, that if our subject is dignity, it is indignity as well. Indignity is, of course, the antonym of dignity, yet there is a lot that we will miss if we approach indignity solely as dignity's opposite or deficient pair. We would be wrong to treat indignity as a simple lack of dignity to be filled or an absence of dignity awaiting presence, because indignity is a rich resource for studying dignity. As I have already mentioned, Ahmed's study of happiness is illuminating in this respect. She writes of the 'assumed transparency of the "un"' in 'unhappiness' – the presumption that unhappiness is the simple non-existence of happiness. What would it be to set aside that presumption, she asks, and 'listen to those who are cast as wretches'? Perhaps we might gain a 'different angle on happiness', and be led to understand it in unaccustomed ways.[68] Equally, we may gain a different angle on dignity by listening to those cast as undignified. With that reorientation may come new knowledge not only about what dignity is, but also about how it functions – its limitations and demarcations, its underpinnings and effects, and its methods and sometimes wily ways.

Katherine Newman conducted research with people employed at fast food outlets in New York City.[69] Newman was interested in the fast food workers as exemplars of the urban working poor, and one of the questions she set out to investigate was how they managed to maintain their dignity while doing a job that paid wages on which they could barely survive, and in some cases actually could not survive, and that was 'the butt of countless parodies and sarcastic

[68] Ahmed, *The Promise of Happiness*, 17.

[69] Katherine Newman, *No Shame in My Game: The Working Poor in the Inner City* (New York: Vintage Books, 2000).

asides'.[70] The answer, for Newman, lay in the 'dignity of work'.[71] As the basis of that contention, she quotes statements from workers such as this: 'I'm not ashamed because I have a job. Most people don't and I'm proud of myself that I decided to get up and do something at an early age. So as I look at it, I'm not on welfare. I'm doing something.'[72] Newman also underscores the supportive role played by colleagues and managers, sharing this story from another worker: 'One night this little boy came in … and cursed me out. He [said], "That's why you are working [here]. You can't get a better job … ". I was upset … I started crying. [My manager] was like, "… [D]on't bother with him. I'm saying, *you got a job*. You know. It's a *job*."'[73] Newman concludes that her nation's working poor 'work hard at jobs the rest of us would not want because they believe in the dignity of work … [W]orking keeps them on the right side of American culture.'[74]

Or does it? Some years after Newman published her study, Carol Cleaveland interviewed welfare recipients in Philadelphia.[75] Her specific interest was in women who had refused work, quitting low-wage, low-status jobs to return to welfare, with supplementary help from charities, relatives and friends. Cleaveland describes hearing of repeated 'confrontations with authority figures at various job sites'. By her interpretation, such confrontations and the walkouts that followed them 'afforded impoverished women the chance … to maintain [at least] the vestiges of a defiant dignity in the face of a hostile social order'.[76] These workers did not have the 'means of mounting a general challenge to the status quo, [but] they could challenge particular representatives of it'.[77] They could challenge the people who gave them enough break time only for a few puffs of a cigarette, or ripped off the sheets of an imperfectly made hotel bed. They could say no to those who offered them nothing other than insecure, dead-end employment at poverty-level wages. Cleaveland argues that, contrary to the assessments of analysts like Newman, 'very low-wage workers are not able to find dignity in virtually any job … Entrance into [the kind of worksites to which the women she interviewed were admitted] did not offer a

[70] Ibid., xiv. [71] Ibid., 304. [72] Ibid., 98.
[73] Ibid., 102 (emphasis in original). [74] Ibid., xv.
[75] Carol Cleaveland, 'A Desperate Means to Dignity: Work Refusal amongst Philadelphia Welfare Recipients', *Ethnography* 6(1) (2005) 35.
[76] Ibid. [77] Ibid., 48.

move to the "right side" of American culture . . .; rather [these women's] work experiences served notice of the chasm between themselves and more affluent Americans'.[78]

If Newman foregrounds the association of dignity with having a job, being self-reliant, and not depending on welfare,[79] Cleaveland's research brings into focus the defiant dignity of those who refuse such an understanding of dignity. The message we receive from her interviewees is that Newman's dignity – a familiar version to people in many societies today that presumably reflects, at least in part, the repudiation of earlier approaches to social protection – is ideology. It is a legitimising manoeuvre designed to mask both the *indignity* of low-wage, insecure, dead-end jobs and the *indignation* that can be witnessed on the part of the poor, mostly non-white, disproportionately female workers expected, and impelled by the lack of alternative employment opportunities, to do them. More than that, the message we receive is that this form of dignity *dignifies* such jobs with a status they do not deserve. 'Dignify' is an interesting word inasmuch as it sounds a note of caution about this noble or ennobling concept, dignity; it encourages a certain scepticism towards what is predicated. Perhaps respectability is just the decorous drapery of power. Perhaps respect is commanded only in the sense of being mandated by a higher authority. I want us to listen to that note of caution, and stay awhile with its reverberations.

The Messy Experiential

The points to be picked up so far are, then, that dignity is not just an idea, but also an embodied performance and interactive practice. Linked to that, it is not just an attitude, property or trait, but also a phenomenon in motion, the unfolding of a process. At the same time, it is not simply a private or individual issue, but also arises as part of a larger history characterised by social conflict and attempts to contain it through ideology. With regard to the uses to which dignity is put, we have seen that it may be simultaneously a principle of practical ethics, a revolutionary rallying cry, and a marketing device for products and services to be consumed in situations where dignity is deemed to be at particular risk. Dignity is a theme of

[78] Ibid., 55. [79] On this, see Chapter 2.

activism, policy and research on matters that include death, personal hygiene, social care, health care, sanitation, refuse collection, state bureaucracy and the conditions of work. The thrust of some of the research is to show how threats to dignity may be effectively defused; in other cases, indignity is called out, and we read of dignity as a depleted substance, unyielding but reduced to its vestigial remains.

The analyses of dignity to which I have referred suggest that it implicates both behaviour and treatment, and both respect for autonomy and conformity with convention. What these analyses also disclose are the deep social divisions – to use Cleaveland's word, the *chasms* of the social-structural landscape – that must be taken into account in any attempt to come to grips with dignity. Arlie Hochschild touches on something of this in *Strangers in Their Own Land*, her 'journey to the heart of the American right' published in 2016 and often cited in discussions of the context in which Donald Trump was elected US President in 2017.[80] Hochschild got to know supporters in Louisiana of the Tea Party movement of that time. After many conversations, she sums up feelings repeatedly expressed to her by white working-class people as follows. 'You are a stranger in your own land ... It is a struggle to feel seen and honoured.' You might 'turn to your workplace for respect – but wages are flat and jobs insecure. So you look to other sources of honor. You get no extra points for your race. You look to gender, but if you're a man, you get no extra points for that either. If you are straight you are proud to be a married, heterosexual male, but that pride is now seen as a potential sign of homophobia – a source of dishonour.'[81] And on it goes.

Hochschild does not use the language of dignity in those passages. Rather, she writes of honour, pride and respect, mindful perhaps of the idea of dignity as an intrinsic form of worth that is distinct from socially conferred worth, and all the more so from the entrenched forms of social privilege ('extra points') to which her account alludes. In a more recent study, Vincent Lloyd also takes up the problem of entrenched social privilege in America, though from the opposite perspective of those struggling to put an end to

[80] Arlie Hochschild, *Strangers in Their Own Land: Anger and Mourning on the American Right* (New York: New Press, 2016), xii.
[81] Ibid., 144.

it.[82] For him, dignity is precisely the right term to use when speaking of their struggle. I will return to Lloyd's work in the final chapter of this book. It suffices to mention now that he recovers a long history of African-American activism and thought which has put the concept of dignity at the centre of movements for Black liberation, whether in the context of abolitionism, civil rights, Black power, Black feminism, or, as today, Black Lives Matter. Drawing together the legacies of that history, Lloyd proposes that '[i]n a world that denies Black humanity and embraces racial domination, dignity names an affirmation of that humanity, which necessarily means struggle against domination'.[83]

Richard Sennett and Jonathan Cobb spent time with working people in Boston, Massachusetts during the early 1970s as part of an investigation into what they termed the 'hidden injuries of class'.[84] The report of their study fixes frequently on the subject of dignity, and its key conclusion in that regard is that there exists a gap between American 'public beliefs' about shared dignity and the equal claim of everyone to respect, on the one hand, and realities that bear little resemblance to the societal picture suggested by those beliefs, on the other.[85] Sennett and Cobb tell of how people on the lower rungs of the social ladder are not denied the 'possibility' of winning respect, but they are denied the 'presumption' of respect. They are denied 'some way of moving through daily life without being defensive and on guard, some way of being open with other people without being hurt'. The authors describe how the 'humbling of inferiors', well known to have been integral to the maintenance of status, hierarchy and order in pre-modern Europe, continues in liberal-democratic America in forms that are similarly oppressive, if 'at once less brutal and more insidious'.[86] Indeed, they characterise humbling as 'the most routine of modern

[82] Vincent Lloyd, *Black Dignity: The Struggle against Domination* (New Haven: Yale University Press, 2022).

[83] Ibid., 2. On this, see also Norman Ajari (Matthew Smith, trans.), *Dignity or Death: Ethics and Politics of Race* (Cambridge: Polity Press, 2023). On the arguments of these books, see Chapter 6.

[84] Richard Sennett and Jonathan Cobb, *The Hidden Injuries of Class* (New York/London: W. W. Norton, 1972). The work of Pierre Bourdieu, and especially Pierre Bourdieu et al. (Priscilla Parkhurst Ferguson et al., trans.), *The Weight of the World: Social Suffering in Contemporary Society* (Cambridge, Polity Press, 1999), pursues a somewhat similar enquiry in a different time and place.

[85] Sennett and Cobb, *The Hidden Injuries of Class*, 251.

[86] Ibid., 248.

occurrences'. They remark, however, that, unlike in the past, the system which sustains and is sustained by such occurrences 'goes itself into hiding', and attention falls squarely on the battle among individuals to become 'personally exempted from shaming and indignity'.[87]

Let me mention one final study, in which Imogen Tyler considers the denigration of working-class people in contemporary Britain. This phenomenon had earlier been described by Owen Jones with reference to the concept of the 'chav' – a term that came into currency during the 2000s to mock people with working-class origins as vulgar and undignified.[88] Tyler observes that one response to that kind of slur, one rebuttal, has been to insist on the reality of 'working-class dignity', and to point out that 'those in jobs paying little more than benefits' have a 'remarkably strong work ethic', that 'carers and cleaners [do] essential work well, despite lack of money or respect', and that so-called 'chav mums' are, in fact, 'willing to work'.[89] While acknowledging that the figure of the 'noble suffering worker' has facilitated the 'articulation of class solidarities' and the repudiation of class contempt, she argues that it has also sustained a distinction between the deserving and undeserving poor, and between 'honest hardworking families' and a 'parasitical, pathological underclass'.[90] To Tyler's mind, the answer to the demonisation of working people is not to provide evidence of a 'mismatch between . . . vilifying class names [chav and so on, on the one hand] and . . . [actual] working-class dignity', on the other. Rather, it is to challenge the 'forms of classificatory violence' that are expressed in, and carried forward by, those names. It is 'to understand how the [relevant] representations of self and other . . . are formed, and how they might be transformed'.[91]

How representations of self and other are formed, and how they might be transformed, is a big question, and a mark perhaps of the distance we have travelled in the foregoing, which is itself a mark of

[87] Ibid., 150 (emphasis omitted).

[88] Owen Jones, *Chavs: The Demonization of the Working Class* (London: Verso, 2nd ed. 2016).

[89] Imogen Tyler, *Revolting Subjects: Social Abjection and Resistance in Neoliberal Britain* (London: Zed Books, 2013), 169–70 (quoting Polly Toynbee and referring also to Owen Jones).

[90] Ibid., 170. [91] Ibid. (quoting Jacques Rancière).

the span and scope of the issues, perspectives and phenomena that come into play when the question is posed of what it is to 'see dignity'. Dignity is a matter of how we are with ourselves, so to speak – the narratives we develop about our identities and our lives. (Remember the English refuse collectors and the Indian security guards.) But it is also a matter of what our encounters are like with others – how others behave towards us day-to-day, what we do, what we are allowed to do and to be. (Remember the psychiatric nurse saying 'I let her keep her dignity'.) Dignity is useless, but also essential. It is an ethical ideal, but also a management strategy and a funeral company. It can be ideological, but it is also defiant and oppositional – the struggle against domination. Dignity is a lofty concept, but, as this introductory chapter has tried to show, also a worldly one that is inextricably bound up (to borrow yet again from Ahmed) with 'the messiness of the experiential, the unfolding of bodies into worlds, and … the drama of … how we are touched by what comes near'.[92]

[92] Ahmed, *The Promise of Happiness*, 22.

2

The Idea of Human Dignity

Intrinsic Dignity, Status Dignity

The English word 'dignity' is traced to the Old French *digneté* and French *dignité,* and through them, to the Latin *dignitas,*[1] meaning merit or worth, and *dignus,* meaning worthy.[2] Discussions of dignity often draw a distinction between two kinds of dignity, corresponding to two forms of merit, worth or worthiness. On one side is put the inherent worth and value of every human being, and the respect that is due to all of us simply by virtue of our being human. In what follows I will refer to that as 'intrinsic dignity'. On the other side there appears the honour that belongs, and the esteem that is owed, to those who hold high office or occupy some other particular status or role. A number of now obsolete meanings of dignity were along those lines – it once denoted an 'honourable office, rank or title', or, by transference, a 'person holding a high office or position', or even, by further transference, the whole collectivity of 'persons of high estate or rank' – but the idea remains recognisable in the inflected term 'dignitary'. That second kind of dignity I will refer to as 'status dignity'.

The common thread is obviously that dignity denotes the condition of being worthy of respect, honour or esteem. A related sense identifies it with conduct befitting the condition of being worthy of respect, honour or esteem. People who comport themselves with

[1] It is actually the accusative form *dignitatem* that is referenced.
[2] The lexical and etymological information in this chapter is taken from the *Oxford English Dictionary.*

dignity, or lend things around them an aura of dignity, exhibit 'stateliness or gravity' and, more generally, an 'elevated aspect, manner or style'; they bring to their situation that distinctive composure, seriousness and decorousness to which we attach the label 'dignified'. Yet there is an important difference to be registered here. For while intrinsic dignity is an egalitarian idea about universal human worth, status dignity is rooted in hierarchy, privilege and rank. This is reflected in a bifurcation of the conduct-befitting sense of dignity, as Daniel Miller observes. In an ethnographic study of life on a London street, Miller contrasts the dignity of 'an aristocratic demeanour which is inherited, ... may put others in awe', and seems to 'come from effortless success', with the 'modest and pleasant' dignity that 'is as respectful of others as it commands respect', and that abides and 'is retained' even in the midst of 'failure' and 'however undignified the circumstances'.[3]

The philosophical literature on dignity mostly converges around an historical narrative which is said to underlie the distinction between what I have termed intrinsic dignity and status dignity. The story begins in classical antiquity, then moves to the Italian Renaissance philosopher Pico della Mirandola, and from him to the sage of eighteenth-century Königsberg, Immanuel Kant, held by many scholars to be the towering figure in the development of the idea of human dignity. A subsequent, unfinished chapter takes up the twentieth-century invocation of human dignity in national constitutions and international human rights instruments, along with the large and ever-growing body of jurisprudence, commentary and other writing which has come with that invocation. Reviewed in the pages to follow, this is a story of which anyone interested in the topic of dignity needs to be cognisant, even if – or perhaps especially if – it turns out to tell us only part of what we need to know about the history of dignity.

Towards Interiorisation

Ancient Roman *dignitas* denoted the rank and prestige of a person who held a particular public office or of a collectivity with a

[3] Daniel Miller, *The Comfort of Things* (London: Polity Press, 2008), 218. 'Defiant dignity', introduced in Chapter 1 of this book, is something different again, as the succeeding chapters will attempt to show.

particular status. It was also used as a generic term for the relevant public offices themselves. The *Notitia Dignitatum* is a catalogue of civil and military dignities in the late Roman Empire.[4] It lists the most important offices that could be bestowed by the governments of different parts of the empire, and indicates how authority was distributed among them. The positions enumerated range from praetorian prefects and generals of the cavalry and infantry to chamberlains, notaries, secretaries and tax collectors. The *Notitia Dignitatum* is thought to have been compiled around the fifth century CE. The *Corpus Juris Civilis,* prepared at the instigation of the Emperor Justinian in the succeeding century, provides further insight into imperial Roman dignities. Book Twelve of Justinian's Code, entitled *De Dignitatibus,* sets out the powers, duties, privileges and immunities of a wide array of dignities, along with the order of precedence that applied to them and the criteria that determined eligibility for appointment.

A general section at the beginning of Book Twelve states in one notable provision that the entrance to, or gate of, dignity – *porta dignitatis* – is barred to those of bad reputation, whose infamy and iniquity exclude them from the society of respectable people. In another provision of that section, the Code declares: 'Let no one who belongs to the lowest class of merchants, brokers or persons engaged in vile or abject pursuits or employments, or who occupy base or dishonourable positions, attempt to enjoy any dignity.'[5] Miriam Griffin explains that *dignitas* included 'the idea of worthiness and the respect inspired by that worthiness'.[6] Quoting a comment by Seneca that *dignitas* is one of the virtues which 'work to make an impression', she highlights that this was linked to an orientation towards 'outward or perceivable behavior'. Griffin observes furthermore that *dignitas* was 'inherently comparative'. An individual or collectivity to which it attached was 'understood as superior to other' individuals or collectivities.[7] For example, the *dignitas* of a family (*gens*) implied that family's superiority over other

4 *Notitia Dignitatum,* available at: www.notitiadignitatum.org/. See esp. appendix 14.

5 *Code of Justinian, Book XII,* available at: https://droitromain.univ-grenoble-alpes.fr/Anglica/CJ12_Scott.gr.html. See esp. title 1, paras. 2 and 6.

6 Miriam Griffin, 'Dignity in Roman and Stoic Thought', in Remy Debes (ed.), *Dignity: A History* (Oxford: Oxford University Press, 2017), 47, 50.

7 Ibid.

families. At the same time, the hierarchy of public offices (*gradus dignitatis*) meant that dignities stood with respect to each other in strict rank order.

Reference to the dignity of human beings in general can be found in the writing of the Roman Republican statesman, jurist and philosopher Marcus Tullius Cicero, and there is a tradition of thought according to which he should be seen as a precursor of our modern notion of intrinsic dignity. In his treatise on public ethics, *De Officiis,* composed in 44 BCE, Cicero proposes that, whereas other living creatures are impelled by 'instinct' and the gratification of sensuous desires, human beings have a 'superiority and dignity [*excellentia et dignitas*]' which consists in the fact that 'man's mind is nurtured by study [and rational contemplation]'.[8] However, Griffin considers that this hardly expresses human dignity as we understand it today. For one thing, the accent still remains on distinctions of rank, in this case between human beings and other animals. For another thing, the context is a Stoic-inspired argument about the virtues of moderation, restraint and decorum. Cicero contends that a life which does not keep impulses under the control of reason is 'quite unworthy of the pre-eminence [or, as the Latin here is sometimes translated, dignity] of man [*non satis esse dignam hominis praestantia*]'.[9] Rather than being a quality that everyone just has, Cicero's human dignity is a 'status we must live up to'.[10]

Giorgio Agamben reminds us that ancient Roman *dignitas* was fundamentally a juridical concept, the concomitant of a system of public administration and military governance.[11] That system imposed duties on office-holders, and it carried expectations about appropriate conduct and appearance – the 'physical appearance

[8] Cicero (Walter Miller, trans.), *De Officiis* (Cambridge, MA: Harvard University Press, 1913), I, 105–6 [30], available at: www.gutenberg.org/files/47001/47001-h/47001-h.htm.

[9] Ibid., I, 106 [30] and 132 [36], available at: www.perseus.tufts.edu/hopper/text?doc=Perseus%3Atext%3A2007.01.0048%3Abook%3D1%3Asection%3D105 and www.perseus.tufts.edu/hopper/text?doc=Perseus%3Atext%3A2007.01.0048%3Abook%3D1%3Asection%3D132. The word 'praestantia' is rendered in this translation as 'dignity'. On Cicero's relation to ideas about dignity, see further Jacob Giltaij, 'Existimatio as "Human Dignity" in Late Classical Roman Law', *Fundamina* 22(2) (2016) 232.

[10] Griffin, 'Dignity in Roman and Stoic Thought', 55.

[11] Giorgio Agamben (Daniel Heller-Roazen, trans.), *Remnants of Auschwitz: The Witness and the Archive* (New York: Zone Books, 1999), esp. 66.

adequate to an elevated condition'.[12] Regarding the concept's subsequent history, Agamben explains that when, much later, dignity reappeared in treatises of moral philosophy as a moral concept, it took on an 'interiorized' character[13] – interiorized not in the sense that the outward appearance and behaviour to which Griffin also refers no longer counted but in the sense that official position and formal rank were no longer determinative. A dignified person became a 'person who, while lacking a public dignity [i.e. an office conferred by the governing authorities], behaves in all matters as if' he or she possessed one. The 'bearing of the individual' became '[liberated from] the possession of a duty' or office,[14] and dignity emerged as something the entrance to which was, in principle, barred to no-one. How did that happen? Let us now pass over many centuries to reach another writer who is sometimes represented as a forerunner of modern thinking about human dignity, the fifteenth-century Italian Giovanni Pico della Mirandola.

Pico's text known as *Oratio de hominis dignitate* is not the most renowned artefact of the Italian Renaissance, but it has some celebrity in writings about the history of human dignity. It was written in 1486 as the introduction to a much longer work in which Pico set out some 900 philosophical theses or *conclusiones.*[15] A conference had been organised to debate the theses with scholars from across Europe the following year in Rome, and the plan was for Pico to deliver an oration introducing his arguments to the learned participants. In the event, the oration was never delivered. Fearing heresy, Pope Innocent VIII cancelled the conference, and ordered a theological enquiry into the 900 theses. While only some of them were found to be heretical, the result was a general papal censure of Pico's text.[16] There exist copies of his introductory oration because it was published two years after Pico's death by his nephew Gianfrancesco. Written in Latin and left untitled by Pico, it acquired the title *Oratio de hominis dignitate* – *Oration on the dignity*

[12] Ibid., 67. [13] Ibid. [14] Ibid., 68.

[15] On the 900 theses, see Stephen Farmer, *Syncretism in the West: Pico's 900 Theses (1486)* (Tempe, AZ: Arizona Center for Medieval and Renaissance Studies, rev. ed. 2008).

[16] See further Pier Cesare Bori, 'Historical and Biographical Background of the Oration', in Francesco Borghesi et al. (eds.), *Pico della Mirandola: Oration on the Dignity of Man, A New Translation and Commentary* (Cambridge: Cambridge University Press, 2016), 10.

of man, in the conventional English rendering – in an edition that appeared in Strasbourg in 1504.

The *Oration* is strikingly obscure, combining Christian themes with Jewish mysticism, natural magic and various other esoteric sources.[17] Also striking is that, despite the title chosen by the Strasbourg editor and retained ever since, the text contains few references to dignity. In a major recent study of the work, Brian Copenhaver argues that it actually has nothing to do with the eponymous concept. According to Copenhaver, 'Pico never wrote an *Oration* about human dignity. Instead, he drafted . . . a speech to promote ascetic mysticism – a way of life incompatible with human dignity, as modern thinkers . . . have used the word "dignity" in English and other vernaculars'.[18] If some scholars have felt able to make sense of the *Oration*'s posthumous title, it seems that they emphasise what they take to be Pico's investment in the distinctively self-creating, self-choosing character of human beings. For John Milbank, Pico carries forward in admittedly syncretic and unorthodox terms the Church Fathers' conception of humanity as 'a proteus' who assumes variously 'the ruling, knowing, and loving functions of the three angelic orders of the Thrones, Cherubim and Seraphim', and whose 'dignity [lies in] our capacity to elect to be united in the love of the Cherubim to God'.[19]

Certainly, in one of its rare usages of the word *dignitas*, the *Oration* proclaims: 'Let us fly off to the otherwordly court that is near to the most eminent Divinity. There, according to the sacred mysteries, seraphim, cherubim, and thrones occupy the first places; let us emulate their dignity *[dignitatem]* and glory, unwilling as we are to yield to them and unable to endure second place.'[20] As Milbank

[17] See Brian Copenhaver, *Magic and the Dignity of Man: Pico della Mirandola and His Oration* (Cambridge, MA: Harvard University Press, 2019). As Copenhaver reads him, Pico was seeking to explain Kabbalah to Christians.

[18] Ibid., 2. See also Brian Copenhaver, *Pico della Mirandola on Trial: Heresy, Freedom, and Philosophy* (Oxford: Oxford University Press, 2022).

[19] John Milbank, 'Dignity Rather than Rights', in Christopher McCrudden (ed.), *Understanding Human Dignity* (Oxford: British Academy/Oxford University Press, 2013), 189, 200–1.

[20] Francesco Borghesi et al. (eds.), *Pico della Mirandola: Oration on the Dignity of Man, A New Translation and Commentary* (Cambridge: Cambridge University Press, 2016), 135. According to Copenhaver, the word 'dignitatem' in this passage should be translated into English not as dignity, but rather as (angelic) 'rank'. See Copenhaver, *Magic and the Dignity of Man*, 27–28.

reads Pico, the latter is signalling that human dignity 'lies finally in the divinely gracious gift', the act of grace that grants us the capacity to emulate the angels, share in their glory, and be close to God.[21] Such an account plainly interiorises dignity; one is no longer in the 'outer' domain of public office or status. Yet it still remains at some distance from a notion of intrinsic dignity, inasmuch as the implication is not that we 'possess dignity in ourselves' or thanks to any 'inalienable property'. Rather, dignity is figured as 'something that we are granted, that we have borrowed' or might copy.[22] Stephen Riley argues that the *Oration* 'provides a point of departure for modern conceptions of human dignity' because it anticipates later, secularised approaches to self-constitution and self-command.[23] Maybe so, but the work of Milbank, Copenhaver and others suggests that properly intrinsic dignity needs to be understood as the outcome of later developments, including, three centuries after Pico, the philosophy of Immanuel Kant.

Elevated above Any Price

In a study of the history and meaning of dignity, Michael Rosen expresses the widely held view that Kant's contribution is indeed of overriding importance. Kant 'should stand at the centre of any historical account of dignity', Rosen writes, as his thought 'has been the inspiration ... of very much of what has come later'.[24] (In passing, we may note that Rosen also, and relatedly, says that it is on Kant's 'giant shoulders [that] the modern theory of human rights largely rests'.[25]) The main text to which attention is directed in this context is the *Groundwork of the Metaphysics of Morals*, first published in 1785. It is well known that this is the work in which Kant identifies his 'categorical imperative', the general ethical

21 Milbank, 'Dignity Rather than Rights', 201.

22 Ibid. For a somewhat similar reading of Pico, see Piet Steenbakkers, 'Human Dignity in Renaissance Humanism', in Marcus Düwell et al. (eds.), *The Cambridge Handbook of Human Dignity: Interdisciplinary Perspectives* (Cambridge: Cambridge University Press, 2014), 86, esp. 92.

23 Stephen Riley, *Human Dignity and Law: Legal and Philosophical Investigations* (London: Routledge, 2018), 19.

24 Michael Rosen, *Dignity: Its History and Meaning* (Cambridge, MA: Harvard University Press, 2012), 19.

25 Ibid.

principle that he states with the formula: 'act only according to that maxim through which you can at the same time will that it become a universal law'.[26] In the discussion of the universal law of nature that follows, Kant also states his famous principle of humanity, the 'practical imperative' that commands: 'So act that you use humanity, in your own person as well as in the person of any other, always at the same time as an end, never merely as a means.'[27] For, as he explains, 'a human being and generally every rational being exists as an end in itself, not merely as a means for the discretionary use of this or that will'.[28]

Kant elucidates the principle of humanity with reference to distinctions between absolute worth and conditional or relative worth, and between persons and things. 'Beings whose existence rests … on nature, if they are non-rational beings, … have only relative worth, as means', he writes, 'and are therefore called *things*'. In contrast, 'rational beings' have absolute worth; they 'are called *persons*, because their nature already marks them out as ends in themselves, i.e. something that may not be used merely as a means, and hence to that extent limits all choice (and is an object of respect)'.[29] This is then further explicated in a way that brings us, eventually, to the concept of dignity. After laying out his idea of persons as self-legislators in a kingdom of ends, Kant avers: 'In the kingdom of ends everything has either a price, or a dignity. What has a price can be replaced with something else, as its equivalent; whereas what is elevated above any price, and hence allows of no equivalent, has a dignity.'[30] He continues: 'What refers to general human inclinations and needs has a *market price*; what, even without presupposing a need, conforms with a certain taste … has a *fancy price* [by which Kant seems to mean an aesthetic value]; but what constitutes the condition under which alone something can be an end in itself does not merely have a relative worth, i.e. a price, but an inner worth, i.e. *dignity*'.[31]

What is it that constitutes the condition under which alone something can be an end in itself? What is it that has dignity?

[26] Immanuel Kant (Mary Gregor and Jens Timmerman, trans. and ed.), *Groundwork of the Metaphysics of Morals* (Cambridge: Cambridge University Press, rev. ed. 2012), 34.
[27] Ibid., 41. [28] Ibid., 40 (emphasis omitted). [29] Ibid., 40.
[30] Ibid., 46 (emphasis omitted). [31] Ibid., 46.

Kant says that 'morality is the condition under which alone a rational being can be an end in itself', as it is 'possible only by this to be a legislating member in the kingdom of ends'. It follows that 'morality and *humanity, in so far as it [and only it] is capable of morality*, is that which alone has dignity'.[32] I need to mention just one more step in his chain of reasoning here. If Kant emphasises the idea of persons as legislating members in the kingdom of ends, that is because he wants to bring out another 'practical imperative' – the principle of autonomy. This invites us to regard 'the will of every rational being as a universally legislating will',[33] and hence to think of human beings as not simply subject to morality, not simply addressees of the moral law, but also, at least potentially, authors of it – agents who are 'free with regard to all laws of nature, obeying only' those maxims that they have themselves laid down, as part of 'a universal legislation (to which [they] at the same time [subject themselves])'.[34] Returning to dignity, Kant adds that the universal but notably self-enacted 'legislation that determines all worth must itself have a dignity, i.e. unconditional, incomparable worth, for which the word *respect* alone makes a befitting expression of the estimation a rational being is to give to it'.[35] By his account, '[a]utonomy is thus the ground of the dignity of a human and of every rational creature'.[36]

The word which Kant used that, from the beginning, got translated into English as dignity, was *Würde*. *Würde* is related etymologically to *Wert*, meaning worth, value or price,[37] and like others of and after his time, Kant saw that latter concept as carrying a salient ambiguity. On the one hand, there was worth in the sense of exchange value, the value of something that is fungible, that has an equivalent, that can be replaced by something else. On the other hand, there was the value of that which has no equivalent, which is irreplaceable, and which, accordingly, does not have merely relative worth, worth as a commodity or object of exchange, but absolute worth or, as he also characterised it, 'inner worth'. That irreplaceable, incommensurable, incomparable worth was what Kant associated with dignity – a kind of value that, as he put it in another

[32] Ibid., 47 (emphasis added). [33] Ibid., 43. [34] Ibid., 47.
[35] Ibid., 47–48 (emphasis in original). [36] Ibid., 48.
[37] See Elmar Seebold (ed.), *Kluge: Etymologisches Wörterbuch der deutschen Sprache* (Berlin and Boston: De Gruyter, 25th ed. 2011).

passage of the *Groundwork*, stands 'infinitely above any price, with which it cannot be balanced or compared at all without, as it were, violating its sanctity'.[38] As we have seen, he presented this dignity that stands infinitely above any price as a property of humanity insofar as it is capable of morality. And he identified as the ground of such dignity the autonomy that is manifest in the self-legislating agency of human beings with respect to moral duties.

The sections from the *Groundwork* to which I have just referred are those foregrounded in discussions of Kant's contribution to the conceptual history of dignity, but it is commonly observed that he also used the word in other ways, or at any rate in contexts that seem to warrant other readings, both in the *Groundwork* and elsewhere. A further complication is that, in his later *Metaphysics of Morals*, he identifies dignity in the sense outlined above with the Latin term *dignitas*, which, as I previously recalled, had mostly to do with office-holding and privileged status, though he then qualifies *dignitas* with the word *interna,* as if to map it onto his idea of 'inner worth'. The relevant passage comes in his treatment of the 'doctrine of virtue', where he evokes the human being's feeling of 'inner worth . . ., in terms of which he is above any price . . . and possesses an inalienable dignity (*dignitas interna*), which instills in him respect for himself'.[39] Oliver Sensen argues that, in fact, the older idea of high office or rank remains integral to Kant's engagement with dignity.[40] When Kant says that the human being is above any price, and that that which is elevated above any price has dignity, for Sensen he is adhering to the classical frame of reference and communicating an idea of dignity as special status or higher standing, dignity as uplift to a loftier, more exalted domain.

Part of Sensen's argument rests on the word which Kant used to express the condition of being above any price: *erhaben.* Translated into English as 'elevated', in the sense of raised or lifted to a higher plane, *erhaben* is also the German term for 'sublime'. Sublimity is, of course, a complicated concept in itself, with particular significance in eighteenth-century aesthetic theory, but its connotations of loftiness and exaltation are clear, even in English where a different

[38] Kant, *Groundwork of the Metaphysics of Morals,* 47.

[39] Immanuel Kant (Lara Denis, ed.; Mary Gregor, trans.), *The Metaphysics of Morals* (Cambridge: Cambridge University Press, 2017), 202.

[40] Oliver Sensen, *Kant on Human Dignity* (Berlin and Boston: De Gruyter, 2011).

word is needed in the phrase 'elevated above any price'. Indeed, Kant explicitly brackets sublimity with dignity, writing in the *Groundwork* of the 'sublimity [*Erhabenheit*] and inner dignity' of the moral law.[41] Rosen likewise notes this linkage of dignity with sublimity. By his assessment, however, it represents 'only a very minor aspect of Kant's use of the term'.[42] Overall, as in most tellings of the conceptual history of dignity, Rosen holds that Kant departs from the tradition in which dignity is a matter of superior status. 'Kant's conception of dignity is ... deeply egalitarian', he writes, for the main point about this priceless worth is that it is 'an intrinsic quality of all human beings', 'something that all human beings have in common'.[43] 'Under the influence of Kant, it has [accordingly] come to be taken for granted that ... dignity and equality go together', just as 'Kant played a significant role in establishing the terminological link between dignity and autonomy'.[44]

In Dignity and Rights

To speak of the influence and role of Kant is, of course, to look back to Kant from the standpoint of later times. Which later times? I have been narrating this story about status dignity and intrinsic dignity, and about the evolution of human dignity, as though it were the accretion of centuries. In actuality, it is itself a twentieth- and twenty-first-century story. The edition of Pico's *Oration* which I have used informs readers that the work was 'rediscovered' only in the 1930s and 1940s,[45] leading to a celebrity that, in the United States, can also be traced to its interwar adoption as set reading for Columbia College's 'Contemporary Civilization in the West' course.[46] The transatlantic explosion of Kant scholarship, and, at any rate, of Kant scholarship on dignity, is a more recent occurrence still. Insofar as one may set store by Google Ngram, a search of the phrase 'human dignity' shows that it started to become significant

[41] Kant, *Groundwork of the Metaphysics of Morals*, 38.
[42] Rosen, *Dignity: Its History and Meaning*, 29–30. [43] Ibid., 29, 24.
[44] Ibid., 31, 25–26.
[45] Massimo Riva, 'Preface: History of the Pico Project and Criteria for the Current Edition', in Francesco Borghesi et al. (eds.), *Pico della Mirandola: Oration on the Dignity of Man, A New Translation and Commentary* (Cambridge: Cambridge University Press, 2016), 3, 9.
[46] See Copenhaver, *Magic and the Dignity of Man*, 452–53.

within Google's corpus of English-language books in the later 1930s and 1940s, with sharp rises in significance occurring during the 1950s and 1960s and at intervals thereafter.[47] To provide a true representation of this story, I should have begun in the twentieth century, when discussions of human dignity brought with them the question of its history and antecedents.

Let us, belatedly then, take up the narrative as it has unfolded over the past hundred years or so. A major context of developments in this period is national constitutional and international human rights discourse. References to dignity can be found in a number of constitutions written before World War II, but there is uncertainty as to what was intended by those references, and most authors consider human dignity a postwar constitutional concept. Dignity is evoked in many postwar constitutions – more than 160, apparently[48] – of which the German Basic Law and the Constitution of South Africa have been among the most influential in this respect.[49] It appears as well in the preamble to the Charter of the United Nations, where we read of a reaffirmation of faith 'in the dignity and worth of the human person'. That reaffirmation is echoed in the Universal Declaration of Human Rights, which also puts dignity in an opening preambular statement that 'recognition of the inherent dignity and of the equal and inalienable rights of all members of the human family is the foundation of freedom, justice and peace in the world', and again in article 1 ('all human beings are born free and equal in dignity and rights'), article 22 (concerning the right to 'realization . . . of the economic, social and cultural rights indispensable for [one's] dignity'), and article 23 (concerning the right of all those who work 'to just and favourable remuneration ensuring for [themselves and their] family an existence worthy of human dignity').

The concept of dignity is equally a component of the human rights treaties that followed the adoption of the Universal Declaration. For example, the opening preambular paragraphs of the International Covenant on Civil and Political Rights and

[47] See https://books.google.com/ngrams/graph?content=human+dignity&year_start=1500&year_end=2019&corpus=26&smoothing=3.

[48] See Doron Shulztiner and Guy Carmi, 'Human Dignity in National Constitutions: Functions, Promises and Dangers', *American Journal of Comparative Law* 62(2) (2014) 461.

[49] Regarding the Constitution of South Africa, see Chapter 5.

the International Covenant on Economic, Social and Cultural Rights repeat the Universal Declaration's statement about recognition of inherent dignity being the foundation of freedom, justice and peace in the world, and go on to affirm that the rights set out in the two Covenants 'derive from the inherent dignity of the human person'. There is then further mention of dignity in article 10 of the International Covenant on Civil and Political Rights (concerning the right of people deprived of their liberty to be 'treated with ... respect for the inherent dignity of the human person') and article 13 of the International Covenant on Economic, Social and Cultural Rights (concerning the right to education 'directed to the full development of the human personality and the sense of its dignity'). Central to the later-twentieth- and twenty-first-century visibility of dignity in this sense of intrinsic dignity is the large jurisprudence which has built up out of interpretations of dignity by national and international courts and tribunals. To that jurisprudence must also be added the considerable body of legal scholarship – doctrinal and theoretical – which has, in turn, built up out of it.

In a survey of judicial interpretations of dignity, Christopher McCrudden reviews cases about topics that include censorship, abortion, peepshows, sado-masochistic sex, so-called 'dwarf-throwing', unwanted life-saving treatments, fertility treatments and assisted suicide.[50] What was human dignity taken to mean in these cases, and is there a common conception of human dignity which emerges, either within a particular jurisdiction or transnationally? McCrudden explains that the various judicial interpretations do not make for any 'coherent judicially interpreted conception of dignity',[51] but they are consistent with an idea of dignity that has a certain 'basic minimum content', viz. the claim that 'every human being possesses an intrinsic worth, merely by being human', that

[50] Christopher McCrudden, 'Human Dignity and Judicial Interpretation of Human Rights', *European Journal of International Law* 19(4) (2008) 655.The book has a reproduction of Velázquez's painting *Las Meninas* (1656), depicting the Infanta Margarita attended by ladies-in-waiting and other court servants including two people with achondroplasia, on its cover. See also Christopher McCrudden, 'On Portraying Human Dignity', in Dieter Grimm et al. (eds.), *Human Dignity in Context* (Baden-Baden: Nomos, 2018), 25.

[51] McCrudden, 'Human Dignity and Judicial Interpretation of Human Rights', 724.

'this intrinsic worth should be recognized and respected by others', and that 'recognizing the intrinsic worth of the individual requires that the state should be seen to exist for the sake of the individual human being, and not vice versa'.[52] With that in mind, how ultimately should we understand dignity's significance in constitutional and human rights adjudication? Despite (or maybe because of) not providing precise content, McCrudden contends that the concept offers important 'institutional' orientation. In ways that he describes, it helps courts and tribunals to deal both with conflicts of rights and with local contingencies.

Recent decades have seen the publication of numerous essay collections devoted to the concept of dignity.[53] While each sets its own distinctive course, *Understanding Human Dignity*, edited by McCrudden, may illustrate something of the general enquiry.[54] With contributions from legal scholars, moral philosophers, theologians and historians of ideas, the book returns to the issue of a minimum core meaning of human dignity, and addresses a range of further and allied questions. What is the foundation of human dignity? Should dignity be assessed subjectively or objectively? Can a person's dignity be waived? How does the dignity of human beings relate to the dignity of nations and of institutions? Do animals and other nonhumans have dignity? A particular focus of many of the essays is on the relationship between human dignity and human rights. Are the International Covenant on Civil and Political Rights and the International Covenant on Economic, Social and Cultural

[52] Ibid., 679.

[53] See, for example, David Kretzmer and Eckhart Klein (eds.), *The Concept of Human Dignity in Human Rights Discourse* (The Hague: Kluwer Law International, 2002); Paulus Kaufmann et al. (eds.), *Humiliation, Degradation, Dehumanization: Human Dignity Violated* (Dordrecht: Springer, 2011); Christopher McCrudden (ed.), *Understanding Human Dignity* (Oxford: Oxford University Press, 2013); Marcus Düwell et al. (eds.), *The Cambridge Handbook of Human Dignity: Interdisciplinary Perspectives* (Cambridge: Cambridge University Press, 2014); Remy Debes (ed.), *Dignity: A History* (Oxford: Oxford University Press, 2017); Amos Nascimento and Matthias Lutz-Bachmann (eds.), *Human Dignity: Perspectives from a Critical Theory of Human Rights* (Abingdon: Routledge, 2018); and Austin Sarat (ed.), *Human Dignity* (Bingley: Emerald Publishing, 2022). Regarding the contribution of international law and international lawyers to the protection of human dignity, see also Andrea Gattini et al. (eds.), *Human Dignity and International Law* (Leiden: Brill Nijhoff, 2021) (giving particular attention to the intersection of human dignity and minority rights).

[54] McCrudden, *Understanding Human Dignity*.

Rights correct to say that human rights derive from human dignity? Is human dignity instead, or concurrently, an outcome of the protection of human rights? What does it mean to guarantee human dignity as a human right in itself? For some of the contributors, human rights not only do not derive from human dignity, but (for better or worse) they are at odds with human dignity, and whereas a variety of different reasons are given for that, one is that dignity is inseparable from ancient and medieval *dignitas.*[55]

It is perhaps an index of the rising prominence of the concept of dignity in constitutional and human rights law that a series of associated neologisms have come into use. Talk of 'dignitarian' jurisprudence, of varieties of 'dignitarianism', and of 'dignity rights', is today a familiar aspect of academic work in these fields (even if the words 'dignitarian' and 'dignitarianism' are so new that they do not yet appear in the Oxford English Dictionary). Thus, for example, Pablo Gilabert outlines what he calls a 'dignitarian approach to human rights', identifying the approach with a programme of 'normative dignitarianism', according to which 'at least some of the central norms concerning the treatment of individual entities depend on their inherent dignity'.[56] Gilabert links such an approach and such a programme to the larger project of 'putting humanity first'.[57] Erin Daly examines the scope and significance of dignity as a right under diverse systems of national constitutional law.[58] Rather than a singular 'right to dignity', she finds in the legal materials a multiplicity of 'dignity rights', encompassing a spectrum of 'interests [that includes] equality, expression, due process, privacy, health, family, work, and virtually every other sphere of life'.[59]

55 See, for example, Milbank, 'Dignity Rather than Rights'.

56 Pablo Gilabert, *Human Dignity and Human Rights* (Oxford: Oxford University Press, 2018), 191.

57 Ibid., 23–24. Regarding the place of human dignity within international law more generally, see Patrick Capps, *Human Dignity and the Foundations of International Law* (Oxford: Hart Publishing, 2009) (arguing that international law is normatively orientated towards respect for human dignity, and that states derive their legitimacy from protection of the dignity of their constituents).

58 Erin Daly, *Dignity Rights: Courts, Constitutions, and the Worth of the Human Person* (Philadelphia: University of Pennsylvania Press, 2012).See also James May and Erin Daly, *Advanced Introduction to Human Dignity and Law* (Cheltenham: Edward Elgar, 2020).

59 Daly, *Dignity Rights: Courts, Constitutions, and the Worth of the Human Person,* 6 (emphasis omitted).

With respect to these interests, Daly proposes that dignity 'reflects and protects the part of each person that is individual'.[60] Courts 'choose to invoke human dignity in order to say something about … what people are entitled to purely by virtue of being human'.[61]

An Upwards Equalisation

If dignity is invoked to say something about the entitlements which people have purely by virtue of being human, scholarly attention has turned to the question of how to make sense of this within the longer history of dignity. What has happened to status dignity? Contributing to a book about European and US constitutionalism, James Whitman emphasises that the ideas about human dignity which inform constitutional and human rights law today 'are the products of a long history'.[62] In Europe, 'elaborate and obnoxious rules' formerly ensured that 'high-status persons would be treated better than low-status persons'. '[W]hether the issue was punishment, privacy, or any other aspect of daily life, only high-status persons received respect and dignified treatment', and even '[w]ell into the twentieth century, only high-status Europeans could expect their dignity to be protected by the law'. Whitman remarks that 'it may seem a clumsy scholarly error to suppose that the old high-status forms of "dignity" bear any real relationship to the new "human" forms'. Yet he maintains that 'the old and new forms are intimately related': '"[h]uman dignity" … has been shaped by a rich and complex collective memory of the obnoxious past'. The 'core idea' is that 'the old forms of low-status treatment are no longer acceptable'. Everyone 'is now supposed to be possessed of a "dignity" protected by law'.[63]

The way Whitman puts this is to posit that the concept of intrinsic or human dignity has been 'formed by a pattern of levelling up, by

[60] Ibid., 8. [61] Ibid., 7.

[62] James Whitman, '"Human Dignity" in Europe and the United States: The Social Foundations', in Georg Nolte (ed.), *European and US Constitutionalism* (Cambridge: Cambridge University Press, 2005), 108, 110. See also James Whitman, 'On Nazi "Honor" and New European "Dignity"', in Christian Joerges and Navraj Singh Ghaleigh (eds.), *Darker Legacies of Law in Europe* (Oxford: Hart Publishing, 2003), 243.

[63] Whitman, '"Human Dignity" in Europe and the United States', 110.

an extension of formerly high-status treatment to all sectors of the population'.[64] That notion of levelling up recurs, and is further developed, in a study of the interconnections of dignity, rank and rights by Jeremy Waldron.[65] Committed as Waldron is to the modern conception of human dignity, he argues that analysis of dignity should nonetheless 'contrive to keep faith somehow with its ancient connection to noble rank or high office'.[66] A 'sea change in the way "dignity" is used' has assuredly occurred, 'enabling it to become a leading concept of universal rights (as opposed to special privileges)'.[67] But while '[i]t might be thought that the old connection of dignity and rank was superseded by a … notion of the dignity of humanity as such, and that this [latter] notion is really quite different in character', he again insists that this is not the case.[68] Rather than being 'obliterated', the 'resources of the older notion … are put to work in the new' one.[69] Specifically, 'the connotation of ranking status remained, and … what happened was that it was transvalued';[70] the high status of a few became the high status of everyone – a universal elevation.

In Waldron's widely quoted formulation, 'the modern notion of human dignity involves an upwards equalization of rank, so that we now try to accord to every human being something of the dignity, rank, and expectation of respect that was formerly accorded to nobility'.[71] Gregory Vlastos is a reference point for Waldron here.[72] From Vlastos, Waldron takes the thought that 'we organize ourselves not like a society without nobility and rank, but like an aristocratic society that has just one rank (and a pretty high rank at that) for all of us'. Expressed differently, 'we are not like a society that has eschewed all talk of caste; we are like a caste society with just one caste (and a very high caste at that). Every man a Brahmin.'

64 Ibid. (emphasis omitted).
65 Jeremy Waldron, *Dignity, Rank and Rights* (Oxford: Oxford University Press, 2012).
66 Ibid., 30. 67 Ibid., 33 (emphasis omitted). 68 Ibid., 31. 69 Ibid., 33.
70 Ibid., 31.
71 Ibid., 33 (emphasis omitted). On Waldron's account, see Stéphanie Hennette-Vauchez, 'A Human *Dignitas*? Remnants of the Ancient Legal Concept in Contemporary Dignity Jurisprudence', *International Journal of Constitutional Law* 9(1) (2011) 32, esp. 53–55 ('drawing from' and 'extending' his line of argument).
72 Gregory Vlastos, 'Justice and Equality', in Jeremy Waldron (ed.), *Theories of Rights* (Oxford: Oxford University Press, 1984), 41.

And again, '[e]very man a duke, every woman a queen, everyone entitled to the sort of deference and consideration, everyone's person and body sacrosanct, in the way that nobles were entitled to deference or in the way that an assault upon the body or the person of a king was regarded as a sacrilege'.[73] Waldron commends this analysis to our attention as a basis on which 'aspects of the traditional meaning of dignity associated with high or noble rank [might be used] to cast light on our conceptions of human rights', and with them, of human dignity.[74]

Arguments along somewhat similar lines are also advanced by other prominent theorists of law, the state, justice and human rights. As part of his exposition of the 'realistic utopia of human rights', Jürgen Habermas asks how we are to understand the seemingly 'paradoxical generalization of a concept of dignity that was originally geared not to any equal distribution of dignity but to status differences' linked to ranks in 'hierarchically ordered traditional societies'.[75] His answer is that '[w]hen these status-dependent dignities ... coalesce into the universal dignity of human beings, this new abstract dignity sheds the particular characteristics of a corporative ethos'. At the same time, however, the new abstract dignity 'retains the connotation of a self-respect that depends on social recognition'. It follows that human dignity still requires anchoring in a status that can confer social recognition, but now the status 'must be an equal one for everybody'.[76] Or rather, there is only one relevant social status: 'democratic citizenship'.[77] Democratic citizens protect their human dignity by 'establishing and maintaining a political order based on human rights'.[78] As Habermas sums up the position, 'the concept of human dignity transfers the content of a morality of [respect and recognition] to the status order of citizens who derive their self-respect

[73] Waldron, *Dignity, Rank and Rights*, 34. See further Vlastos, 'Justice and Equality', 54. Vlastos highlights a likeness between 'our society' and 'a caste society', save insofar as there is only 'first-class citizenship' in the former. He then writes: '[T]he fact that first-class citizenship, having been made common, is no longer a mark of distinction does not trivialize the privileges it entails. It is the simple truth, and not declamation, to speak of it as a "rank of dignity" in some ways comparable to that enjoyed by hereditary nobilities of the past.'

[74] Waldron, *Dignity, Rank and Rights*, 34.

[75] Jürgen Habermas, 'The Concept of Human Dignity and the Realistic Utopia of Human Rights', *Metaphilosophy* 41(4) (2010) 464, 471–72.

[76] Ibid., 472 (emphasis omitted). [77] Ibid., 475. [78] Ibid., 473.

from the fact that they are recognized by all other citizens as subjects of equal actionable rights'.[79]

Jack Donnelly describes the conceptual shift from status dignity to intrinsic dignity in different but again convergent terms that revolve around a distinction between two conceptions of human being – 'normative' and 'taxonomic'. He writes: 'A normative human being is a creature with certain qualities (e.g. virtue, reason, or a soul) that demand recognition and respect. A taxonomic human being is a creature with certain biological features (e.g. Aristotle's featherless biped).' Internationally recognised human rights are premised on the idea that 'these two classes are identical and that all taxonomic humans are normative humans (and vice versa)'. Yet '[h]istorically the class of taxonomic humans [was] much larger than that of normative humans – or [as those latter would have been called] men of dignity'. So there has been an 'expansion of the class of normative humans to include all taxonomic humans'. Donnelly wants us to register that this expansion is '[e]ven more radical than the idea that all human beings have equal and inalienable rights',[80] though he also wants us to keep in mind that the prospects for enjoyment of human rights are, to varying degrees, tied to citizenship. Rather like Habermas, Donnelly concludes that 'equal citizenship is the honorable status accorded to human dignity in the contemporary world'.[81]

I referred earlier to observations by Giorgio Agamben about ancient *dignitas* and the subsequent development of an interiorised concept of dignity. The context for those observations is his meditation on the testimonies of Holocaust survivors and the fate of dignity in conditions of bare life (or, as Donnelly might term it, taxonomic humanity), *Remnants of Auschwitz*.[82] For Agamben, '[t]he atrocious news that the survivors carry from the camp ... [is] that it is possible to lose dignity ..., that there is still life in the most extreme degradation. And this new knowledge now becomes the touchstone by which to judge and measure all morality and all

[79] Ibid., 472 (emphasis omitted). While setting out an argument that is broadly convergent with Waldron's, Habermas takes issue with some aspects of Waldron's account: see 473–74.

[80] Jack Donnelly, 'Normative Versus Taxonomic Humanity: Varieties of Human Dignity in the Western Tradition', *Journal of Human Rights* 14(1) (2015) 1, 2.

[81] Ibid., 13.

[82] Agamben, *Remnants of Auschwitz: The Witness and the Archive.*

dignity.'[83] That dignity may be best approached negatively, through scrutiny of circumstances in which people are deprived of it, is also the suggestion of Avishai Margalit.[84] In Margalit's influential account of the 'decent society', a decent society is one 'in which every person is accorded due honor', and 'the concept of honor that is relevant to the decent society is the concept of human dignity'.[85] In turn, human dignity is a matter of treating people with respect for their humanity, and we understand what that means 'basically through the negative sense of not treating humans as humans'.[86] Margalit identifies this 'negative sense' with humiliation. Thus, he affirms, a 'decent society is a nonhumiliating one'.[87]

Mixed with No Anthropology

Humanity and equality, respect and self-respect, recognition, non-humiliation, autonomy and honour – these are the leitmotifs of philosophical and legal engagement with dignity. No less recurrent across the literature is this narrative arc that moves from status dignities to intrinsic dignity, almost invariably pausing over Immanuel Kant along the way, whether the pause is long and detailed or more cursory. To round out our survey, it will be instructive to spend a little more time with that pivotal figure. I have quoted passages from his *Groundwork of the Metaphysics of Morals*. The idea of a metaphysics of morals which animates this text is, of course, the idea of a 'pure' moral philosophy, a moral philosophy that detaches itself from the sphere of empirical knowledge and relies entirely on *a priori* reasoning. '[A]ll moral

83 Ibid., 69.

84 See Avishai Margalit (Naomi Goldblum, trans.), *The Decent Society* (Cambridge, MA: Harvard University Press, 1996) and Avishai Margalit, 'Human Dignity between Kitsch and Deification', *The Hedgehog Review* (Fall, 2007) 7. For the claim that we understand dignity through analysis of humiliation, see Ute Frevert (Adam Bresnahan, trans.), *The Politics of Humiliation: A Modern History* (Oxford: Oxford University Press, 2020).

85 Margalit, *The Decent Society*, 41, 43–44.

86 Margalit, 'Human Dignity between Kitsch and Deification', 18. (Margalit's main argument in this text is that human dignity in the sense of 'moral honour' has its justification in pure humanity, and one should avoid alternative justifications that turn either on the pathos of potential victimhood ('kitsch'), or on the heroism of rationality and moral self-legislation ('deification').)

87 Margalit, *The Decent Society*, 41.

concepts have their seat and origin completely *a priori* in reason', he writes.[88] Kant explains that, seeing as 'moral laws are to hold for every rational being as such', it is necessary 'to derive them from the universal concept of a rational being as such'; it is necessary 'to set forth all moral science – which for its application to human beings needs anthropology – first independently as pure philosophy, i.e. metaphysics'.[89] Moral science corresponds, then, to the 'rational part' of ethics, and anthropology, to the 'empirical part'.[90] Kant is emphatic that an adequate explication of issues which include (as we have seen) human dignity has to remain 'completely isolated', 'mixed with no alien addition of empirical stimuli'. In particular, it must be 'mixed with no anthropology'.[91]

These references to anthropology are interesting because Kant was among the pioneers of that field. He taught a course on anthropology at the University of Königsberg annually from the 1772–73 academic year until his retirement in 1796. His *Anthropology from a Pragmatic Point of View*, published in 1798, is said to have had the largest first print run of any of his works. Well before all of this, he taught anthropology as part of a similarly pioneering course on geography. Kant began teaching geography in the 1756–57 academic year, and after introducing his stand-alone course on anthropology, he alternated between the two-lecture series, normally offering geography in the summer semester and anthropology in the winter semester. While he never produced a book on geography like his *Anthropology* text, the contents of his courses are known from surviving notes taken by students and other auditors. He also wrote a number of essays linked to his geography lectures, and arranged for the publication of an edited version of them, which appeared in 1802 under the title *Physical Geography*. Framed as issues of aesthetics, topics he covered were additionally addressed in his *Observations on the Feeling of the Beautiful and Sublime*, published in 1764.

Is there anything in these various writings which is relevant to, or at any rate worth bringing to bear upon, a discussion of human dignity? To read the contemporary philosophical and legal

[88] Kant, *Groundwork of the Metaphysics of Morals*, 25.
[89] Ibid., 26 (emphasis omitted). [90] Ibid., 4. [91] Ibid., 25.

literature on dignity, one would assume that there is not, as it makes no mention of them. However, investigations into Kant's anthropological and geographical thought, and into previously understudied aspects of *Observations on the Feeling of the Beautiful and Sublime,* may prompt us to wonder about that. It is hardly surprising that Kant's notions of anthropology and geography were different from our notions of them today. As he presents the two areas of study, they form a 'two-fold field' concerned with 'nature and the human being'. 'I call the first instruction [nature] physical geography . . ., the second one [the human being] I call anthropology', he writes in an essay announcing the courses in 1775.[92] On the other hand, since the human being is part of nature, Kant's geography was also concerned with human beings. Mindful of an eighteenth-century spatial trope, some scholars have suggested that, according to his way of thinking, geography had to do with the 'outer' or 'external' nature of human beings – their physical characteristics and (to use a much later term) environmental situation – and anthropology, with 'inner' or 'internal' aspects – the psychological and moral life of human beings.[93] Other scholars are less convinced of this.[94] Either way, Kant goes on to say that both fields 'must be considered cosmologically', that is, 'with respect to . . . the relation as a whole in which they stand and in which everyone takes his place'.[95] How is such an enquiry to proceed?

One of the more famous biographical facts about Kant is that he never left Prussia, and remaining closer to home still, almost never left his native city of Königsberg – today's Kaliningrad. By all accounts, he was, however, a voracious reader of travel literature, and, as an inhabitant of a bustling Baltic seaport, he was also well placed to pick up the stories of sailors, merchants, missionaries, explorers and adventurers, which, in his time, were a prime source

92 'Of the Different Races of Human Beings', in Immanuel Kant (Günter Zöller and Robert Louden, eds.), *Anthropology, History, and Education* (Cambridge: Cambridge University Press, 2007), 84, 97 (emphasis omitted).

93 See, for example, Emmanuel Chukwudi Eze, 'The Color of Reason: The Idea of "Race" in Kant's Anthropology', *The Bucknell Review* 38(2) (1995) 200, 202–3.

94 See Robert Louden '"The Play of Nature": Human Beings in Kant's *Geography*', in Stuart Elden and Eduardo Mendieta (eds.), *Reading Kant's Geography* (Albany, NY: State University of New York Press, 2011), 139, esp. 145–46.

95 'Of the Different Races of Human Beings', 97 (emphasis omitted).

of information in Europe about distant lands. Thomas McCarthy observes that Kant repeatedly warned his students about the unreliability of sources of that kind. Yet, as McCarthy further observes, 'rely on them [Kant] did', recycling in the process 'the racist commonplaces of the age'.[96] Thus, to give just a couple of examples, we read in *Observations on the Feeling of the Beautiful and Sublime* that the 'Negroes of Africa have by nature no feeling that rises above the ridiculous', and that 'the difference between [Negroes and white people] . . . seems to be just as great with regard to the capacities of mind as it is with respect to color'.[97] In a later essay, the native Americans are put before us as a 'race, which is too weak for hard labor, too indifferent for industry and incapable of any culture – although there is enough of it as example and encouragement nearby – [a race which] ranks still far below even the Negro, who stands on the lowest of all the other steps that we have named as differences of the races'.[98]

But Kant's contribution to sustaining racial hierarchies was not simply a matter of recycling racist commonplaces. For Kant was an early and highly influential *theorist* of race. One of the 'central figures in the birth of modern "scientific" racism',[99] he provided an account thanks to which (and this is where McCarthy's observations ultimately lead) 'these commonplaces were naturalized through being biologized'.[100] Indeed, the argument has been made that it is Kant who should be regarded as the 'inventor' of the concept of race, in the sense of the one who 'gave the concept sufficient definition for subsequent users to believe that they were addressing something [the] scientific status [of which] could at

[96] Thomas McCarthy, *Race, Empire, and the Idea of Human Development* (Cambridge: Cambridge University Press, 2009), 49. See also David Harvey, 'Cosmopolitanism and the Banality of Geographical Evils', *Public Culture* 12(2) (2000) 529, esp. 533.

[97] 'Observations on the Feeling of the Beautiful and Sublime', in Immanuel Kant (Günter Zöller and Robert Louden, eds.), *Anthropology, History, and Education* (Cambridge: Cambridge University Press, 2007), 23, 59. (David Hume is quoted in the passage of which this is a part.)

[98] 'On the Use of Teleological Principles in Philosophy', in Immanuel Kant (Günter Zöller and Robert Louden, eds.), *Anthropology, History, and Education* (Cambridge: Cambridge University Press, 2007), 195, 211.

[99] Charles Mills, *Black Rights/White Wrongs: The Critique of Racial Liberalism* (Oxford: Oxford University Press, 2017), 95.

[100] See McCarthy, *Race, Empire, and the Idea of Human Development*, 49.

least be debated' – the one who secured the concept's 'status and influence',[101] initiating the idea 'that the question of race should be put upon a . . . scientific footing'[102] and producing the first 'theory of race worthy of the name'.[103] Kant's thinking about race[104] was informed by the classificatory work of Carl Linnaeus and the Comte de Buffon, as well as by writings on physiology, anthropology and craniometry of the younger Johann Friedrich Blumenbach, who himself, in turn, drew on work by Kant. Kant's thinking about race also developed in response to criticisms by his student Johann Gottfried Herder, and by Georg Forster, whose perspective was grounded in the experience of accompanying James Cook on the latter's second voyage to the South Pacific in 1772–75.

[101] Robert Bernasconi, 'Who Invented the Concept of Race? Kant's Role in the Enlightenment Construction of Race', in Robert Bernasconi (ed.), *Race* (Oxford: Blackwell, 2001), 11.

[102] David Harvey, 'Cosmopolitanism in the *Anthropology* and *Geography*', in Stuart Elden and Eduardo Mendieta (eds.), *Reading Kant's Geography* (Albany, NY: State University of New York Press, 2011), 267, 274.

[103] Bernasconi, 'Who Invented the Concept of Race?', 11, 14. See also, for example, Eze, 'The Color of Reason'; Tsenay Serequeberhan, 'Eurocentrism in Philosophy: The Case of Immanuel Kant', *The Philosophical Forum* 27(4) (1996) 333; Mark Larrimore, 'Sublime Waste: Kant on the Destiny of the "Races"', *Canadian Journal of Philosophy*, Supplementary vol. 25 (1999) 99, and 'Antinomies of Race: Diversity and Destiny in Kant', *Patterns of Prejudice* 42(4–5) (2008) 341; McCarthy, *Race, Empire, and the Idea of Human Development*, chap. 2; Wulf Hund, '"It Must Come From Europe": The Racisms of Immanuel Kant', in Wulf Hund et al. (eds.), *Racisms Made in Germany* (Racism Analysis Series B: Yearbook, vol. 2) (Berlin and Vienna: LIT Verlag, 2011), 69; *Mills, Black Rights/White Wrongs*, chap. 6; Norman Ajari (Matthew Smith, trans.), *Dignity or Death: Ethics and Politics of Race* (Cambridge: Polity Press, 2019), esp. 27–30; and Kehinde Andrews, *The New Age of Empire: How Racism and Colonialism Still Rule the World* (London: Penguin Books, 2021), esp. 2–7.

[104] The question of whether Kant changed his mind about race in the final decade of his life – he lived to be 79 – has provoked considerable debate. For the claim that he did, see Pauline Kleingeld, 'Kant's Second Thoughts about Race', in Katrin Flikshuh and Lea Ypi (eds.), *Kant and Colonialism* (Oxford: Oxford University Press, 2014), 43. For a refutation of that claim, see Robert Bernasconi, 'Kant's Third Thoughts on Race', in Stuart Elden and Eduardo Mendieta (eds.), *Reading Kant's Geography* (Albany, NY: State University of New York Press, 2011), 291. For the claim that it was not only the case that Kant did not lose interest in race or repent of what he had said about it, but that his 'view of race' actually 'took flight', gained 'philosophical traction', and 'came into its own' in the final decade of his life, see Larrimore, 'Antinomies of Race', 351, 357–58.

In his early discussions of human variety, Kant dwells mostly on differences of temperament, understood along the lines of the medieval theory of 'humours'.[105] His turn to racial theorising seems to have been, at least in part, an effort to defend the idea of monogenesis – the idea that, as depicted in the Creation story, humanity has a single origin – against the polygeneticist (multiple origin) claims that had been advanced by Voltaire, Lord Kames, and others. I have referred to the essay which Kant wrote in 1775 announcing his lectures in the coming academic year on physical geography and anthropology. The title under which that announcement was published is *Of the Different Races of Human Beings*. It has been pointed out that, in Kant's time, a specific word for race – *Rasse* – had only relatively recently entered the German language, and was initially used mostly in relation to animal breeding.[106] That is helpful to know because the propagation of animal species is his starting-point in this essay. Kant writes that, just as there exist distinct species of animals, so too 'all human beings on the wide earth belong to one and same natural species'. And just as animal species exhibit variations of diverse kinds, including variations that 'persistently preserve themselves in all transplantings . . . over prolonged generations . . . which . . . are called races', the same applies to human beings.[107] The bulk of the essay is then devoted to examining the causes and consequences of the division of the human species into different races.

Kant writes that there are four races, distinguished here and throughout his subsequent writing by reference to skin colours, which he identifies as 'white', 'red', 'black' and 'yellow'.[108] His explanation for how these races arose goes something like this.[109] As it was the destiny of human beings to people the whole earth, they had to be made suitable, *in potentia*, for living in 'all climates and . . . every soil'.[110] To enable this, they were implanted with a set

[105] That is, choleric, melancholic, phlegmatic and sanguine. See, for example, 'Observations on the Feeling of the Beautiful and Sublime', 23, esp. 32.

[106] See Larrimore, 'Sublime Waste', 101, and Larrimore, 'Antinomies of Race', 343–44.

[107] 'Of the Different Races of Human Beings', 84–85.

[108] See, for example, ibid., 95.

[109] See ibid., 89. The theory is reiterated in, for example, 'On the Use of Teleological Principles in Philosophy', 208.

[110] 'Of the Different Races of Human Beings', 90.

of seeds (*Keime*, sometimes translated as 'germs'), each containing different natural characteristics (*Anlagen*, sometimes translated as 'dispositions'). In different climatic conditions, the seeds appropriate to that particular climate became activated, and with that, the natural characteristics corresponding to those seeds developed. These processes happened at some point in the remote past, and they were permanent. Even where further migration occurred, the activation of one set of seeds blocked the further activation of another set of seeds. The four races are a reflection of the fixed natural characteristics that thereby came into existence, and Kant portrays the natural characteristics as bringing with them a fixed and differentiated set of capacities and prospects. Such is the differentiation that the races stand with respect to one another in rank order of 'perfectibility'. In one notorious passage, Kant raises the question of why the inhabitants of Tahiti 'in their tranquil indolence ... exist at all, and whether it would have been just as good to have this island populated with happy sheep and cattle'.[111] In another text, he expresses a belief that all except the white race will eventually 'be extinguished'.[112]

How Cherished an Icon

Although (as in the passage I just quoted) Kant refers to one of the four races as white, Mark Larrimore points out that he always portrayed white people as not just superior to, but qualitatively different from, the other three races. Whites, as Kant depicted them, were 'distinguished from the [other races] as balance is from imbalance',[113] and it is Larrimore's argument that, in inventing race, Kant also 'invented "whiteness" as an escape from [race]', the 'summation and circumvention of race' – a race that was simultaneously 'beyond race'.[114] Kant's Königsberg students would come to learn that a unique and highly consequential place had been assigned to them; '[p]repared for transplantation anywhere,

[111] 'Review of J.G. Herder's *Ideas for the Philosophy of the History of Humanity* Parts 1 and 2', in Immanuel Kant (Günter Zöller and Robert Louden, eds.), *Anthropology, History, and Education* (Cambridge: Cambridge University Press, 2007), 124, 142.

[112] Note 1520 of *Reflexionen zur Anthropologie*, quoted in Robert Bernasconi, 'Will the Real Kant Please Stand Up?', *Radical Philosophy* 117 (2003) 13.

[113] Larrimore, 'Antinomies of Race', 362. [114] Ibid., 350.

they must and could make something of themselves'.[115] This message indeed aligns with Kant's pitch in *Of the Different Races of Human Beings*, where the instruction on offer is commended as 'knowledge of the world'. By that, Kant says he means a kind of knowledge which 'serves to procure the pragmatic element for all otherwise acquired sciences and skills', and hence to furnish the means by which all other knowledge becomes 'useful not merely for the school but . . . for life'. Those taking his course in geography, along with his linked course in anthropology, would be equipped with the intellectual resources needed in order that 'the accomplished apprentice' may go out into the world, including the wider world beyond Europe, and be 'introduced to the stage of his destiny'.[116]

And if this knowledge to be imparted is pragmatic, Kant emphasises that it is also, importantly, theoretical, in the sense of explanatory. For the mere 'description of nature . . . is far from sufficient to indicate the ground for the manifold variations' that characterise humanity, so central to knowledge of the world. Rather, explanatory theory – 'natural history', in the terminology of his time – is required. The account of race to be laid out in his courses comes from an awareness that 'one must venture a history of nature, which is a separate science and which could gradually advance from opinions to insights'.[117] Kant's pseudo-science of race would, of course, take off in the succeeding century, even if his seed theory would be displaced by versions of the social Darwinism more familiar to us today.[118] Rather later, when the history of ideas about dignity came to be written, we have seen that his work on the metaphysics of morals would assume groundbreaking significance in the development of a conception of human dignity. What now comes into focus is the way this body of scholarship repeats and reenacts Kant's gesture of 'completely isolating' his work on dignity and related matters, and refraining from the 'alien addition of empirical stimuli'.

As another of Kant's phrases might have it, these writers 'mix' their analyses of dignity with 'no anthropology'. To mix analysis

115 Ibid.

116 'Of the Different Races of Human Beings', 97 (emphasis omitted).

117 Ibid. (emphasis omitted). On the 'scientific, providential and pragmatic significance' of the concept of race, see Larrimore, 'Antinomies of Race', 342.

118 On this, see Chapter 3.

with no anthropology is to abstract it from social realities. Thus, philosophers and legal scholars set aside the actual conditions of the world, with its inequalities, hierarchies and practices of domination, to declare the emergence of a 'new abstract dignity', an 'intrinsic dignity' realised in equal citizenship and counterposed to all heteronomy. They report on the 'interiorisation' of status dignities, and on the 'coalescence of status-dependent dignities' into the 'universal dignity of human beings'. They describe a dynamic of 'levelling up', and celebrate a conceptual 'expansion', 'transfer' or 'transvaluation' that has brought about an 'upwards equalization of rank' somehow present in its patent absence. Moreover, in doing so, they set aside not only their own 'anthropologies', but also Kant's. Writing in 2021, Kehinde Andrews remarks that '[i]n the history of European thought we are presented with all the positive aspects of the sainted philosophers and none of the negative', and '[t]here is perhaps no better example of this Whitewashing of the record than Immanuel Kant'. Andrews continues: 'I never realized how cherished an icon Kant was until I pointed out he was a racist on television.'[119]

Already in the 1990s, Emmanuel Chukwudi Eze and Tsenay Serequeberhan called the attention of English-speaking readers to Kant's relatively neglected work on anthropology and geography and, within that, his raciological thought. For Eze, the 'interrelatedness of geography and anthropology and moral philosophy is evident throughout Kant's lectures'.[120] Kant's moral philosophy 'presupposes' his geography and anthropology, so that far from being 'peripheral' to his critical philosophy, his writing about race is fundamental to it.[121] As thematised in the *Groundwork* and other texts, 'the "essence" of humanity, that which one ought to become in order to deserve human dignity', is a quality possessed by the 'white race' alone. It follows that the 'so-called primitives surely ought to be leary of such Kantian "universalist-humanoid abstraction", which colonizes humanity' and belongs with the ideology of

[119] Andrews, *The New Age of Empire*, 2. For the claim that Kant is being 'scapegoated' by those whose 'single-minded focus [is] on one major Enlightenment figure', see Katrin Flikshuh and Lea Ypi, 'Introduction: Kant on Colonialism – Apologist or Critic', in Katrin Flikshuh and Lea Ypi (eds.), *Kant and Colonialism* (Oxford: Oxford University Press, 2014), 1, 2. See also other essays in the same volume for a defence of Kant in this context.

[120] Eze, 'The Color of Reason', 204–5. [121] Ibid., 205.

European empires.[122] Serequeberhan likewise rejects the idea that Kant's racial theorising can be excised from his wider theorising, as an 'indiscretion' unworthy of notice.[123] Analysts may choose not to ask 'whose humanity is at stake' in Kant's philosophical writings, but his anthropological and geographical writings, along with *Observations on the Feeling of the Beautiful and Sublime*, make 'the answer to [that question] ... rather simple and straightforward'.[124] On the other hand, as Charles Mills emphasises in more recent work on Kant, the thinking behind this was itself not at all simple and straightforward: 'we are not ... talking about a mere "empirical" belief but a sophisticated and elaborated theoretical position'.[125] Kant's 'view of personhood' was shaped by a theory of race that involved ambitious causal and providential claims.[126]

Neither Mills nor any of the other authors on whose work I have just touched finally resolves the matter of how Kant's raciology relates to his conception of dignity. Yet if the person who 'should stand at the centre of any historical account of dignity' is also one of the people – or even *the* person – who should stand at the centre of any historical account of race, then the question of what these two histories have to do with one another cannot be easily dismissed. Perhaps, as some contend, 'race science did not have to build bridges to the human sciences [and] philosophy', inasmuch as 'it was in large part constituted by them'.[127] Perhaps, as is again contended, the 'nobility of Kant's ... ethical vision' only makes sense when it is tempered by recognition of the 'banality of his ... geographical knowledges'.[128] To read the great philosopher's writings about dignity without reference to his profoundly and fatefully inegalitarian account of human diversity is to forestall consideration of the 'normative violence of his discourse'.[129]

[122] Ibid., 232. [123] Serequeberhan, 'Eurocentrism in Philosophy', 333, 334.
[124] Ibid., 339. [125] Mills, *Black Rights/White Wrongs*, 104–5 (emphasis omitted).
[126] Ibid., 91.
[127] Sara Eigen and Mark Larrimore, 'Introduction', in Sara Eigen and Mark Larrimore (eds.), *The German Invention of Race* (Albany, NY: State University of New York Press, 2006), 1, 7. On this, see also Todd Hedrick, 'Race, Difference, and Anthropology in Kant's Cosmopolitanism', *Journal of the History of Philosophy* 46(2) (2008) 245, esp. 267–68.
[128] Harvey, 'Cosmopolitanism and the Banality of Geographical Evils', 529, 536.
[129] Nikita Dhawan, 'The Canary Who Sings in a Predictable Monotone: Kant and Colonialism', *Postcolonial Studies* 22(2) (2019) 257, 259.

Larrimore warns that it might prove impossible to uproot the ideology of race which Kant helped legitimate without both 'tracing its connections to [his metaphysics of morals] and providing pragmatic as well as theoretical counter-knowledge'.[130] In the spirit of providing such counter-knowledge, let us now begin the exploration of what a different telling of the history of dignity might involve.

130 Larrimore, 'Antinomies of Race', 362–63; see also 361: 'Immanuel Kant was not singlehandedly responsible for the spread of the ideology of race, but his work giving scientific and philosophical cachet to this term with roots in the world of breeding was indispensable.'

3

Regarding Trucanini's Dignity

The 'Last of the Tasmanians'

Our story begins in colonial Australia with a photograph taken in 1866 (Figure 3.1). The photograph was taken in Hobart, the city that was to become the state capital of Tasmania, and it depicts a woman of the Nuenonne people named Trucanini.[1] Born and raised south of Hobart on Bruny Island (Alonna-Lunawanna, in the language of the Nuenonne), and around fifty-four at the time of this photograph, Trucanini is shown facing the camera, against a blank background, with only her head and shoulders in view. She wears a buttoned cloth jacket and a shell necklace of a kind traditional among her people.

The occasion for the photograph was that year's Melbourne Intercolonial Exhibition. Charles Woolley, a professional photographer with a studio in Hobart, had been commissioned to take a series of photographs of Tasmanian Aboriginal people for the exhibition, and Trucanini was one of his sitters. After the exhibition, the photographs he made for it, and especially this and other photographs of Trucanini, circulated widely. They were sold as card-sized prints, they appeared in albums and books, and they

[1] Trucanini's name has been transcribed in a variety of ways. (See further below.) The spelling I use is based on advice given by Gregory Lehman and on the following text which Professor Lehman considers relatively reliable in this respect: John Woodcock Graves, 'Trucanini's Story of Herself', *The Mercury*, 6 June 1876, 3. I am immensely grateful to Professor Lehman for his advice on this and other questions of Tasmanian Aboriginal referencing practice relevant to the present chapter.

Figure 3.1 Truganini, 1866. Photograph by Charles Woolley.

found their way into museum collections, both in Australia and elsewhere. I first came across the photograph in a publication of the Pitt Rivers Museum in Oxford, which acquired it in 1895.[2]

A major part of the reason why Woolley's photographs of Trucanini achieved such success is that she was said to be the 'last of the Tasmanians'. When she died ten years after this photograph was taken, her death was said to mark the extinction of Tasmanian Aboriginal people. That claim is today falsified by the existence of

[2] Elizabeth Edwards and Lynne Williamson, *World on a Glass Plate: Early Anthropological Photographs from the Pitt Rivers Museum, Oxford* (Oxford: Pitt Rivers Museum, 1981), 38.

a large and flourishing Indigenous community in Tasmania. Yet in the nineteenth century and for much of the twentieth century, extinction discourse, as it has been termed, had substantial currency as the idiom for discussions and representations of Indigenous peoples. And to purveyors of extinction discourse, Tasmania presented a notable instance of what they called a dying race actually becoming extinct, with Trucanini as the unfortunates' final survivor and the eventual symbol of their collective demise.

Trucanini's countenance in the photograph to which I have referred has been seen in this light. We read of her 'haunting stare'[3] and 'piercing gaze',[4] and of the 'tragic' look in her 'expressive' eyes.[5] For one commentator, this is a 'portrait of an elderly woman in despair'.[6] Several others remark that the vignette form in which it was originally printed – the form that blurs or darkens the image at its periphery – serves 'to isolate and dissolve the portrait into the surrounding emptiness',[7] and communicate the message that 'the Aborigines were literally fading out'.[8] Even so, we are invited to consider that, '[a]lthough [Trucanini's] face is deeply etched, she wears the lines without regret, [and] without disdain'.[9] Her 'stoic and level'[10] regard is held to evince 'pathos and dignity'.[11]

What is it to be a dignified sitter for such a photograph? This chapter takes up the question of dignity in the context of Woolley's and other images of the period and the discourses that informed

[3] James Ryan, *Picturing Empire: Photography and the Visualization of the British Empire* (London: Reaktion Books, 1997), 142.

[4] Andrys Onsman, 'Trucanini's Funeral', *Island* 96 (2004) 39, 50.

[5] Vivienne Rae-Ellis, 'The Representation of Trucanini', in Elizabeth Edwards (ed.), *Anthropology and Photography 1860–1920* (New Haven and London: Yale University Press, 1992), 230, 233.

[6] Ibid., 233. [7] Ryan, *Picturing Empire,* 142.

[8] Anne Maxwell, *Colonial Photography and Exhibitions* (London and New York: Leicester University Press, 1999), 138. See also Leigh Astbury, 'Constructing the Other: Race and Representation', in Blair French (ed.), *Photo Files: An Australian Photography Reader* (Sydney: Power Publications and Australian Centre for Photography, 1999), 183, 187.

[9] Onsman, 'Trucanini's Funeral', 50.

[10] Judy Annear, *The Photograph and Australia* (Sydney: Art Gallery of NSW, 2015), 47.

[11] Margaret Maynard, 'Review of Anne Maxwell, Colonial Photography and Exhibitions', *Journal of Australian Studies* 61 (1999) 202, 203.

them.[12] And since a photograph is not only a visual representation to be scrutinised and interpreted, but also a material object, our investigation will follow the pictures that interest us from their production to their subsequent passages across time and space. In order to maintain focus, we will stay with Trucanini. If the photographs that were taken of her were meant to capture an end, they can equally initiate enquiry into the mutual determinations of colonial photography, Victorian race theory and ideas about dignified life.

Epitome of the Noble Savage

The earliest extant photographs of Indigenous Australians are believed to be a set of daguerreotypes of members of the Kulin nation – the First Nation of the area around Melbourne – made in 1846 and 1847,[13] along with a daguerreotype of three Tasmanian Aboriginal people made in 1847 or 1848.[14] These photographs were taken in studio settings, often with props such as spears, and they show their subjects wearing tribal dress. Or rather, as Julie Gough explains with reference to the Tasmanian image, they show their subjects wearing 'pseudo-tribal' dress at a time when European clothing would already have been more normal.[15] The studio settings were a requirement of the photographic technology that was used, but the props and dress seem to have reflected pictorial codes for the representation of Indigenous peoples that were carried over from painting, drawing, engraving and sculpture.[16] Before turning to later photographs where Trucanini is the subject or among the subjects, let us touch on some portraits of her made in other media which will serve to illustrate this.

[12] On the dignity of Indigenous people in colonial Australia, see also Shane Chalmers, 'Native Dignity', *Griffith Law Review* 29(2) (2020) 175. On Chalmers's work, see Chapter 6.

[13] See Jane Lydon, 'Photographing Kooris: Photography and Exchange in Victoria', in Jane Lydon (ed.), *Calling the Shots: Aboriginal Photographies* (Canberra: Aboriginal Studies Press, 2014), 103, esp. 107.

[14] See Julie Gough, 'Forgotten Lives – The First Photographs of Tasmanian Aboriginal People', in Jane Lydon (ed.), *Calling the Shots: Aboriginal Photographies* (Canberra: Aboriginal Studies Press, 2014), 20, esp. 23–24. The three subjects are Walter George Arthur, Maryann Bruny and David Bruny.

[15] Ibid., 21, 32.

[16] See Helen Ennis, *Photography and Australia* (London: Reaktion Books, 2007), 18.

Figure 3.2 Benjamin Duterrau, *The Conciliation*, 1840. Oil on canvas. Tasmanian Museum and Art Gallery.

Benjamin Duterrau's *The Conciliation*, dating from 1840, is perhaps the best-known Tasmanian painting of the era (Figure 3.2).[17] A preliminary study for a larger work entitled *The National Picture* (now lost), it commemorates an important episode in the colony's history that had recently occurred. After a decade of war between British settlers and First Nations – the so-called 'Black War' – the governor of the colony had appointed George Augustus Robinson to 'conciliate' the members of the First Nations. Robinson had gained relevant experience on Bruny Island, and his appointment led to an extensive, multi-year journey undertaken with the aim of persuading the Indigenous peoples of Tasmania – or Van Diemen's Land, as the colonists then called it – to give up armed resistance in exchange for official protection and temporary exile on Flinders Island in Bass Strait, north-east of the Tasmanian mainland.[18]

[17] See Greg Lehman, 'Benjamin Duterrau: The Art of Conciliation', *Journal of War and Culture Studies* 8(2) (2015) 109.

[18] Robinson documented his 'friendly mission', as he termed it, in a detailed journal. See N. J. B. Plomley, *Friendly Mission: The Tasmanian Journals and*

While some of those living in mainland Tasmania and on other islands in Bass Strait did not succumb, Robinson's mission led to the displacement of most Tasmanian Aboriginal people to Flinders Island. To help him in this work, he enlisted as interpreters, guides and co-negotiators a number of Aboriginal people he had come to know on Bruny Island, among them Trucanini. *The Conciliation* celebrates Robinson as the 'pacifier' of Tasmanian Aborigines and the saviour of Van Diemen's Land. Inspired by the tradition of great European history paintings, the work depicts fifteen Aboriginal people arranged around Robinson on a grassy slope, with three dogs and a wallaby in the foreground. Trucanini and the others from Bruny Island who accompanied him on his journey can be seen in the background of the picture, watching a tense encounter believed to have involved members of the Big River nation from central Tasmania.[19]

Around five years before he painted *The Conciliation*, Duterrau made one of the first representations we have of Trucanini (Figure 3.3). It's an etching that shows a young woman standing in a vaguely sketched outdoor landscape. She has a round face, close-cropped hair, and strong legs planted firmly on the ground. Her arms are folded across her waist, and she wears a kangaroo skin draped around her body in a way that leaves her breasts partly exposed. Around her neck are four strands of maireener shells – the distinctive and often iridescent spiral-shaped shells of a sea snail native to the waters of southern Australia that have long been used to form women's jewellery in Tasmania. She looks forward, her gaze directed straight at the viewer, and though we do not see much of her facial features, which are left largely undefined, her expression is made clear by a pleasant smile.

This rudimentary picture of a contented innocent is, and in those years was, often contrasted with another work made in the early-mid 1830s, a watercolour portrait of Trucanini by Thomas Bock

Papers of George Augustus Robinson 1829–1834 (Hobart: Queen Victoria Museum and Art Gallery, Launceston, and Quintus Publishing, 2008). For recent discussion of this text, see also Anna Johnston and Mitchell Rolls (eds.), *Reading Robinson: Companion Essays to George Augustus Robinson's Friendly Mission* (Melbourne: Monash University Publishing, 2012).

19 Earlier commentary that identified Trucanini with a figure in the foreground of the picture is now considered to be mistaken.

Figure 3.3 Benjamin Duterrau, *Truggernana*, 1835. Etching on paper.

(Figure 3.4).[20] Here Trucanini is rendered in considerable detail, and with a pose that does not suggest contentment, but instead anxiety or at any rate disquiet. She again wears a maireener shell necklace, along with a fibre neck ornament, and has exposed

[20] Bock's portraits of Trucanini and another woman named Wutapuwitja have been re-identified to correct an earlier confusion. See curator's comments at www.britishmuseum.org/collection/object/E_Oc2006-Drg-56 and www.britishmuseum.org/collection/object/E_Oc2006-Drg-58.

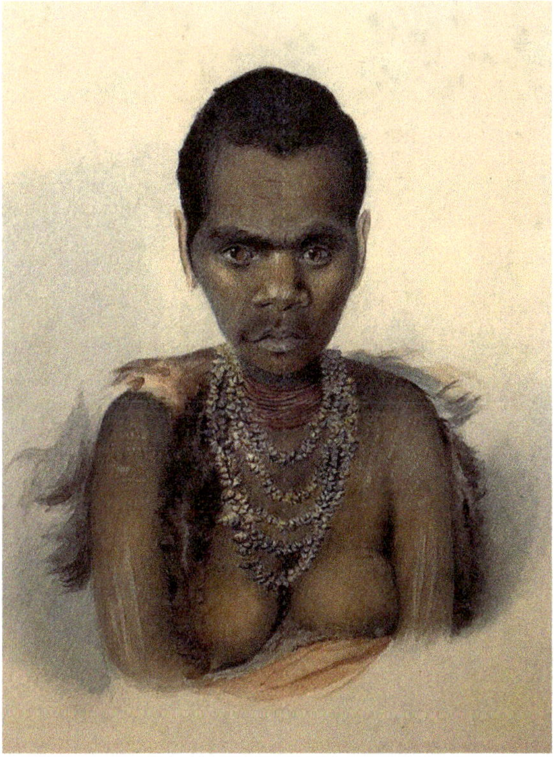

Figure 3.4 Thomas Bock, *Truganini*, 1831. (Previously identified as Wutapuwitja.) Drawing, graphite and watercolour.

breasts and signs of scarification on her arms. Tufts of kangaroo fur around her shoulders again lead us to imagine a skin cloak. Yet she has a smaller frame than in Duterrau's picture. She seems less sturdy and more vulnerable, and rather than looking ahead, her eyes do not meet the viewer's gaze. She is evidently preoccupied, and her brow is furrowed.

Trucanini's association with Robinson brought her to the attention of a number of artists seeking to prove their skill and generate commissions in colonial Hobart. A further work of this time which is standardly bracketed with the two I have just described is a nearly contemporaneous portrait bust by Benjamin Law (Figure 3.5). Law made portrait busts of both Trucanini and her husband, whom Robinson appears to have considered his leading Aboriginal guide,

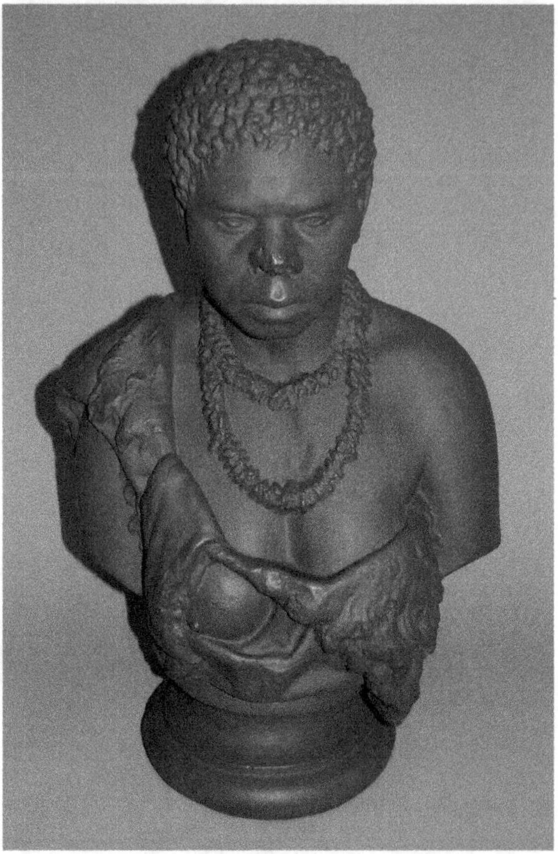

Figure 3.5 Benjamin Law, *Trucaninny, wife of Woureddy*, 1835. Plaster bust. The Trustees of the British Museum

Wooredy. Imbuing the pair with a classical gravity, the sculptures depict Wooredy as resolute and proud, while, following convention, the face of the female figure is assigned to bear the imprint of suffering and sorrow.[21] Each is shown wearing an animal skin and a neck ornament – in Trucanini's case, another maireener necklace. In Wooredy's case, Robinson informed his contemporaries that '[t]he drapery is in imitation of the kangaroo skin worn by

[21] On this, see Gareth Knapman, 'The Art of Conciliation' (2017), available at: www.portrait.gov.au/magazines/57/the-art-of-conciliation.

the aborigines in their primitive state', and the 'necklace is also aboriginal and is made of the sinews of the kangaroo tail'.[22]

Returning to the question of pictorial codes, it is plain that, despite their differences, these works by Duterrau, Bock and Law predicated and developed a shared visual language for the representation of Tasmanian Aboriginal people. Tribal garments, exotic jewellery and semi-nakedness are clearly part of this. So too is the unaffected simplicity and mode of life in harmony with nature evoked in Duterrau's etching. And whereas his smiling Trucanini evades the brutal realities of invasion and resistance, also part of the shared visual language is the sense we get from the more refined works of Bock and Law that Wooredy was a worthy adversary in war, and that, as the embodiment of the vanquished, Trucanini deserved compassion. Dispossession is tinged with pathos in these men's portraits of Trucanini, which commemorate the 'saving' of Van Diemen's Land in a manner that registers also loss.

What is this language that informs and is informed by these works? For Lyndall Ryan, Bock represented Trucanini as the 'epitome of the "noble savage", a primitive with a "noble countenance"'.[23] Elizabeth Edwards also writes of the representation by Bock of 'gentle noble savages'.[24] At the same time, Tim Bonyhady notes the relevance of the noble savage to the work of Duterrau and Law, arguing that 'Law's neo-classical busts', in particular, 'amply demonstrate that [the idea of] the noble savage flourished in Tasmania in the 1830s … as the Black War was being won', and the men and women 'conciliated' by Robinson were being removed

[22] Quoted in N. J. B. Plomley, 'Thomas Bock's Portraits of the Tasmanian Aborigines', in Dianne Dunbar (ed.), *Thomas Bock, Convict Engraver, Society Portraitist* (Launceston: Queen Victoria Museum and Art Gallery, 1991), 16.

[23] Lyndall Ryan, 'The Struggle for Trukanini 1830–1997', *Tasmanian Historical Research Association: Papers and Proceedings* (1997) 153, 155 (partly quoting Plomley, 'Thomas Bock's Portraits of the Tasmanian Aborigines'). Note that the work to which Ryan refers has subsequently been identified as a portrait of Wutapuwitja, not Trucanini (see n 20). For the purposes of a consideration of pictorial codes for the representation of Tasmanian Aborigines, however, this work is also relevant, and we may reasonably infer that Ryan's assessment would have applied equally to the portrait of Trucanini.

[24] Elizabeth Edwards, 'Evolving Images: Photography, Race and Popular Darwinism', in Diana Donald and Jane Munro (eds.), *Endless Forms: Charles Darwin, Natural Science, and the Visual Arts* (New Haven/London: Yale University Press, 2009), 166, 185.

to Flinders Island.[25] Mark McKenna likewise remarks that there is 'dignity and pride' in Law's works.[26] If so, the thrust of these scholars' commentaries is that what is being depicted is the distinctive dignity of the noble savage – the 'dignified bearing with an air of freedom' which, to contemporaries, made for a contrast with 'low class Europeans'.[27]

The concept of the noble savage has a long and complicated history. Ter Ellingson traces the idea to Marc Lescarbot, the French lawyer and author remembered for his participation in a colonial expedition to eastern Canada in 1606–7, and for the book he wrote upon returning home, *Histoire de la Nouvelle France.* Highlighting that Lescarbot described the native Americans among whom he travelled as 'truly noble', Ellingson maintains that what led Lescarbot to that view was that they practised hunting, and that, in Europe, hunting was a privilege restricted by law to members of the nobility.[28] In Ellingson's account, then, the indigenes seemed 'noble' to the Frenchman because they resembled the European nobility in this respect.[29] As Ellingson also discusses, the English expression 'noble savage' first appeared later in the seventeenth century, in a play by John Dryden which included the lines: 'I am as free as Nature first made man, / 'Ere the base Laws of Servitude began / When wild in woods the noble Savage ran.'[30]

Rather than projecting onto native peoples a model drawn from European nobility and the systems of law that defined it, Dryden lends the noble savage a contrary association here with freedom from that model's constraints – the freedom enjoyed by all humankind in the state in which 'Nature first made man', the freedom said to have subsisted before 'the base Laws of Servitude began'. Out of

25 Tim Bonyhady, 'The Uncritical Culture', *Eureka Street* (October 1997) 24, 30.

26 Mark McKenna, 'The National Picture: The Art of Tasmania's Black War', *Australian Historical Studies* 50(1) (2019) 117, 122.

27 George Taplin (1878), quoted in Henry Reynolds, *The Other Side of the Frontier: Aboriginal Resistance to the European Invasion of Australia* (Sydney: UNSW Press, 2006), 210.

28 Ter Ellingson, *The Myth of the Noble Savage* (London: University of California Press, 2001), chap. 2, esp. 22–23.

29 Ibid., 23.

30 John Dryden, *Almanzor and Almahide, Or, The Conquest of Granada, The First Part* (first published 1672), in Vinton Dearing (ed.), *The Works of John Dryden, Vol. XI* (Berkeley: University of California Press, 1978), 30, quoted in Ellingson, *The Myth of the Noble Savage,* 8.

this came in the eighteenth and nineteenth centuries the familiar idea of the noble savage as the personification of life uncorrupted by 'civilisation'. Conceptualised along those lines, the noble savage served as a foil to colonial culture, deployed to criticise its vices, degeneracies and flaws. Equally, and once again contrarily, the noble savage became identified with the propagation of a romantic myth, which was itself criticised as an obstacle to clear-eyed views of social progress. In yet another usage, the noble savage played a part in the project of glorifying colonial 'exploits' and gains, while also invoking pity for the populations thereby dispossessed and displaced.

Throughout these and other twists and turns, Ellingson shows how one relatively constant theme in the concept's history going right back to Lescarbot was the idea that native peoples were a vital source of information both about human variety and about the natural history of humankind, including the prehistory of Europeans. This came with the further message that that information would not be available indefinitely; it needed to be gathered before the 'inevitable destruction [of native peoples] had been achieved'.[31] The concept of the noble savage thus converged with the contention that native peoples would inevitably be destroyed and 'die out'. It also converged with the longstanding literary trope of the 'last of the race', in which the story is told of individuals identified as the final representative of their kind, perhaps most famously exemplified in the nineteenth century by James Fenimore Cooper's novel *The Last of the Mohicans.*[32]

The phrase 'doomed race theory' has been applied to this way of thinking about native peoples.[33] At the beginning of this chapter, I used the term 'extinction discourse' – a phrase coined by Patrick Brantlinger to incorporate reference also to the wider ideological frameworks, modes of communication and systems of knowledge production within which the theory emerged, developed, and was

[31] Ellingson, *The Myth of the Noble Savage*, 32.

[32] James Fenimore Cooper (John McWilliams ed.), *The Last of the Mohicans* (Oxford: Oxford University Press, 2008).The text was first published in 1826. On the 'last of the race' trope, see Fiona Stafford, *The Last of the Race: The Growth of a Myth from Milton to Darwin* (Oxford: Oxford University Press, 1994).

[33] See, for example, Russell McGregor, *Imagined Destines: Aboriginal Australians and the Doomed Race Theory, 1880–1939* (Melbourne: Melbourne University Press, 1997).

sustained.[34] According to Brantlinger, extinction discourse was a pervasive feature of colonial culture. Wherever in the world Europeans encountered Indigenous peoples, there existed a 'massive', 'rarely questioned' and hence 'extremely potent' consensus over the idea that some or all of those peoples were destined to disappear.[35] This was 'sometimes celebrated as necessary' for societal advancement, but it 'also inspired mourning'.[36] Indeed, Brantlinger observes that celebration and mourning were often fused in a distinctive discursive register which he calls 'proleptic elegy'.[37]

An elegy is, of course, a poetic lament, typically for the dead, and prolepsis is the rhetorical device of anticipation. Brantlinger explains that proleptic elegy operates in a 'future perfect mode', which mourns native peoples not because they 'are already extinct but because they will sooner or later [have] become extinct'. It expresses the 'confidence of self-fulfilling prophecy', summoning up a vision of a world in which new nations will arise, are arising, as the original ones 'recede'.[38] Proleptic elegy is thus simultaneously epic and melancholic – a paean to nation-building as supersession in a sentimental key. Underscoring the potency of extinction discourse, Brantlinger writes that, even the 'most ardent humanitarians' – and he gives the example of the British Aborigines' Protection Society, founded in 1837 – 'could speak only of preventing future violence', and of rescuing 'by civilizing the sad remnants of the dying races'.[39]

Certainly, that seems to have been how Robinson perceived his mission in Tasmania, with the added element of exile. He wrote of his plans to instil 'civilisation' and Christianity in those whose souls he was evidently determined to save, even if, and presumably in part because, received opinion held out limited expectations for their physical survival.[40] That Robinson himself shared that opinion is reflected in another of his writings, where he reveals that he

[34] See Patrick Brantlinger, *Dark Vanishings: Discourse on the Extinction of Primitive Races, 1800–1930* (Ithaca and London: Cornell University Press, 2003), 1.

[35] Ibid., 1–2. [36] Ibid., 2.

[37] Ibid., 3. On the related phenomenon of 'imperialist nostalgia', in which people retrospectively mourn the passing of what they have themselves destroyed, see Renato Rosaldo, *Culture and Truth: The Remaking of Social Analysis* (Boston, MA: Beacon Press, rev. ed., 1993), 69.

[38] Brantlinger, *Dark Vanishings*, 3–4. [39] Ibid., 3.

[40] See Plomley, *Friendly Mission*, 57. On the idea of saving 'at least of the souls of the last members of perishing races', see Brantlinger, *Dark Vanishings*, 5.

undertook his earliest 'conciliation' work on Bruny Island both for 'missionary' reasons and in order 'to become acquainted with the history manner and language of this interesting portion of the human race ... especially as I had entertained an impression that [it] would ultimately and at no distant period become extinct'.[41] It is from this perspective that one contemporary critic was led to compliment Law on his portrait busts of Wooredy and Trucanini. 'They are of full size, perfect likenesses; in fact altogether a respectable work', the critic writes in an essay on Van Diemen's Land art published in 1839. He goes on: 'As the race of the natives of this island is nearly extinguished, these [sculptures] will retain a constant historical value.'[42]

A Comprehensive Scientific Record

Let us now look at some photographs. Deplorable conditions at the settlement set up by Robinson on Flinders Island eventually compelled its closure, and in 1847, those still remaining there were taken to Oyster Cove in the south-east of mainland Tasmania, just across from Bruny Island. Around ten years after their arrival there, the Anglican Bishop of Tasmania, Francis Nixon, visited the community. Nixon was a keen amateur photographer, and by this point it had become possible to travel with photographic equipment and undertake photography outdoors, so Nixon came with his camera, and took a series of photographs.

In one of the photographs, nine Aboriginal people – eight women and one man – are arranged in front of a building, with a dog in the foreground (Figure 3.6). As the site at Oyster Cove had formerly been used to house convicts, it may be that the building dates from that time. Nixon did not provide any information about the identities of the people he photographed, simply labelling the picture 'Aborigines of Tasmania', but we now have their names.[43]

41 Plomley, *Friendly Mission*, 971 (quoted in Patrick Brantlinger, *Taming Cannibals: Race and the Victorians* (Ithaca and London: Cornell University Press, 2011), 53).

42 John Lhotsky, 'The State of the Arts in New South Wales and Van Diemen's Land' (July 1839), reprinted in Bernard Smith, *Documents on Art and Taste in Australia: The Colonial Period 1770–1914* (Oxford: Oxford University Press, 1975), 71, 74. (Lhotsky refers to 'Mr Low', but clearly intends reference to Benjamin Law.)

43 See Gough, 'Forgotten Lives', 20, figure 1.

Figure 3.6 *Aborigines at Oyster Cove, Tasmania*, 1858. Photograph by Francis Nixon.

Trucanini is on the extreme right of the photograph. Like most of the others, she has reached middle age, and like all of the others, she wears European-style clothing. Gough reports on evidence that 'Western clothing was worn in practical but unconventional ways at Oyster Cove, particularly when outsiders were not present'.[44] From a recent biography of Trucanini by Cassandra Pybus, one also learns that, in Trucanini's case, she 'was issued a blue serge petticoat to be worn under an ankle-length woollen sack dress', along with a knitted jacket and scarf, and liked to cover her head with a 'red peaked cap'[45] – as perhaps in this photograph.

It seems that the community at Oyster Cove received many visitors during these years. Day trips from Hobart by steamer were advertised in the city's newspaper with the message: 'To those who have never visited the aboriginal establishment at this pretty

[44] Ibid, 43.
[45] Cassandra Pybus, *Truganini* (Sydney: Allen & Unwin, 2020), 240–41.

little bay, we should say that the trip will be more than usually interesting.'[46] In a published account of a voyage he had made to Flinders Island and the surrounding archipelago in Bass Strait a few years earlier, Nixon made clear something of the basis of his own interest.[47] Noting the dwindling numbers at Robinson's mission station, as now again at Oyster Cove where living conditions were scarcely less wretched and poor provisions did little to offset the early depletion of local food sources,[48] he informs his readers that the Tasmanian Aborigines are 'fast disappearing from the face of the earth; and in all probability the lapse of a few years will find the race extinct'.[49]

Were the nine individuals he photographed aware that this is what he and others believed, and why they came? The subjects look straight into the camera lens, positioning themselves to scrutinise those who would scrutinise them. The dog seems to have wandered into the picture, but creates no distraction. It may be imagined that the subjects have fallen in with Nixon's instructions or, at any rate, suggestions as to how they should arrange themselves for the camera. Some sit on the ground, others sit along benches or to one side, and the rest stand in a row at the back. Within that pleasing triangular composition, their expressions give little away. Even allowing for the long camera exposure times of this time which always occasioned a certain rigidity, Pybus judges the group to be 'stiff as mannequins' in their multiple layers of clothing.[50] Gough writes that they held 'poses that they surely knew marked an end point for [the person] bringing the photographic apparatus'.[51]

Nixon's sixteen or so photographs were the work of several visits he made to Oyster Cove between 1858 and around 1860. It is germane to recall that those years coincide with the publication, on 24 November 1859, of Charles Darwin's groundbreaking book, *On the Origin of Species*. *Origin* and especially Darwin's later companion study, *The Descent of Man* (published in 1871), laid a basis for

[46] 'Miscellaneous Shipping', *Hobart Town Mercury*, 25 November 1859, 2, available at: https://trove.nla.gov.au/newspaper/page/837757. See Gough, 'Forgotten Lives', 51, n. 53.

[47] Francis Nixon, *The Cruise of the Beacon* (London: Bell and Daldy, 1857).

[48] See *Companion to Tasmanian History: Oyster Cove*, available at: www.utas.edu.au/tasmanian-companion/biogs/E000732b.htm.

[49] Nixon, *The Cruise of the Beacon*, 18.

[50] Pybus, *Truganini*, 267.

[51] Gough, 'Forgotten Lives', 39.

reshaping extinction discourse – the postulate of the 'end point', 'fast disappearance from the face of the earth' and 'probable extinction of the race with the lapse of a few years' – in ways that were to make it more potent and pervasive than ever. For, according to the Darwinian theory (as formulated and developed also through the work of others), the inevitable destruction of Indigenous peoples was not simply a matter of divine providence and the sometimes harsh natural order of things. It could be explained scientifically, as an outcome of the process of human evolution, that is to say, progress.

The basic idea was, of course, that, like all biological forms, human beings are engaged in a Malthusian struggle for existence, in which survival depends on adaptation to changing conditions, and development occurs by natural selection, as less well-adapted forms succumb to, and are superseded by, better-adapted ones. Already in *Origin,* Darwin signals that there exist, as he puts it, 'favoured races in the struggle for life',[52] and in *Descent,* he elaborates on this aspect. Or rather, he elaborates on its corollary, the disfavoured races. Broaching the topic of the 'extinction of the races of man', Darwin explains that the 'partial or complete extinction of many races and sub-races of man is historically known'.[53] He then gets to the point with the pronouncement that '[w]hen civilised nations come into contact with barbarians the struggle is short'.[54] His primary example of such a situation is Tasmania, as to which he cites statistics about population decline among Aboriginal people since colonisation that he took from two publications of the previous year, *Daily Life of the Tasmanians* and *The Last of the Tasmanians,* both by James Bonwick.[55]

One effect of Darwinian thought was to add impetus to endeavours aimed at the production and dissemination of knowledge about Indigenous peoples. The consolidation of anthropology as a 'salvage' discipline focused on investigating and documenting the so-called 'vanishing native' was part of that. In James Clifford's telling, anthropologists of the time made it their business to save

[52] See, for example, the full title which Darwin gave the work: *On the Origin of Species by Means of Natural Selection, or the Preservation of Favoured Races in the Struggle for Life.*

[53] Charles Darwin, *The Descent of Man, and Selection in Relation to Sex* (London: Penguin, 2004), 211.

[54] Ibid., 212. [55] Ibid., 213–14.

'in the text' facets of human diversity which they saw as imminently or eventually to be lost in the actuality.[56] But so too, and relatedly, was photography part of the heightened profile of these endeavours. From its origins earlier in the century, photographic technology grew in importance and sophistication in step with the Darwinian project,[57] quickly becoming a key instrument of salvage anthropology and racial 'science'. Darwin's friend and ally in the promotion of evolutionary theory, Henry Huxley, played an influential role in this respect.

In 1868, Huxley was elected president of the Ethnological Society of London (an offshoot of the Aborigines' Protection Society, which aligned itself with Darwin in debates that followed the publication of *Origin*). This was a time when papers presented to the Society were starting to be illustrated with photographs, and Huxley seems to have been keen to promote more systematic use of photography within the discipline of anthropology. Thus, one of his initiatives as president was to launch a scheme for a large-scale photographic survey that would comprise 'measurable' and 'comparable' photographs of the 'various races of men comprehended within the British Empire'.[58] The scheme gained the support of the Colonial Office, which sent out requests to colonial governors to cooperate. According to the protocols laid down by Huxley, four photographs of each exemplary subject were to be taken – front-facing and side-on, close-up to the face and showing the whole naked body – in each case, against a neutral background and at a fixed distance

[56] James Clifford, 'On Ethnographic Allegory', in James Clifford and George Marcus (eds.), *Writing Culture: The Poetics and Politics of Ethnography* (Oakland: University of California Press, 1986), 98, 112. See also James Clifford, *Returns: Becoming Indigenous in the Twenty-First Century* (Cambridge, MA: Harvard University Press, 2013), chap. 4 ('Ishi's story'), for an account of a story with some parallels to Trucanini's.

[57] On the parallel histories of photography and Darwinian thought, see Philip Prodger, *Darwin's Camera: Art and Photography in the Theory of Evolution* (Oxford: Oxford University Press, 2009), xxiii. On the relatedly 'doubled history' of photography and anthropology, see Christopher Pinney, *Photography and Anthropology* (London: Reaktion Books, 2011), chap. 1.

[58] Correspondence between Thomas Henry Huxley and Lord Granville, 12 August 1869, *Huxley Papers*, vol. 30, folio 75, 1 (quoted in Prodger, *Darwin's Camera*, 71). On this scheme, see also Elizabeth Edwards, *Raw Histories: Photographs, Anthropology and Museums* (London: Bloomsbury, 2001), chap. 6.

from the camera, so that 'the relative proportions' could easily be apprehended.[59]

It is known that not all colonial governors responded positively to the Colonial Office's request, but that the Governor of Tasmania was among those who did. However, instead of having new photographs taken, he submitted the photographs that had already been made by Charles Woolley for the Melbourne Intercolonial Exhibition three years earlier, to which I referred at the beginning of this chapter. The Governor was able to assume that these more or less met the stated specifications because Woolley's brief for the exhibition had been to make three photographs of each of his Indigenous sitter's faces – one facing the front, the second in profile, and the third a three-quarter view. The brief reflected, and Huxley encouraged, a kind of photographic practice that was linked to the emergent anthropological subdiscipline of anthropometry, which studied human diversity through the measurement and observation of physical features, including, but not limited to, cranial shapes and sizes.

Concurrently with Huxley's project, the Assistant Secretary of the Ethnological Society of London, Jones Lamprey, devised a measuring grid as an aid to anthropometric photography. The grid consisted of two-inch squares made by stretching silk thread over a wooden frame, in front of which photographers were advised to place their subjects. In *Notes and Queries on Anthropology, for the Use of Travellers and Residents in Uncivilized Lands*, the British Association for the Advancement of Science later recommended the use of a ruler 'in the same plane as the body of the subject'. As if to suggest that object's salience as a metonym for anthropological enquiry itself, the cover of the publication was embossed in gold with two rulers – one marked out in inches, the other in centimetres.[60] *Notes and Queries* also provided detailed guidance on other issues pertaining to the production of standardised photographic data.[61] For example, it was suggested that the camera 'lens should be on a level with the face, and the eyes of the subject looking straight from the

[59] *Huxley Papers* (quoted in Prodger, *Darwin's Camera*, 72).

[60] British Association for the Advancement of Science (John Garson and Charles Read eds.), *Notes and Queries on Anthropology, for the Use of Travellers and Residents in Uncivilized Lands* (London: Anthropological Institute, 3rd ed., 1899), 239 and cover page.

[61] Ibid., 239. See also generally 235 (no. LXXVII).

head should be fixed on a point at their own height from the ground'.

The Governor of Tasmania may have felt confident to submit Woolley's photographs as contributions to Huxley's project for reasons that also have to do with the prestige associated with the Melbourne Intercolonial Exhibition and the fact that Woolley received a prize for his work at it.[62] The Melbourne event of 1866 (which was 'intercolonial' in the sense that it brought together exhibits from the various colonies of Australia) was one of many large-scale, high-profile exhibitions that took place after the Great Exhibition in London of 1851, to put on show attractive, impressive or simply 'interesting' features of imperial life. Photographic displays and live exhibits involving Indigenous people are said to have been particularly popular features of them.[63] Nixon's group photographs taken at Oyster Cove were accepted for display at the second world fair held in London in 1862, leading to sales to British and European institutions and collectors, and it was in the wake of that success that Woolley received his commission from the organisers of the Melbourne intercolonial show.

By August 1866, there were only five Aboriginal people still living in the former convict settlement at Oyster Cove, and these five were brought to Woolley's studio in Hobart to be photographed. I have already described one of the resulting photographs – the portrait of Trucanini in which we see her in a buttoned cloth jacket and a maireener shell necklace facing the front.[64] Another two were taken, which show her, as required, in profile and three-quarter view. Anticipating Huxley's instructions, Woolley has used a neutral background and placed Trucanini at the same distance from the camera in each photograph. Consistently also with the British Association for the Advancement of Science's later guidance document, Woolley has set the camera lens on a level with Trucanini's face, and she is looking directly forward. A selection of Woolley's photographs of Trucanini and the others from Oyster Cove was displayed at the Tasmanian stand in Melbourne under the heading 'The Last of the Tasmanians'. As already mentioned, the photographs of Trucanini were subsequently reprinted and disseminated

[62] On Woolley's prize, see Jane Lydon, *Eye Contact: Photographing Indigenous Australians* (Durham: Duke University Press, 2005), 91.

[63] See Maxwell, *Colonial Photography and Exhibitions*.

[64] See Figure 3.1.

in numerous forms and publications. Darwin would have seen etching copies of the front-facing and profile photographs of her in James Bonwick's *The Last of the Tasmanians*, where they appear before the penultimate page of the book.

Another professional photographer who made photographs of Trucanini around this time was Henry Frith. Quite different from Woolley's photographs, Frith's are group portraits, which differ also from Nixon's group photographs inasmuch as they were not taken where the subjects lived, but rather at some very grand interior locations in Hobart.[65] In one image, four Aboriginal people dressed in genteel Victorian clothing can be seen posing on an elegant checkerboard floor, with Corinthian columns behind them and ornamental parapets to the side (Figure 3.7). The subjects are disposed across the picture plane in a manner that calls to mind the originally informal, but by the mid-nineteenth century highly formalised 'conversation piece' genre of group portraiture. Frith later produced copies of this and other photographs from the series in a range of marketable formats. Like Nixon, he did not provide the names of the individuals he photographed. However, the sitters have been identified as, from the left to the right of the picture I have described, Pangernowidedic, William Lanne, Mary Ann and, seated with her hands on her lap, Trucanini.[66]

The male figure in the photograph, William Lanne, was said in colonial circles to be the last surviving Tasmanian Aboriginal man. As such, he became the object of intense post-mortem interest when he died in 1869, with a major scandal erupting around the mutilation and removal of parts of his mortal remains while they were still held in a morgue.[67] Trucanini followed him to the grave in 1876, spending her final years in Hobart. One of the last extant photographs to be taken of her was made by another of the city's studio photographers, Henry Hall Baily (Figure 3.8). The picture shows a formidable woman with a solemn and stately demeanour in apparently vigorous older age. She wears a dark dress with a loose white ruffle over the collar and a single-stranded maireener shell

[65] Frith's photographs were apparently taken at Hobart's Theatre Royal and in the Tasmanian Governor's residence, Government House; see Elizabeth Edwards, 'Early Cross-Cultural Photography', *History of Photography* 29(4) (2005) 379, 380.

[66] See Gough, 'Forgotten Lives', 45.

[67] See Helen MacDonald, *Human Remains: Dissection and Its Histories* (New Haven and London: Yale University Press, 2006), chap. 5.

Figure 3.7 The Last of the Tasmanian Natives, 1864. Photograph by Henry Frith.

necklace looped over the ruffle. Were it not for the shell necklace, Lyndall Ryan suggests that one might almost consider Trucanini in this picture a 'look-alike Queen Victoria'.[68] Indeed, Baily reprinted the image in 1888 with the caption 'Queen Trucanini, Last Aborigine of Tasmania'. And just as William Lanne was frequently referred to as 'King Billy', so too, when Trucanini died, reports told of the death of 'Queen Trucanini',[69] the 'queen of the dead tribes'.[70]

These photographs by Nixon, Woolley, Frith and Baily are plainly far removed from the portraits of Trucanini in other media on which I previously touched. There is no (pseudo-) tribal garb and no semi-nakedness. The figures we see are neither happy innocents,

[68] Ryan, 'The Struggle for Trukanini 1830–1997', 159.

[69] 'Funeral of Queen Trucanini', *Hobart Town Mercury*, 12 May 1876, 2, available at: https://trove.nla.gov.au/newspaper/article/8944992/792715.

[70] Robert Dudley Adams (aka Alpha Crucis), *Trucanini's Dirge* (1876), available at: https://en.wikisource.org/wiki/Trucanini%27s_Dirge.

Figure 3.8 *Queen Trucanini, Last Aborigine of Tasmania*, 1888. Photograph by Henry Hall Baily.

nor proud warriors, nor yet sorrowing victims of empire. To my knowledge, no-one has applied the term 'noble savage' to the mode of representation in these pictures. Rather, what Gough discerns in Nixon's photographs taken at Oyster Cove are the 'aggrieved faces' of 'desperate hopeless people whose wants were never met'.[71] Where Woolley's portraits are concerned, Anne Maxwell points to the objectification of Trucanini, in the context of an attempt to

[71] Gough, 'Forgotten Lives', 37–38.

'create a comprehensive scientific record' for a taxonomy of human evolutionary forms.[72] As for the 'conversation piece' photographs by Frith, the long shadow of ambitions to 'rescue' surviving native Tasmanians by 'civilising' them is not difficult to make out. Helen Ennis explains that professional photographers like Woolley and Frith 'keenly felt the momentousness of what they considered to be the final chapter in human evolution and history'. With these 'immensely troubling' photographs, she invites us to notice that such men produced images that are, at the same time, 'grand statements, technically superb and laden with gravitas'.[73]

To speak of gravitas is to speak of seriousness, importance and dignity. Yet at least part of what makes these pictures so troubling is the sense that, for the photographers and their presumptive audiences, the dignity of the sitters did not count. All that counted was the fraudulent and calamitous 'dignity' of a colonial power which set about destroying Indigenous life under the pretence that it was doomed to self-destruction, and then subjected Indigenous individuals to photographic sessions purporting to document the last survivors for posterity. This is especially evident in the photographs taken by Woolley for the Melbourne Intercolonial Exhibition. As Jane Lydon observes, the conventions of anthropometric photography 'challenge our ideas about human dignity' inasmuch as they discounted the dignity that we hold to belong to all human beings, and turned those photographed into 'biological specimens laid bare for scientific appraisal'.[74] And if Woolley paid no heed to Trucanini's dignity and rendered, or tried to render, her a biological specimen for scientific appraisal, he also, and in the process, made her serve as an exemplar of a racial category.[75] For racial scientists, an exemplar of a racial category was a body and especially a face, the outward appearance of which encoded racial information.

Patricia Spyer highlights the effort in this context to reduce people to a set of corporeal and especially facial features, and fabricate 'anonymous generic masks of "types" . . . of different racial

[72] Maxwell, *Colonial Photography and Exhibitions*, 140.
[73] Ennis, *Photography and Australia*, 33–34.
[74] Jane Lydon, *Photography, Humanitarianism, Empire* (London: Routledge, 2016), 45.
[75] On this process, see Edwards, 'Evolving Images', 169.

groups'.[76] The concept of the 'type' had a central role in racial science. Disregarding human individuality, it was premised on the production of exemplary forms that could be deployed '[i]n the popular sphere … as a generalising and distancing conceit, and in "science" [as a means of bringing about the] visibility of the specimen' and creating 'units of comparative analysis'.[77] Hence the 'shockingly impersonal treatment' involved in photography such as Woolley's.[78] Set alongside his images, the other photographs on which I have touched are plainly less 'scientific' and less objectifying. They neither portray their sitters as biological specimens to be appraised, nor seek to provide analysts with units that can be compared. Nonetheless, they likewise represent their sitters as exemplars of a racial type – 'Aborigines of Tasmania', rather than (except in the case of Baily's picture) named individuals. They also share with Woolley's work the presupposition of a natural-historical scheme according to which Indigenous Tasmanians are evolutionarily disfavoured, and soon to be trampled in the onward march of human progress.

Viewers could clearly see this in Nixon's bleak scene. But no less clearly could they discern it in Frith's image of 'civilised' survival and Baily's portrait of 'Queen Trucanini, Last Aborigine of Tasmania'. As well as evoking the 'conversation piece' genre to which I have referred, Frith's highly choreographed composition may have put contemporary viewers in mind of the popular Victorian entertainment known as *tableau vivant* – the enactment of silent, static scenes in costume, with props.[79] If so, this would have reinforced the idea that Indigenous prospects belonged to the realm of simulation, that is to say, fantasy. Regarding Baily's photograph, Lydon reports that it was not uncommon for the epithets 'King' and 'Queen' to be used by colonists in Australia with reference to Indigenous individuals, whether because those individuals

[76] Patricia Spyer, 'Photography's Framings and Unframings', *Comparative Studies in Society and History* 43(1) (2001) 181, 186.

[77] Edwards, 'Evolving Images', 169.

[78] Maxwell, *Colonial Photography and Exhibitions*, 42.

[79] Regarding the staging of *tableaux vivants* in Tasmania, see Jane Lydon, 'The Frontier Land: Photography, Colonialism and Living Pictures', in Kate Darian-Smith and Penelope Edmonds (eds.), *Conciliation on Colonial Frontiers: Conflict, Performance and Commemoration in Australia and the Pacific Rim* (New York and London: Routledge, 2015), 95, esp. 100.

were believed to have high status among their people, or as a sarcastic gesture which the speaker found amusing, or for other reasons. Whatever the intention, a widely understood subtext was apparently that those concerned were 'bearers of an authentic but disappearing tradition',[80] which had a past, but, again, no future.

Subjecting Indigenous people to the indignity of being treated as exemplars of a racial category, and moreover of a racial category that needed to be recorded because it constituted an inferior form of life and had no future, was, of course, part of the violence of invasion and of the dehumanisation integral to colonial relations. Equally obviously, however, the colonised were not dehumanised exemplars from their own perspective. This raises the question of whether there is more that can be said about what is captured in these photographs. Peter Andersson notes that 'portrait photographs of the indigenous peoples of European colonies [are] generally interpreted as pacifying the sitter and exposing him or her to the prejudiced view of Western culture', but that such photographs are increasingly also 'credited with giving the colonized subject a tool for self-presentation'.[81] Relevant here is the 'random inclusivity' or 'visual excess' that is a feature of all photographic image-making – the fact, emphasised by scholars of photography, that a photograph can never be fully controlled by its maker;[82] it invariably and necessarily includes more than its maker intended, something caught in the camera lens that was not set up to be there. One consequence of this is that the influence of the sitter on the outcome of a photographic portrait can never be completely negated, so that even the most abusive practices of photographic representation coexist with some element of self-representation.

In Frith's work, the sitters arrange themselves in a composition which suggests very extensive intervention by the photographer. Frith has used for the picture an ornate space at a major colonial building, quite unlike anything in the built environment of the place where the sitters live. He has furnished it with items appropriate to that space, and has positioned the furniture in a way that is suitable for the particular style of group portraiture at which he

80 Lydon, *Photography, Humanitarianism, Empire*, 24.
81 Peter Andersson, *Silent History: Body Language and Nonverbal Identity, 1860–1914* (Montreal: McGill-Queens University Press, 2018), 34.
82 See, for example, Edwards, 'Evolving Images', 169.

aims. He has surely also managed the configuration of the figures and their posture – where they sit and stand, how they sit and stand, what they do with their hands. He may have organised as well for them to be wearing the particular clothes, hats and shoes they wear. However, not everything has come under his control. Most obviously, he has not been able to obliterate his subjects' evident uncertainty in the situation. He has not been able to make them look any less ill at ease than they do. Self-presentation is especially vivid in Baily's portrait, where, far from appearing uncertain, Trucanini adopts a pose that projects will, personality and self-possession. Frith's photograph contains nothing of the original material culture of the sitters, but in Baily's picture, Trucanini accessorises her conventional Victorian dress with a shell necklace that signals her independence and draws into the frame criteria of beauty, respectability and value which do not only come from the coloniser.

Linked to the idea that a photographic portrait can never be fully controlled by its maker and, in particular, can never be controlled to the extent that the sitter's influence on it is negated, Edwards reminds us that a photograph is not just a process of producing images. It is a site of interaction and experience. A 'photograph is a moment, positive or negative, happy or terrifying, that someone lived through', she writes.[83] 'Subjects are never passive – they think, they experience', and in the context of colonial photography of the kind we have been considering, Edwards proposes that that active presence is inscribed on the photographic surface in details visible to those willing to notice and explore them.[84] It follows that 'photographs mark not only the photographer's standpoint', but always also, and at least to some degree, 'a point of view of those in front of the camera'.[85] In Nixon's photograph, Trucanini sits against the back wall and slightly to one side, with her fingers interlaced on her lap – might she be seeking to hold the photographer at a distance? The only man in the picture occupies the central position at the front – might he have assumed the role of spokesperson for the

[83] Elizabeth Edwards, 'Anthropology and Photography: A Long History of Knowledge and Affect', *Photographies* 8(3) (2015) 235, 240. In turn, Edwards draws on Ulrich Baer, *Spectral Evidence: The Photography of Trauma* (Cambridge, MA: MIT Press, 2002), esp. 8.

[84] Edwards, 'Anthropology and Photography', 241.

[85] Ibid.

group?[86] And what of this dog that enters the scene, and is calmly ignored by those present? Gough reports that, 'after thousands of years of isolation, my people successfully incorporated [*inter alia*] dogs . . . into their daily existence within a decade of invasion'[87] – might that incorporation form part of what is recorded here?

Such details are harder to find in Woolley's photographs of Trucanini. Guided by scientific standards of reliability and reproducibility, Woolley has done his best to exclude all traces of the particular moment. His pictures have a blurred and bare setting designed to cast Trucanini's head and shoulders in relief. She directs her gaze straight ahead, and maintains the same facial expression in all three photographs. How did that come about? What instructions did Woolley give, and what explanations did he offer? What reactions did Trucanini disclose, and what concerns did she express? Did he make small talk about her journey to his studio in Hobart? Did she enquire as to why he was taking the photographs and what would be done with them? It goes without saying that we cannot know what passed between Woolley and Trucanini in the photographic sessions that brought them together. If 'a photograph is an experience that someone lived through',[88] we can only guess at what Trucanini's experience was like – what she thought and felt in posing for these pictures, how she hoped to be represented to those who would eventually see them, whether indeed she cared how Woolley, with his preposterous method, represented her. What we can know, when we look at this set of images today, is that that experience was hers to signify (or not signify) in ways that no would-be fabricator of 'anonymous generic masks' of racial 'types' could wholly eliminate or occlude.

Subverting the Colonial Symbol

In the years after Trucanini's death in 1876, Woolley's photographs of her, or engraved reproductions of them, could be seen in books

86 This figure has been identified as Calamarowenye (also known as Tippo Saib). See Gough, 'Forgotten Lives', 20.

87 Julie Gough, 'History, Representation, Globalisation and Indigenous Cultures: A Tasmanian Perspective', in Claire Smith and Graeme Ward (eds.), *Indigenous Cultures in an Interconnected World* (Sydney: Allen & Unwin, 2000), 89, 91.

88 Elizabeth Edwards, 'Der Geschichte ins Antlitz blicken: Fotografie und die Herausforderung der Präsenz', in Herta Wolf (ed.), *Zeigen und/oder Beweisen? Die Fotografie als Kulturtechnik und Medium des Wissens* (Berlin: De Gruyter, 2016), 305, 307 (with thanks to the author for an earlier English version of this).

such as the multivolume *Picturesque Atlas of Australasia*, produced under the editorship of Andrew Garran between 1886 and 1888,[89] and Henry Ling Roth's *The Aborigines of Tasmania*, published in 1890.[90] Roth's book also contained an illustration based on a copy of Thomas Bock's watercolour portrait of Trucanini from the 1830s, with a caption informing readers that, while Bock's work 'possibly [gives] a good representation of the "get up" of the natives, the features are not correctly drawn, as a comparison with the photographs [by Woolley, reproduced in an appendix] will indicate'.[91] In another appendix, Roth reproduced a magazine article from 1834 reporting on the portraits of Trucanini and other Tasmanian Aboriginal people made by Benjamin Duterrau. To that he appended the comment that, again, Duterrau's 'portraits do not bear comparison with Mr. Woolley's photographs, that is, they fail in the same way as do those of Bock, namely, in not catching that sinister form of expression which is so characteristic of the late owners of the island'.[92] A 'sinister form of expression' may have been, for Roth, a malevolent one, as in the modern usage of the word, though it is worth noting that in the nineteenth century, 'sinister' additionally had the sense of ill-starred.

Among the many museums that acquired Woolley's photographs of Trucanini was the Tasmanian Museum and Art Gallery in Hobart. Between 1904 and 1947, his photographs of her formed part of a larger display there that also included Trucanini's skeleton. The skeleton could be seen in a glass case fitted with a measuring tape to indicate its height. It seems that Trucanini's body had been unlawfully exhumed shortly after her burial, and that her bones had been found in a crate at the museum some decades later, after which they had been articulated and exhibited, first in Melbourne at another Intercolonial Exhibition and then back at the museum. The skeleton was eventually removed from public display in 1947 following criticism that, in the words of one newspaper article, '[s]o truly royal a character should have been

89 See Andrew Garran (ed.), *Picturesque Atlas of Australia, Vol. 2* (Sydney, Melbourne, London and Springfield (Mass): The Picturesque Atlas Publishing Company, 1886), 497. (An account of Trucanini and her life is given on page 508.)

90 See Henry Ling Roth, *The Aborigines of Tasmania* (Cambridge: Cambridge University Press, 2009, reprint of 2nd ed., 1899), appendix G.

91 Ibid., illustration facing 17.

92 Ibid., appendix I.

preserved from the indignity of [becoming] a mere anatomical exhibit'.[93] In 1976, the centenary of Trucanini's death, her mortal remains were handed over by the Tasmanian Museum and Art Gallery to representatives of Tasmania's Aboriginal community and officials of the state's government, and cremated. The hand-over was the result of a long campaign by Indigenous activists that led to the re-solemnisation of Trucanini's funeral and the scattering of her ashes in the waters lying between mainland Tasmania and Bruny Island.

Yet the point for the activists was not just the indignity of making Trucanini an anatomical exhibit. It was not just the failure to allow her the dignified death that (as we saw in Chapter 1) looms so large in modern conceptualisations of dignity. It was also that Trucanini was being presented in the museum as the last Tasmanian Aboriginal person. That is to say, the museum authorities were helping to perpetuate the idea that Indigenous Tasmanians had become 'extinct' – and hence that there could exist none in the present. The basis for this was an investment in racial thinking which carried forward earlier scientific racism through the identification of authentic Aboriginality with so-called 'full-blood' Aboriginality, lineage that could include no non-Aboriginal ancestry. A misrecognition of the descendants of Tasmania's original inhabitants as inauthentic 'half-bloods' or 'hybrids' thereby became possible and even justifiable.[94] As Ros Langford summed up the situation of those descendants, '[s]cience . . . proved that we did not exist'.[95] For her and other Indigenous Tasmanians, the indignity of the museum exhibit was continuous with, and part of the context for, the everyday indignity they experienced of having their Indigenous identity denied, and with that, their place in history erased and their rights – indeed their very right to have rights – as Aboriginal people annulled.

If culture worked in tandem with science to sustain the misrecognition of Indigenous Tasmanians, the photographs and other

[93] Bernard Cronin, 'One Great Tribal Queen, Now Exhibit in Hobart Museum', *The Queenslander*, 15 December 1937.

[94] See, for example, N. J. B. Plomley, *The Tasmanian Aborigines* (Launceston: Adult Education Division, 1977), 66.

[95] Ros Langford, 'Our Heritage – Your Playground', *Australian Archaeology* 16 (1983) 1, 2.

portraits of Trucanini on which we have touched were never far from view. In 1978, a poster could be seen throughout Australia advertising the release of a film by Tom Haydon entitled *The Last Tasmanian.* The poster reproduced in large format the front-facing photograph of Trucanini taken by Woolley in 1866. In some versions, it also had other images in the background, including a man throwing a spear and a Thomas Bock portrait of a woman named Wutapuwitja, for a long time mistakenly believed to be a portrait of Trucanini.[96] The subtitle of the film was 'A Story of Genocide', and the poster trailed it as 'presenting a search by [the archaeologist] Rhys Jones to discover the life and death of the Tasmanian Aborigines'. The idea that the Indigenous inhabitants of Tasmania were the victims of a genocide had begun to circulate in Australia some decades earlier,[97] and it is known that Raphael Lemkin, who gave that name to the concept, planned a chapter on Tasmania in the history of genocide which he was still writing at his death in the late 1950s. Lemkin's main source for the chapter was apparently James Bonwick's *The Last of the Tasmanians*[98] – one of two studies by Bonwick that, as I have already noted, also served as the basis of Darwin's account of the 'extinction' of native Tasmanians.

Haydon's film exposed the brutality of the Tasmanian frontier wars, but otherwise followed colonial convention in portraying Trucanini as the eponymous 'last Tasmanian'. In retrospect, Lyndall Ryan suggests that it served as the 'catalyst for a public confrontation' between that 'old interpretation' of Trucanini and a 'new [interpretation]' which was 'competing for public space at this time'.[99] As articulated by the Tasmanian Indigenous leader Michael Mansell in a debate about the film on national television, the new interpretation '[claimed Trucanini] as an antecedent of

[96] For this image, see www.britishmuseum.org/collection/object/E_Oc2006-Drg-58.

[97] See especially, Clive Turnbull, *Black War: The Extermination of the Tasmanian Aborigines* (Melbourne: Lansdowne Press, 2nd ed., 1965), first published in 1948 (the year in which the UN Convention on the Prevention and Punishment of the Crime of Genocide was signed).

[98] See Ann Curthoys, 'Raphael Lemkin's "Tasmania": An Introduction', *Patterns of Prejudice* 39(2) (2005) 162, 167.

[99] Ryan, 'The Struggle for Trukanini 1830–1997', 169. On this, see also Rebe Taylor, 'The National Confessional', *Meanjin* 71(3) (2012) 22.

the modern Aboriginal community'.[100] Ryan writes that Mansell's statement marked 'a historic moment in the displacement' of Trucanini as the 'last Tasmanian'.[101] Even so, the themes of extinction and extermination were not easily swept aside. In 1980, the art historian Bernard Smith delivered a prominent public lecture series entitled *The Spectre of Trucanini,* in which he argued that 'a spectre has haunted Australian culture, the spectre of Trucanini'. He went on: '[w]hen she died in 1876, ... [i]t was the end of a war ... a complete victory. None of the original Tasmanians survived.'[102] The question Smith invited his audience to consider was: '[h]ow shall we redeem [contemporary Australia] from the guilty awareness that' its beginnings co-occurred with, and were predicated upon, Indigenous 'termination'?[103] On the cover of his published lectures was a picture of Benjamin Law's dolorous portrait bust of Trucanini from 1835.[104]

Smith used Trucanini, and more generally Tasmania, as a symbol for the original sin of Australia's post-colonial nationhood. From a Tasmanian Aboriginal perspective, this was yet another turn in the cycle of misrecognition, inasmuch as such a usage depended for its rhetorical force on a narrative about the ending of Indigenous life in Tasmania. In an essay published in 1993, Ian Anderson lent his voice to the rising chorus engaged in reclaiming Trucanini from those who would press her into the service of that narrative.[105] The text begins with a personal memory. 'When I was a kid', he writes, 'we were told that we were TRUCANNINI's descendants. In actual fact we are not. But colonialism had extinguished a tapestry of history and offered in return an emblem of extinction: TRU-GEE-NAN-NER.'[106] As this opening passage already indicates, Anderson chose not to keep to any single spelling of Trucanini's name, but rather to reflect something of the variety of ways in which her name had been rendered by colonial chroniclers, along with the

[100] 'The Last Tasmanian', *Monday Conference,* ABC TV, Sydney, 4 September 1978, quoted in Ryan, 'The Struggle for Trukanini 1830–1997', 153, 169.

[101] Ryan, 'The Struggle for Trukanini 1830–1997', 169.

[102] Bernard Smith, *The Spectre of Trucanini: 1980 Boyer Lectures* (Sydney: Australian Broadcasting Corporation, n.d.), 9.

[103] Ibid., 10. [104] See Figure 3.5.

[105] Ian Anderson, 'Re-Claiming Tru-ger-nan-ner: De-Colonising the Symbol', *Art Monthly Australia* 66 (1993/94) 10.

[106] Ibid., 10.

capitalised orthography used in the diary entries of the 'conciliator' George Augustus Robinson. Reflecting on this in a later essay, he comments that 'I refused, in [that] particular paper, to be restricted to any particular convention for spelling Trukanini's name. Every version was mediated by a colonial ear – so I used them all in a gesture towards the epistemological difficulty of engaging with my precolonial Aboriginal history through the static colonial discourse.'[107]

Anderson observes that '[a]s a colonial symbol TRUG-ER-NAN-NE signifies the land empty of natives, and declares the colonial period over'. She stands for the 'end of authenticity', and asserts the status of present-day Indigenous Tasmanians as not 'the "real thing"'. In this context, he continues, reclaiming Trucanini entails 'de-colonising the symbol' of her – repudiating the 'essentialised notions of race and culture' that were mobilised to construct 'the "authentic" Aborigine', and re-inserting 'TRU-GAN-NAN-NER back into the Aboriginal landscape of history'.[108] As an example of how that might be pursued, Anderson refers to an artwork by Clinton Naina (formerly Clinton Peterson) entitled *Don't Fence Me In* (Figure 3.9). In the middle of a canvas with a bold composition painted in red ochre and black and white ink, Naina had stuck an original-sized copy of a postage stamp containing a reproduction of Woolley's familiar, front-facing photograph of Trucanini.[109] The image's tiny size meant that a viewer would need to squint to make it out in detail, and the artist then compounded the difficulty by slightly splattering it with ink. Anderson remarks that, in this work, 'TRU-GER-NAN-NA is barely perceptible. The colonial symbol of TRUGER-NANNER' is thus restored to its location within 'an Aboriginal history which has many other significant figures, both before and after. We remember her pain, but she is no full-stop. In subverting the colonial symbol of TRUGGENNE, our connections with our past are enabled.'[110]

[107] Ian Anderson, 'A People Who Have No History?', in Anna Johnston and Mitchell Rolls (eds.), *Reading Robinson: Companion Essays to George Augustus Robinson's Friendly Mission* (Melbourne, Monash University Publishing, 2012), 59.

[108] Anderson, 'Re-Claiming Tru-ger-nan-ner', 11, 14.

[109] The stamp was part of a series issued in 1975 under the title *Australian Women.*

[110] Anderson, 'Re-Claiming Tru-ger-nan-ner', 12.

Figure 3.9 Clinton Naina, *Don't Fence Me In*, 1993. Mixed Materials. © Clinton Naina.

The subversion of colonial symbols, and of the photographic representations associated with them, can, of course, assume many different forms. Ricky Maynard takes photographs that document Indigenous lives, communities and histories. *Broken Heart*, from his series *Portrait of a Distant Land*, shows a man standing knee-deep and fully clothed in the sea (Figure 3.10). The photograph was taken in 2005 on Flinders Island, the site to which Robinson removed Aboriginal people from mainland Tasmania in 1833, and the man in the photograph is Maynard himself, an Indigenous Tasmanian whose ancestors lived there. Accompanying the photograph is an

Figure 3.10 Ricky Maynard, *Broken Heart* (from the series *Portrait of a Distant Land*), 2005. Gelatin silver photograph, selenium toned. © Ricky Maynard/Copyright Agency.

excerpt from a petition sent by the displaced Aboriginal leaders to Queen Victoria in 1846, protesting their ill-treatment and neglect at the hands of Robinson's final successor as superintendent, Henry Jeanneret: 'When we left our own place we were plenty of People, we are now but a little one.'[111] In 1847, the decimated community was relocated to Oyster Cove, where its remaining members were photographed by Francis Nixon. You will recall that in Nixon's

[111] See www.mca.com.au/artists-works/works/2010.32.9/.

photograph, nine individuals sit or stand to face the camera. Maynard literally turns this around, making the subject the photographer and standing with his back to the camera. Now sovereign with respect to his own representation, he puts his face out of sight, so that, instead of looking at him, viewers of the picture look with him[112] – directing their gaze where he directs his, and contemplating the horizon he contemplates.

The title of Maynard's work was echoed shortly afterwards in remarks about Nixon's Oyster Cove photographs by Darlene Mansell. In a television series entitled *First Australians* that had its original release in 2008, Mansell said: '[y]ou look at those photos and these beautiful Aboriginal women, who have just experienced so much despair in their life and they're sitting there in strange clothing, their *hearts broken*'.[113] Highlighting these remarks, Jeni Thornley writes of how Mansell re-presents the women in Nixon's photographs so that they are 'no longer frozen in past time – observed, captured and taken [in Nixon's luggage] to London' for display at the International Exhibition of 1862 and subsequent inclusion in ethnographic collections. Rather, they become 'linked by Mansell to her community and held tenderly' in the present.[114] It has been suggested with reference to the Indigenous Australian artist Brook Andrew – much of whose art involves repurposing photographs from the colonial-era archives of European museums – that his work 'gives [the Aboriginal subjects of colonial photography] back their personhood', 'resurrecting the dead and enlivening them with dignity and grace'.[115] Of Mansell and her intervention concerning Nixon's photographs, Thornley writes something similar: 'In a powerful sequence, Darlene Mansell, from the Tasmanian Aboriginal community, restores dignity to her Elders as she recuperates the women in the photographs back into her care.'[116]

[112] See Jeni Thornley, '"Islands of Possibility": Film-Making, Cultural Practice, Political Action and the Decolonization of Tasmanian History', *Studies in Australasian Cinema* 7 (2–3) (2013) 126, 131.

[113] Quoted in Thornley, '"Islands of Possibility"', 130 (emphasis added).

[114] Ibid.

[115] Marcia Langton, 'Brook Andrew: Ethical Portraits and Ghost-Scapes', *Art Journal* (National Gallery of Victoria) 48 (2014).

[116] Thornley, '"Islands of Possibility"', 130.

Trucanini's Stare

If dignity is restored, are we to infer that it was lost? If personhood is given back, was it previously taken away? According to those who made the photographs which we have examined in this chapter, Indigenous Tasmanians were casualties of natural history, doomed not by the misguided savagery of their ways (as the earlier artists on whose work we first touched seem to have believed), but for reasons of evolutionary deficiency. Anthropology and Darwinian 'race science' came together to repackage destruction as 'extinction', and to announce the need to salvage knowledge before it was too late. Photography became a privileged collaborator in that endeavour insofar as it was seen to overcome the subjectivity and unreliability of earlier technologies of representation, such as painting and etching.[117]

What may have been under-appreciated was the 'ineradicable surfeit' that always accompanies the photographic process.[118] These high-tech image-makers did not fully control the images they produced. As Christopher Pinney explains, '[n]o matter how precautionary and punctilious the photographer is in arranging everything that is placed before the camera, the inability of the lens to discriminate will ensure a substrate or margin of excess, a subversive code present in every photographic image that makes it open and available to other readings and uses' than those originally envisaged.[119] At the beginning of this chapter, I referred to some of the ways in which Woolley's now iconic front-facing photograph of Trucanini has been read. One reading picks up the trope of the 'spectre of Truganini', said by Bernard Smith to have 'haunted Australian culture', to tell of her 'haunting stare'.

Yet if Trucanini appears to stare in Woolley's picture, Rebe Taylor raises the question of whether that was just 'to keep still for the camera's slow exposure'. 'I don't want to ... presume to know her mind', Taylor declares. 'To do that is to try to own her once again.'[120] For Greg Lehman too, Trucanini's gaze is best described

[117] See Christopher Pinney, 'Introduction', in Christopher Pinney and Nicolas Peterson (eds.), *Photography's Other Histories* (Durham, NC: Duke University Press, 2003) 1, 6.

[118] Ibid. [119] Ibid. [120] Taylor, 'The National Confessional', 36.

as 'enigmatic'.[121] Nicolas Peterson observes that '[i]t is a commonplace that ethnographic photography in the colonial period encodes power relations, and that Aboriginal people were not only subjects of but were also subjected to the camera'. On the other hand, protracted exposure times and elaborate procedures for setting up photographic equipment meant that almost '[a]ny photographic encounter required a significant level of cooperation'. Peterson suggests that 'the Aboriginal people concerned ... [will] have had a wide range of reasons for cooperating', as to which we might conjecture but cannot claim to know in any particular case.[122]

The recognition that we cannot finally know Trucanini's thoughts and feelings is perhaps part of a subversive code that reads dignity back into Woolley's picture, even as he inflicts on her the indignity of being made a specimen of a racial type, and moreover one traduced in a scheme of human evolution. Writing of other photographs of Tasmanian Aboriginal people who sat for early photographers in colonial Hobart and Oyster Cove, Julie Gough observes that '[t]he rapidity of many of our ancestors' dispersal and deaths is cruelly countered by the impossible longevity of these images'.[123] As she experiences it, '[t]he stare of ... the Old People, our Tasmanian Aboriginal forebears, is relentless, accusatory, unwavering. Captured in the nineteenth century lenses of at least eight colonial photographers ... their gaze is ... something uncanny and uncomfortable, downright painful to be subjected to.' Gough continues: 'We live on and these images seem to find us, like some kind of episodic haunting, we face them and remember.'[124]

[121] Greg Lehman, 'Interest and Truth in History: A Review of Truganini: Journey through the Apocalypse by Cassandra Pybus', *Aboriginal History* 45 (2021) 161, 166.

[122] Nicolas Peterson, 'The Changing Photographic Contract: Aborigines and Image Ethics', in Christopher Pinney and Nicolas Peterson (eds.), *Photography's Other Histories* (Durham, NC: Duke University Press, 2003), 119, 123–24.

[123] Gough, 'Forgotten Lives', 21–22.

[124] Ibid.

4

Gandhi and the Undignified Loincloth

Dignified Self-Assertion

Continuing our investigation into dignity's worldly past, this chapter shifts the focus to early twentieth-century India, where the language of dignity featured prominently in the campaign for non-cooperation and independence led by M. K. Gandhi (or *Mahatma* – the great-souled – Gandhi, as his followers dubbed him). For Gandhi, non-cooperation was 'an attempt to awaken the masses to a sense of their dignity and power'.[1] He called on the Indian people to '[r]ealise [their] own dignity',[2] and maintained that, through 'dignified self-assertion',[3] they could finally put an end to economic exploitation and political domination, and redefine their country's relations with Britain in a manner consistent with 'self-respect and dignity'.[4] 'Self-confidence, dignity and the power of continuously bettering their own position'[5] would then be restored to all.

Central to Gandhi's programme of dignified self-assertion was the achievement of economic self-reliance by means of a boycott of British and other foreign goods and the re-establishment of Indian

[1] *Collected Works of Mahatma Gandhi*, vol. 22 (15 November 1920–5 April 1921), 41. References in this and subsequent footnotes to the *Collected Works of Mahatma Gandhi* are references to the digitised version, available at: www.?gandhiashram sevagram ?.org/gandhi-literature/collected-works-of-mahatma-gandhi-volume-1-to-98.php.

[2] Ibid., vol. 22, 463. [3] Ibid., vol. 26 (24 January 1922–31 December 1923), 10.

[4] Ibid., vol. 23 (6 April 1921–21 July 1921), 64.

[5] Ibid., vol. 71 (25 February 1937–5 July 1938), 244.

manufacturing traditions. In particular – and this will be our main interest here – he promoted the production and use of *khadi* (or *khaddar*), a type of cloth, hand-woven from homespun cotton, that had once been made and worn by peasants and artisans in the subcontinent, but had been displaced during the nineteenth century by imported Lancashire-produced textiles. From the launch of his movement in 1918 until his death in 1948, Gandhi never tired of urging Indians to 'discard this [English] apparel . . . to keep up our dignity as Indians'.[6] All Indians, including 'the so-called cultured classes', needed to learn to 'see dignity in wearing *khadi*'.[7]

More than that, all Indians needed to contribute to the fabrication of *khadi* by engaging in the 'dignified labour'[8] of spinning. If 'our love of foreign cloth . . . ousted the [spinning] wheel from its position of dignity',[9] the pursuit of domestically-based (*swadeshi*) manufactures, and of freedom from foreign rule (*swaraj*), should now impel the 'reinstatement of the spinning wheel in all its ancient dignity'.[10] Famously appealing to his countrymen and -women to allocate a portion of every day to spinning cotton yarn, Gandhi was careful to set an example by doing so – and being seen to do so – himself. Indeed, some of the most abiding images of him show a bespectacled man in a white *khadi* loincloth, sitting at the spinning wheel (Figure 4.1) .[11]

Images of that kind challenged prevailing conceptions of the dignity of a great man in a way that reinforced Gandhi's speeches and writings. *Khadi* was a practical programme and a valuable good, but it was also a visual symbol standing for (among other things) the repudiation of colonial criteria of honour and esteem and their replacement by new criteria rooted in old traditions proper to India. Yet, as we shall see, *khadi* was not embraced by everyone engaged in the struggle for liberation. Perhaps most notably, B. R. Ambedkar kept on his suit and tie – garments that were out of reach or even formally forbidden to most of those who, like him, were born into a Dalit (then known as Untouchable) family – and presented to colonial dignity a different challenge.

[6] Ibid., vol. 23, 51. [7] Ibid., vol. 31 (22 March 1925–15 June 1925), 259.
[8] Ibid., vol. 74 (9 September 1938–29 January 1939), 278.
[9] Ibid., vol. 24 (22 July 1921–25 October 1921), 415. [10] Ibid., vol. 23, 28.
[11] See especially the photographs taken by Margaret Bourke-White for *Life* magazine in 1946, available at: www.life.com/people/gandhi-and-his-spinning-wheel-the-story-behind-an-iconic-photo/.

Figure 4.1 *Mahatma Gandhi*, 1946. Photograph by Margaret Bourke-White.

Clothing and Being Unclothed

'Whoever says Industrial Revolution says cotton', goes the often quoted line from Eric Hobsbawm's *Industry and Empire.*[12] Until the late eighteenth century, write Giorgio Riello and Tirthankar Roy, 'India clothed the world'.[13] To understand the importance that *khadi* was able to assume in the decades leading up to Indian independence, it is necessary to touch, as Gandhi himself frequently did, on the history of cotton textile production in India and the impact of British industrialisation and imperialism upon it. It is also instructive to give attention to some aspects of the significance of clothing, both in the earlier years of the British Raj, and in the preceding period of the late Mughal Empire, when Mughal

[12] Eric Hobsbawm, *Industry and Empire* (London: Pelican, 1969), 56.

[13] Giorgio Riello and Tirthankar Roy, 'Introduction: The World of South Asian Textiles, 1500–1850', in Giorgio Riello and Tirthankar Roy (eds.), *How India Clothed the World: The World of South Asian Textiles, 1500*–1850 (Leiden: Brill, 2009), 1, 6.

rituals of homage and incorporation that revolved in part around textiles and clothing were emulated and adapted by the (British) East India Company.

There is, I think, little doubt about the fact that South Asia was an early centre of cotton textile production, and for a very long time the most important one. Evidence of cotton growing and use has been found in various parts of the ancient tropical and subtropical world, but it was in the Indian subcontinent that manufacturing processes – processes of carding, spinning, weaving, dyeing, painting, embroidery and printing – developed to a level that could foster a transoceanic trade in cotton cloth. That trade began in the Indian Ocean, and grew to encompass eventually the entire globe. Riello and Roy report that, by the late eighteenth century, cotton textiles made in the subcontinent accounted for 'approximately a quarter of the world's textile output and almost certainly a larger percentage' of the seaborne textile trade.[14] In his global history of cotton, Sven Beckert likewise highlights the area's pre-eminence, averring that from antiquity 'until well into the nineteenth century the people of the Indian subcontinent were the world's leading cotton manufacturers'.[15]

Of particular economic importance were the three regions of Gujarat in the west, the Coromandel Coast in the south and Bengal in the east, where traders arranged for the supply of muslins, calicoes, chintzes and distinctive blue cloths dyed with indigo to customers stretching from Southeast Asia to West Africa, and from the Americas to Europe. The European market appears to have been among the slowest to take off. Possessed of a climate in which the cotton plant was unknown, Europeans initially used cotton only for candle wicks, or mixed cotton with linen to make coarse 'fustian' fabric. And when pure cotton textiles began to appear, protectionist measures widely curbed their penetration to support local wool, linen and silk industries. Early European manufacturers of cotton cloth received similar protection against better quality and less expensive Indian imports. In Britain, cotton textiles were first commercially produced at sites near Bristol, Glasgow and Liverpool – port cities that would allow easy access to raw cotton – though with time, of course, the industry became concentrated in the

14 Ibid.
15 Sven Beckert, *Empire of Cotton: A Global History* (New York: Vintage, 2014), 7.

hinterlands of the lastmentioned of those cities, in the county of Lancashire.

Hobsbawm writes of the 'tussle' to which the new enterprise gave rise in Britain 'between industry and commerce (represented most dramatically by the East India Company)'.[16] By the seventeenth century, cotton cloth had become the 'most important manufactured commodity in world trade',[17] and it was the East India Company's own most important trading good. By the second half of the eighteenth century, it is believed to have 'constituted more than 75 percent of the ... Company's total exports'.[18] Yet, as Hobsbawm goes on to explain, that coexisted with an emergent cotton manufacturing sector in Britain which successfully evaded competition from South Asia.[19] And if industry won the tussle with commerce 'in the home market [as early as] 1700', it prevailed also 'in the foreign market [around a century later], when the East India Company was deprived of its monopoly in India, and [the] subcontinent opened to deindustrialization and the massive import of Lancashire cottons'.[20] The story of the mechanisation of cotton textile production in Lancashire, which is part of the backdrop to that development, need not detain us. Inasmuch as Britain's cotton-centric Industrial Revolution was ineliminably an Indian affair as well, a few related points are, nonetheless, worth noting.

To begin with, there is the very fact of the East India Company inserting itself into the Indian cotton textile trade. Established in 1600, the Company initially worked in partnership with local merchants, who arranged for the manufacture of cloth by independent professional weavers. As time passed, however, Company agents exerted increasing control, both over production processes and with respect to export networks. Weavers were coerced to work exclusively for the Company and for prices they did not themselves set. Royal Navy support was enlisted to capture new markets – outlets for the Company's subcontinental fabric range that could, and would, later become markets for Lancashire goods. In that

[16] Hobsbawm, *Industry and Empire*, 49.

[17] Prasannan Parthasarathi, 'Cotton Textiles in the Indian Subcontinent, 1200–1800', in Giorgio Riello and Prasannan Parthasarathi (eds.), *The Spinning World: A Global History of Cotton Textiles, 1200–1850* (Oxford: Oxford University Press, 2009), 17.

[18] Beckert, *Empire of Cotton*, 33.

[19] Hobsbawm, *Industry and Empire*, 49.

[20] Ibid., 49.

connection, it is significant that the Company also stimulated and facilitated efforts to gather knowledge about Indian textile manufacturing technologies. South Asian artisans had developed world-leading techniques in all aspects of cotton textile production, along with exceptional capacity to meet the requirements of particular sartorial customs and tastes. Thousands of varieties of cotton cloth were made in the region, and, in the eighteenth and nineteenth centuries, British observers went to considerable lengths to catalogue them and make Indian products available for copying.

An evident precondition to the establishment of a cotton textile manufacturing industry in a country that is climatically unsuitable for growing cotton is the importation of that raw material. The earliest British producers of cotton cloth obtained their cotton from the slave plantations of the Caribbean. From the 1790s, it was the slave plantations of the American South that became the primary source.[21] After the American Civil War, British cotton industrialists turned for the supply of raw cotton to India. India produced mostly short-staple cotton, whereas American-style medium- and long-staple cotton was what was wanted for spinning mills. Added to that, Indian peasants were resistant to the growing of cotton as a cash crop, disconnected from the activities of spinning and weaving. So it represented a very considerable attempt to transform the South Asian countryside when British cotton manufacturers sent out medium- and long-staple cottonseed for distribution to growers, and persuaded their government – which by then exercised direct rule in India – to clear fields, build infrastructure, and enclose land such that there would exist a landless labour force to work for wages on cotton plantations.

I have mentioned the East India Company's capture of long-distance markets that could, and would, later become markets for Lancashire goods. In the event, the Lancashire mills had the capacity to produce far greater quantities of yarn and cloth than could be absorbed by British domestic consumption and those export markets. New markets were needed, and just as cotton industrialists

[21] As African slavers often demanded cotton cloth in payment for slaves, Beckert calls attention to the 'complex commercial web' that tied together weavers in India, slavers in Africa, enslaved men and women in the Americas, and those in Europe engaged in the construction of a new 'empire of cotton'. See Beckert, *Empire of Cotton*, 36, x.

turned to India as a source of raw cotton, so too they turned to India as an outlet for finished goods. With reference to what then transpired, Beckert comments that '[o]nce Indians began using British-manufactured yarn and cloth, it signaled to all that the world's cotton industry had been turned on its head'.[22] Historians in our own time debate the precise mix of factors that brought about this situation, but whatever it was, Prasannan Parathasarathi and Ian Wendt recall that '[i]n the space of a few decades, India went from exporting voluminous quantities of cloth to losing markets around the world, then importing cheap cotton yarn, and finally importing the cloth itself'.[23] To draw again on Beckert's account, the subcontinent experienced 'a tsunami of deindustrialization',[24] which, to contemporaries, seemed the result of a deliberate colonial strategy to destroy Indian cotton manufacturing and cause Indians to become suppliers of raw cotton and consumers of cotton textiles made in Britain.[25]

What were the consequences of this in India? Already in the 1830s, the senior British official in the country spoke, in terms that famously caught the attention of Karl Marx, of the desperate plight of Indian weavers. 'The misery hardly finds a parallel in the history of commerce', he said. 'The bones of the cotton-weavers are bleaching the plains of India.'[26] With the great famines of the second half of the nineteenth century and the turn of the twentieth century, that misery deepened and expanded to engulf also others. South Asian peasants traditionally cultivated cotton alongside food crops; the phenomenon of a cotton monoculture did not exist. At the same time, whereas weaving was mostly a professional occupation, spinning was a spare-time activity that could generate supplementary income and be stepped up during lean years.[27] It was an effect of the developments mentioned above that both those measures of

[22] Ibid., 67.

[23] Prasannan Parthasarathi and Ian Wendt, 'Decline in Three Keys: Indian Cotton Manufacturing from the Late Eighteenth Century', in Giorgio Riello and Prasannan Parthasarathi (eds.), *The Spinning World: A Global History of Cotton Textiles, 1200*–1850 (Oxford: Oxford University Press, 2009), 397.

[24] Beckert, *Empire of Cotton*, 328. [25] Ibid., 75.

[26] Sir William Bentick, quoted in Karl Marx (Ben Fowkes, trans.), *Capital Volume 1* (London: Penguin, 1990), chap. 15, section 5.

[27] See Parthasarathi, 'Cotton Textiles in the Indian Subcontinent, 1200–1800', 17, 29–30. On weaving as also, for some people or in some contexts, a subsidiary occupation that could take up the slack at lean times, see Ramachandra

food security broke down. The rural populations of India widely lost the means of assuring that they would always survive, and to compound their vulnerability, British colonial policy followed the Smithian *laissez-faire* dogma according to which state action to prevent famine when bad harvests occurred and food prices rose was ill-advised.

Writing about the famines he terms the 'late Victorian holocausts', Mike Davis refers to estimates of Indian famine mortality in 1876–79 and 1896–1902 that range from 12.2 to 29.3 million people.[28] Districts such as Berar in the south-central Deccan, which had been identified by the Lancashire cotton manufacturing lobby as sites for intensive cotton growing, especially suffered. Needless to say, deficits of rainfall were part of the problem, but as the British Government's Famine Commission later acknowledged with regard to Berar in 1899–1900, the 'famine was one of high prices rather than scarcity of food'.[29] More specifically, the famine was one of high food prices, low cotton prices and lack of work, rather than scarcity of food. For the fate of Beraris was now tied to global markets over which they had no control, and to trade policy framed in the interests of distant others. Notoriously, at the same time as they starved, the export of Indian grain reserves for consumption in Britain went on. In Davis's words, 'Londoners were in effect eating India's bread'.[30] Given that Londoners were also wearing India's clothes, Davis remarks furthermore on the striking reversal whereby '[a] society formerly celebrated for its rich cotton fabrics was virtually unclothed' – literally reduced to nakedness and rags – 'by poverty'.[31] Meanwhile, colonial authorities disparaged as 'Oriental despotism' the steps once taken by local rulers to prevent life-threatening destitution.[32]

What of the issue I foreshadowed earlier of clothing as an element in Mughal ritual and later British practice? The presentation of items of cloth and clothing known as *khilats* (also transliterated as *khelats*) appears to have been an important feature of courtly

Guha, *Gandhi: The Years That Changed the World 1915*–1948 (London: Penguin, 2019), 86.

28 Mike Davis, *Late Victorian Holocausts: El Niño Famines and the Making of the Third World* (London: Verso, 2011), 7.

29 Ibid., 19, quoting *Report on the Famine in the Hyderabad Assigned Districts in the Years 1899 and 1900* (1901), 2.

30 Davis, *Late Victorian Holocausts*, 26. 31 Ibid., 315. 32 Ibid., 286.

ceremonies in early modern South Asia.[33] Generally translated as 'robes of honour', *khilats* were garments and other valuable gifts that were bestowed on persons of high rank during formal audiences with emperors (*durbars*),[34] both to honour those persons and to make manifest the emperors' own authority. Bernard Cohn tells of an early seventeenth-century English ambassador to the Mughal court who tried to avoid receiving *khilats,* plainly aware of the 'act of incorporation' in which he would thereby become involved.[35] Unsurprisingly, *khilat* rituals proved more appealing to English officials once they had themselves seized governing authority in India. The presentation to territorial rulers of special clothes at *durbar*-like events was one of a number of methods used by the East India Company and the early Raj to reward loyalty and cement power. But if British officials seemed to be adopting and perpetuating a Mughal tradition, Cohn emphasises that 'the meanings had been changed'.[36] Incorporation was now simple submission, and 'robes of honour' scarcely pretended to be other than 'mantles of subordination'.[37]

Naked Brutality

This history of clothing the world and then being virtually unclothed forms the context in which Gandhi initiated his

[33] *Khilats* were part of a complex ceremony that involved also *nazar,* a gift presented by the recipient of *khilats.*

[34] The term *'durbar'* referred originally to the emperor's noble court. By extension, it came to mean also the audiences that took place there. The *durbars* held by the British administrators of India were formal assemblies designed to put participants and spectators in mind of that practice; in the case of the early twentieth-century 'Delhi *durbars*', they were mass public events.

[35] See Bernard Cohn, 'Cloth, Clothes, and Colonialism: India in the Nineteenth Century', in Annette Weiner and Jane Schneider (eds.), *Cloth and Human Experience* (Washington, DC: Smithsonian, 1989), 303, 311. According to Cohn, the idea was that the emperor would originally take off his own robe and put it on the recipient, and once that practice ceased, the robe of honour still symbolically communicated to the recipient something of the emperor's corporeal essence; it followed that recipients were incorporated into the imperial order in some quite literal or mystical sense, and made, not just the emperor's subordinates, but also his companions.

[36] Bernard Cohn, 'Representing Authority in Victorian India', in Eric Hobsbawm and Terence Ranger (eds.), *The Invention of Tradition* (Cambridge: Cambridge University Press, 1983), 165, 172.

[37] See Cohn, 'Cloth, Clothes, and Colonialism', 316.

campaign to realise dignity through *khadi* and gained substantial support for it. Someone of his age was a child at the time of India's first 'late Victorian holocaust'. By the time he and his generation had reached thirty – if they reached thirty – many millions of Indians had died from starvation and related disease, 'with fatalities concentrated in the tracts ... that had recently been recast to produce cotton for export'.[38] In Berar, life expectancy fell to 'less than ten years' in 1900.[39] Romesh Chunder Dutt, whose two-part *Economic History of India* appeared in 1902 and 1904, had no doubt about the explanation for this. It was the outcome of economic and fiscal policies introduced by the East India Company, and not discontinued but rather extended after Company rule was abolished, that treated India as 'a vast estate or plantation, the profits of which were to be withdrawn from India and deposited in Europe'.[40] 'So great an Economic Drain out of the resources of a land would impoverish the most prosperous countries on earth', he writes. '[I]t has reduced India to a land of famines more frequent, more widespread, and more fatal, than any known before in the history of India, or the world.'[41]

The effort to 'make India subservient' to the textile industry of Britain, and to 'make the Indian people grow raw produce only, in order to supply material for the [British] looms', was very much part of this argument.[42] Dutt did not invent the theory of the economic drain,[43] but his work on it came at a key moment in the history of anti-colonial resistance in India. In 1905, the Viceroy, George Curzon, announced that Bengal was to be partitioned. Strenuously opposing the partition, nationalists in the province responded with a boycott of British goods, including first and foremost cloth and clothing. British-made garments were publicly burned, and activists committed themselves thenceforth to wear

[38] Beckert, *Empire of Cotton*, 337, referring to a study published in *The Lancet*.
[39] Davis, *Late Victorian Holocausts*, 315.
[40] Romesh Dutt, *The Economic History of India under Early British Rule* (London: Kegan Paul, 1902), xiv.
[41] Ibid., 420. See further Romesh Dutt, *The Economic History of India in the Victorian Age* (London: Kegan Paul, 1904).
[42] Dutt, *The Economic History of India under Early British Rule*, x (and elsewhere).
[43] Regarding the theory's application to India, see especially the work of Dadabhai Naoroji, including *Poverty and Un-British Rule in India* (London: Swan Sonnenschein, 1901).

only Indian-made cotton fabrics.[44] The movement became known as *Swadeshi,* a term that pointed to the domestic production (as opposed to reliance on imports) through which adherents sought to stop the drain, revive Indian manufacturing, and restore economic independence to the country. While the *Swadeshi* movement of Bengal always remained a largely provincial endeavour and petered out by 1910, its concepts and practices would resurface and take on all-India significance in Gandhi's later programme tying *swadeshi* to *swaraj,* or national self-government.

Among the many modes of communication which Gandhi used to promote *khadi* was *Young India,* the weekly English-language magazine he set up in 1919. And one thing made plain in the pages of *Young India* was that, compared to the Bengal *Swadeshi* movement, the scope of Gandhi's ambitions was wide, but his conception of *swadeshi* – and with that, of *khadi* – was narrow. For the Bengali activists, it did not matter how cloth was produced, provided it was produced in India. (Most commonly, Indian cloth was a product of the textile mills that had operated in Ahmedabad and a number of other cities since the 1860s, and supplied limited segments of the domestic market.) By contrast, Gandhi laid emphasis on manual production – hand-weaving, but soon also (and this would become his chief preoccupation) the use in hand-weaving of hand-spun yarn. Thus, one reads in his essay entitled 'The Music of the Spinning Wheel' that '[n]ot on the clatter of arms depends the revival of [India's] prosperity and true independence. It depends most largely on the reintroduction ... of the music of the spinning wheel.'[45] And again, in 'The Secret of *Swaraj*', 'India was enslaved for satisfying the greed of the foreign cloth manufacturer ... But we ought not to be dependent ... In [hand-spinning] is the hidden secret of *Swaraj.*'[46]

[44] The Bengali activists likewise did not invent these tactics, which had been used sporadically during the nineteenth century in various parts of India, and especially in the Bombay Presidency, which was the centre of industrialised cloth production in India. On an episode from 1896, see Susan Bean, 'Gandhi and Khadi, the Fabric of Indian Independence', in Annette Weiner and Jane Schneider (eds.), *Cloth and Human Experience* (Washington, DC: Smithsonian, 1989), 355, 364.

[45] *Collected Works of Mahatma Gandhi,* vol. 21 (1 July 1920–14 November 1920), 71–72.

[46] Ibid., vol. 22, 221, 223.

Referencing the analysis of Dutt,[47] Gandhi maintained that 'India cannot be free so long as India voluntarily encourages or tolerates the economic drain which has been going on for the past century and a half'. And since '[f]oreign cloth constitutes the largest drain voluntarily permitted by us', he called on his countrymen and -women to boycott foreign cloth and burn the foreign cloth already in their possession.[48] Gandhi proposed that the Indian 'mills do not and cannot immediately manufacture all the cloth we want'. By his reckoning, there still remained sufficient handloom weavers to supply the deficit; the limiting factor was yarn. The spinning-wheel had practically disappeared from India. Yet no boycott could be successful without boosting the country's output of cotton yarn, and that could 'only be done by hand-spinning'. Indeed, it could only be done by a huge collective effort of hand-spinning, with 'every one spinning during spare hours either for love or money'.[49] This claim received endorsement from the Indian National Congress, which put the spinning-wheel at the centre of its flag, and also, for a time, made voting and office-holding conditional on spinning certain quantities of cotton yarn.

Gandhi's project of reinstating the spinning-wheel 'in all its ancient dignity'[50] drew, as just indicated, on the drain theory of British rule in India. Inasmuch as a more general theme was the regeneration of cottage industries and the revalidation of traditional handicrafts, historians have also linked his project to the Arts and Crafts movement of the later nineteenth and early twentieth centuries in Britain itself. Gandhi had translated John Ruskin's *Unto This Last* into Gujarati some years earlier,[51] and his outlook certainly resonated with William Morris's anti-industrialism. 'A life of labour, i.e. the life of the tiller of the soil and the handicraftsman, is the life worth living', Gandhi wrote, referencing Ruskin.[52] In common with Morris, Gandhi decried as wretched and

47 Ibid., vol. 24, 14. 48 Ibid., vol. 22, 221. 49 Ibid., vol. 22, 222.

50 Ibid., vol. 23, 28.

51 Retranslated into English, Gandhi's text was presented as a *paraphrase* of Ruskin's work. On the irony of Gandhi's fascination with this Tory imperialist whose 'views on India were thoroughly Orientalist', see Patrick Brantlinger, 'A Postindustrial Prelude to Postcolonialism: John Ruskin, William Morris, and Gandhism', *Critical Inquiry* 22(3) (1996) 466, 468.

52 Mahatma Gandhi, *An Autobiography or The Story of My Experiments with Truth* (New Haven, CT: Yale University Press, 2018), 471.

inauthentic the form of existence associated with factory production. The challenge he urged upon nationalists was to revitalise village culture – the culture of the 'seven hundred thousand villages' which he famously held to be where 'India lives'[53] – and the meaningful, creative and sustaining work that once flourished within it. From this perspective, spinning could be represented as a humble, traditional toil of rural India that would epitomise 'the supreme dignity of labour'.[54]

If Gandhi attached importance to spinning as dignified labour that would stand for, and testify to, the dignity of labour in general, he was no less emphatic about the practical significance of spinning as famine protection – a means of making ends meet when food prices rose. As he declared, 'if the millions are to be saved from starvation, they must be enabled to reintroduce spinning in their homes, and every village must repossess its own weaver'.[55] The sale of thread to local weavers would provide crucial additional income for those who lived from agriculture, especially (though, given the seasonal character of agricultural work, not only) during bad years. Gandhi's advocacy for spinning also had another dimension. Going beyond the various arguments to do with the economic drain, the customary culture of the villages, and the practical necessity of supplementary work as insurance against famine, he characterised time spent at the spinning-wheel as 'holy work'.[56] To his way of thinking, it was a 'sacramental rite'[57] that brought meditative and spiritual benefits unique to 'those who work [the spinning-wheel] regularly'.[58] For '[s]pinning is such restful work that, as we make the hand one with the yarn, we can attune our hearts to God'.[59]

I have reviewed something of Gandhi's ideas about the production of homespun cloth, but, of course, his campaign was not just for the production of *khadi*, but also for its use. To be clothed in *khadi* was to be clothed in fabric that was rougher and more coarsely woven than most other available fabrics. What additionally set it apart was that it was plain white, and had no decoration of any kind.

53 *Collected Works of Mahatma Gandhi*, vol. 30 (27 December 1924–21 March 1925), 397.
54 Ibid., vol. 24, 243.
55 Ibid., vol. 21, 73. See further *Collected Works of Mahatma Gandhi*, vol. 23, 142, 479 ('Spinning as Famine Relief').
56 Ibid., vol. 25 (27 October 1921–22 January 1922), 154.
57 Ibid., vol. 23, 39.
58 Ibid., vol. 23, 175.
59 Ibid., vol. 25, 33.

In re-dressing the nation in *khadi,* Gandhi sought to create a new national costume that would bespeak simplicity, self-discipline and patriotic sacrifice. At the same time, he deployed caste-based imagery to portray foreign cloth as dirty and polluting, so that the wearing of *khadi* could appear as an act of self-purification. As Christopher Bayly puts it, homespun cloth was to 'transform the moral fiber of the nation in a quite literal sense'.[60] According to Bayly, such a project gained potency from the history of transactions in cloth in India, which attests to a perception that cloth could transform the wearer or recipient by retaining and imparting to them another's spirit or essence. In the Mughal context, it was the emperor's spirit that *khilats* imparted. Where *khadi* was concerned, its loose, porous weave 'seemed almost to be able to capture and retain the spirit of the land itself'.[61]

At the least, Emma Tarlo notes that the peculiar proximity of clothing to bodies gives it a 'special potential for symbolic elaboration'.[62] Gandhi seems to have been intensely aware of this, as his own frequent and increasingly spectacular wardrobe changes amply demonstrate. Tarlo tells of how Gandhi started life wearing both Indian and European styles. Photographs show that, as a child, his habitual dress was a *dhoti* with a shirt and sometimes also a coat. When he went to England to study law, he switched to full European garb, 'anxious not to look out of place', yet immediately embarrassed to find that his dress was somehow still not quite right.[63] Arriving later in South Africa to serve as legal counsel to an expatriate-Indian merchant, he appeared in court during his first week in a European frock coat and an 'imitation Bengali turban'.[64] The combination of European clothes and Indian headwear was favoured by many men of his class at the time in India, but the presiding magistrate asked Gandhi to remove his turban.

60 Christopher Bayly, 'The Origins of Swadeshi (Home Industry): Cloth and Indian Society, 1700–1930', in Arjun Appardurai (ed.), *The Social Life of Things: Commodities in Cultural Perspective* (Cambridge: Cambridge University Press, 1986), 285, 312.

61 Ibid., 289.

62 See Emma Tarlo, *Clothing Matters: Dress and Identity in India* (London: Hurst and Company, 1996), 16.

63 Ibid., 65 (mentioning also Gandhi's arrival at Southampton 'to find that he was the only person in white flannels').

64 Ibid., 67.

He refused to do so on the grounds that the removal of headwear was a gesture of disrespect for Indians, and left the courtroom. Tarlo suggests that this incident 'marked a turning-point in Gandhi's attitude to dress'. From then on, 'instead of wearing only what was socially acceptable and obligatory, he began to adopt clothes which he knew to be socially unacceptable and provocative'.[65]

Throughout his subsequent and increasingly politically active sojourn in South Africa, as well as after his return to India in 1915, there unfolded 'a period of sartorial experimentation . . . [in which] Gandhi began to convert his embarrassment at being wrongly dressed into a strategy for exposing injustice and embarrassing others'.[66] His final experiment, which was to continue for the remaining twenty-seven years of his life, began in 1921. One of the difficulties of the *khadi* programme was the limited availability of homespun cloth and its high cost relative to imported fabrics. On 22 September 1921, Gandhi announced that he would discard his *topi* (cap) and vest, and content himself with 'only a loin-cloth', along with 'a *chaddar* [shawl] whenever found necessary for the protection of my body' until 31 October of the same year – though, as indicated, that time-frame came to be extended permanently. He explained that this decision had been taken to lead the way and 'make it easy for those who could not afford' to buy enough homespun cloth to replace all the foreign cloth which he was enjoining them to burn. Furthermore, he wrote, 'I consider the renunciation to be also necessary for me as a sign of mourning [that self-government has not yet been achieved] and a bare head and a bare body is such a sign in my part of the country.'[67]

In September 1931, Gandhi travelled to England to represent the Congress at the Second Round Table Conference, convened by the British Government to discuss India's constitutional future. Ramachandra Guha reports that the Indian leader was given police protection in London, as 'Scotland Yard feared actions "such as students dressing up in loin cloths"' – something that did, in fact, occur, and that the police judged 'innocuous' in England, but likely to be widely 'resented' in India.[68] On 5 November, King George V hosted a reception at Buckingham Palace for delegates to the

[65] Ibid., 67. [66] Ibid. [67] *Collected Works of Mahatma Gandhi*, vol. 24, 303.
[68] Guha, *Gandhi*, 398.

Round Table Conference. Another detail mentioned by Guha regarding Gandhi's visit is that the invitation to this event 'specified that those attending should wear "Morning Dress"'; however, 'after much to-ing and fro-ing between the palace officials and Mahadev Desai' (Gandhi's private secretary), an exception was finally made for Gandhi, and he attended the reception in his familiar attire.[69] There is an anecdote about a journalist asking him whether he did not feel cold in his loincloth and sandals, in response to which Gandhi is supposed to have quipped, '[t]he king has on enough for the two of us', but Guha says that he has not been able to verify the exchange.[70] Even so, it is not difficult to imagine that, as Tarlo observes, Gandhi's nakedness would have made, and been intended to make, a 'powerful contrast to the pedantically clad' British guests and their still more pedantically and elaborately clad monarch.[71]

Gandhi seems to have hesitated for some years before adopting his final form of dress. While he may not have minded being mistaken for a Hindu ascetic, he could not fail to be aware that exposure of the body has a different significance outside its normal contexts.[72] He wrote of the worry that his appearance 'would be labelled as "indecent"', and of how he had reached the view that the risk was nonetheless one 'I think it right' to take.[73] In truth, however, and most especially during that visit to London, Gandhi *owned* the indecency of the loincloth. Subverting accepted dress-codes, he used his nakedness as a metonym for his country's reduction to naked impoverishment, itself a token of the 'naked brutality'[74] of British rule in India. With his indecency, he held a mirror up to the indecency of imperial policy that treated the subcontinent as an estate from which to extract profits and resources. When he

[69] Ibid., 409.

[70] Ibid., 410. Guha does, however, confirm a related anecdote, according to which Gandhi was asked by a journalist on arrival at Marseille whether he would continue to wear the loincloth in England, and joked in response: 'In your country you put on plus-fours; I prefer minus-fours.'

[71] Tarlo, *Clothing Matters*, 82.

[72] On this, see Sandra Dudley, 'Material Visions: Dress and Textiles', in Marcus Banks and Jay Ruby (eds.), *Made to Be Seen: Perspectives in Visual Anthropology* (Chicago, IL: University of Chicago Press, 2011), 45, 65–66.

[73] *Collected Works of Mahatma Gandhi*, vol. 28 (22 May 1924–15 August 1924), 369.

[74] Lisa Trivedi, *Clothing Gandhi's Nation: Homespun and Modern India* (Bloomington, IN: Indiana University Press, 2007), 68.

rejected Lancashire-produced cloth, Gandhi also rejected the ideology that made it possible to consider such exploitation proper. Conversely, when students or others then poked fun at him by dressing up in loincloths, they brought home the tenacity of that ideology, though also the absurdity of Gandhi's having to resort to self-humiliation to advance the cause of Indian freedom and self-rule. Through the visual message of his clothing or lack of it, Gandhi returned India's embarrassment to those who ate its bread and wore its clothes, and deployed his indignity to expose their shame.

The Haughty Face

In the event, Gandhi had only limited success at persuading fellow Indians to join his *khadi* movement, at least as he envisaged it. Perhaps his most high-profile critic was the poet and writer Rabindranath Tagore, who expressed dismay at the 'burning of cloth, heaped up before the very eyes of our motherland shivering and ashamed in her nakedness'. 'What is the nature of the call to do this?', Tagore rhetorically asks. He goes on: 'The question of using or refusing cloth of a particular manufacture belongs mainly to economic science ... But far from this, we take the course of ... relying on the magical formula that foreign cloth is "impure". Thus economics is bundled out and a fictitious moral dictum is dragged into its place.'[75] Tagore was concerned that Gandhi had fostered a 'cult of the *charkha*' (spinning-wheel). Yet the 'root cause' of India's poverty was 'complexly ramified', and to address it, what was needed was rational decision-making based on careful investigation into the various contributing factors, not 'blind faith'. 'For the whole country to fall upon only one of [its poverty's] external symptoms with the application of one and the same remedy will not serve to fight the demon away.' Indeed, it only '[distracts] attention from other more important factors in our task of all-round reconstruction'.[76]

[75] Rabindranath Tagore, 'The Call of Truth', reproduced in Sabyasachi Bhattacharya (ed.), *The Mahatma and the Poet: Letters and Debates between Gandhi and Tagore 1915*–1941 (New Delhi: National Book Trust, 1997), 74, 88.

[76] Rabindranath Tagore, 'The Cult of the *Charkha*', reproduced in Sabyasachi Bhattacharya (ed.), *The Mahatma and the Poet: Letters and Debates between Gandhi and Tagore 1915*–1941 (New Delhi: National Book Trust, 1997), 103, 106, 115.

Further to his effort to refocus nationalist policy on economic science, Tagore also took issue with Gandhi's account of the time-honoured dignity and spiritual benefits of spinning. Citing Ruskin's intellectual associate and mentor Thomas Carlyle, Tagore writes of how 'Carlyle may have proclaimed the dignity of labour in stentorian accents, but a still louder cry has gone up from humanity, age after age, testifying to [the] indignity' of repetitive rural labour. Operating a spinning-wheel was stupefying, mind-numbing work, 'undignified drudgery', and anyone suggesting otherwise was making a 'cruel joke' to those for whom spinning was the only alternative to death by starvation.[77] This was a view shared by others including Anilbaran Ray, who remarked that if there was no shortage of people ready to spin, and to do it for the extremely modest sums which they could thereby earn, then that 'shows only the deep poverty of the masses but not the capacity of the *Charkha* [spinning-wheel] to remedy it'.[78] Moreover, spinning-wheels could be worked almost nowhere on an 'independent cottage industry basis'; they depended on public subscriptions, and were being maintained 'at great expense'.[79] Like Tagore, Ray believed that Gandhi's campaign stood 'in the way of true constructive village work', just as it stood in the way of the further development of industrialised production, without which 'the poverty of our people [cannot] be removed'.[80]

Tagore recalled that the design of a new national costume had already been attempted in the 1870s by one of his own elder brothers, Jyotirindranath Tagore.[81] Evidently amused by the memory, the younger Tagore describes how Jyotirindranath deemed the Indian *dhoti* 'not .. business-like', and European-style trousers 'too foreign', 'so he hit upon a compromise which considerably detracted from the *dhoti* while failing to improve the trousers': 'the trousers were decorated with the addition of a false *dhoti*-fold in front and behind'. Jyotirindranath also came up with hybrid headwear, the style of which his younger brother declares to have been similarly unfortunate. And whereas '[n]o person of ordinary

[77] Ibid., 103, 107–8.

[78] Anilbaran Ray, *The Illusion of the Charkha* (Calcutta: Arya Sahitya Bhawan, 1929), 6–7.

[79] Ibid., 3. [80] Ibid., 9, 8.

[81] Rabindranath Tagore (Devabrata Mukherjee, trans.), *My Reminiscences* (New Delhi: Niyogi Books, 2017), 137.

courage could have dared it', we learn that Jyotirindranath 'unflinchingly wore the complete suit in broad day-light, passing through the house of an afternoon to the carriage waiting outside, indifferent alike to the stare of relation or friend, door-keeper or coachman'. Tagore quips that '[t]here may be many a brave Indian ready to die for his country, but there are but few, I am sure, who even for the good of the nation would face the public streets in such pan-Indian garb'.[82] As the reference to his brother's waiting carriage, watchful door-keeper and staring coachman clearly confirms, Tagore belonged to an immensely privileged family, whose life was far removed from that of ordinary Indians. Nonetheless, Jyotirindranath Tagore's failed experiment may have been an early indication of the difficulty of finding a mode of dress that could unite the nation in colonial India.[83]

Gandhi's pan-Indian dress-code – by which I mean the dress-code he asked others to adopt, not the dress-code he adopted for himself – was likewise supposed to offer a compromise between different sartorial styles. However, in his case, the compromise was not between South Asian and European styles; it was between the myriad different traditions of South Asian dress. As Gandhi seems to have conceived it, *khadi* would visually erase the distinctions that existed between people of different regions, religions, classes and castes, and fuse the nation together to bring down British ascendancy. The practice of dressing in white homespun cloth and of spinning the yarn needed for its production would level the gap between rich and poor, while also overriding social divisions of all other kinds in favour of a new, unified, national identity. If that was the aim, significant strains emerged almost immediately. Alongside disparities with regard to spinning, there was a problem of elite nationalists wearing more finely woven, higher thread-count and sometimes also richly decorated artisanal fabrics which they had had made for them. Thus, Lisa Trivedi explains that *khadi* did not 'erase evidence of class and status'. 'Rather, the ways in which class was marked changed. No longer marked through European styles and Lancashire-produced cloth, class identification was maintained

[82] Ibid., 137.

[83] On this point, see Tarlo, *Clothing Matters*, 59. See also Tara Mayer, 'From Craft to Couture: Contemporary Indian Fashion in Historical Perspective', *South Asian Popular Culture* 16(2–3) (2018) 183, 189.

through [variants of] *khadi* clothing that only elites could afford to wear.'[84]

But the main problems with the *khadi* programme were revealed by less affluent nationalists, and especially the women among them. The nationalist uniform in which Gandhi hoped to re-dress the nation consisted of a *khadi dhoti* or *kurta pajama* and *khadi* cap (the so-called 'Gandhi cap') for men and *khadi sari* for women. Inasmuch as this demanded a very substantial change of women who, by regional or religious tradition, dressed in garments other than the *sari*, Gandhi's compromise appeared, from their perspective, distinctly skewed. Its implementation called for a level of negotiation between community standards of dignified raiment on the one hand and solidarity with the nationalist cause on the other that was difficult, and outside elite circles often impossible, to manage. Even for those accustomed to wearing a *sari*, difficulties arose. Gandhi reproduces in *Young India* a letter from a woman who writes of her predicament as a poor person living in a locality where *saris* were conventionally nine yards in length. As *khadi* was costly, she could afford to wear it only by reducing her *sari* to six yards – the length that the *khadi* movement was trying to popularise as a means of dealing with the price differential between *khadi* and imported (or local) mill-made cloth – 'but the elders will not hear of any such reduction'.[85] Gandhi's reflection on this is that 'sticking to old customs' will not bring India closer to *swaraj*. A 'spirit of self-sacrifice' has to be cultivated, including the 'sacrifice of provincialism'.[86]

The re-Indianisation of dress through *khadi* has been characterised as an 'essentially male-dominated' phenomenon, the counterpart of the equally male-dominated Europeanisation of dress that it was supposed to supplant.[87] To be sure, there were prominent exceptions, and some of Gandhi's most important allies in the promotion of *khadi* were women. Yet what he termed the sacrifice of provincialism may not have been an option for the vast majority of South Asian women. Trivedi observes that, in contradistinction to

[84] Trivedi, *Clothing Gandhi's Nation*, 94. This is also a key argument of Emma Tarlo. See Tarlo, *Clothing Matters*, esp. 105.

[85] *Collected Works of Mahatma Gandhi*, vol. 41 (2 December 1927–1 May 1928), 156. On this, see further Trivedi, *Clothing Gandhi's Nation*, 81, 83.

[86] *Collected Works of Mahatma Gandhi*, vol. 41, 156.

[87] Tarlo, *Clothing Matters*, 321.

'elites whose respectability could be established in other ways, [poorer] families ... relied upon the dress of women to establish and maintain status'.[88] The point is presumably that social standing and the respect which came with it were less secure for such families, and (gendered) notions of propriety loomed correspondingly larger. In this regard, a further difficulty associated with the *khadi* sari was its white colour. It was apparently the case in many parts of South Asia at the time that a white homespun *sari* constituted the usual dress of widows. This made it complicated for young women in those regions to wear *khadi*, and all the more so as widowhood was a socially marginal status freighted with a range of undesirable connotations.[89] Despite these and other issues, Charu Gupta writes of how the 'perceived anti-*swadeshi* woman' was often shamed and admonished as a 'bad housewife' or selfish would-be '*memsahib*'.[90]

Gupta also highlights the particular position of Dalits with regard to *khadi*. Dalits lived under a brutal system of social exclusion which confined them to the peripheral zones of rural and urban settlements, and imposed on them a multiplicity of other privations, proscriptions, obligations and afflictions. This system did not operate in the same way everywhere and for all Dalit communities, and nor had its operation always been the same,[91] but restrictions on dress were a widely established feature of it. Though definitely not the most damaging of the exclusionary practices to which Dalits were subjected, dress restrictions served to make visible, and contributed to perpetuating, their outcaste status. So, for example, it was often stipulated that Dalits could not wear head-coverings, footwear, clean clothes, or clothes with fashionable embellishments. Dalit men were forbidden from wearing *dhotis* of the full length worn by their non-Dalit contemporaries. Dalit women were not

[88] Trivedi, *Clothing Gandhi's Nation*, 83.

[89] On this, see further Lisa Trivedi, 'Making Women (In)visible? Homespun in the Nationalist Politics of Dress and Identity in Modern India 1917–1935', in Dede Fairchild Ruggles (ed.), *Woman's Eye, Woman's Hand: Making Art and Architecture in Modern India* (New Delhi: Zubaan Books, 2014), 114, 126–29 and 132.

[90] Charu Gupta, '"Fashioning" Swadeshi: Clothing Women in Colonial North India', *Economic and Political Weekly* 47(42) (2012) 76, 79–80.

[91] On the history of caste and its relation to colonial practices of governance, see Nicholas Dirks, *Castes of Mind: Colonialism and the Making of Modern India* (Princeton, NJ: Princeton University Press, 2001).

allowed to wear a bodice or chemisette under their *saris*, as had long since become the norm among non-Dalit women. In this context, Gupta observes that *khadi* 'did not make much sense to dalits'.[92] A campaign framed in the language of simplicity, authenticity and abstention from consumption hardly reckoned with their circumstances. On the contrary, Gupta suggests that Dalits 'implicitly turned [the *swadeshi* ideal] upside down' to the extent that their aspiration was to 'transcend their position' and 'garner dignity' precisely through the 'power of "foreign" dressing'.[93]

Guha seems to have something similar in mind when he remarks that '[w]hereas portraits of Gandhi usually show him in his loincloth, [the jurist and Dalit leader, B. R.] Ambedkar is always represented by his admirers as wearing a suit and tie'. That is because '[f]or the upper-caste Gandhi, the loincloth signifies sacrifice; were Ambedkar to wear a loin-cloth . . . it would attract no notice, since by custom and tradition he was permitted only to wear the scantiest of garments. It is his wearing of a suit that signifies [his] successful storming of the upper-class citadel.'[94] What makes this juxtaposition noteworthy is, of course, that if Tagore was Gandhi's most high-profile critic, Ambedkar was his most unsettling opponent.[95] The oppositional nature of their relationship arose partly from differences relating to the arrangements that should be put in place for the political representation of Dalits after independence. However, it also ranged a lot more broadly and deeply than that, and Ambedkar's *Annihilation of Caste* (the text of a speech which he prepared for a meeting of Hindu caste-reformers but could not deliver, as the organisers considered aspects of his argument too controversial and cancelled the meeting) illustrates that one area of difference between the two men pertained to dignity.

This comes into view at a point where Ambedkar makes brief reference to two stories about which he had recently read in newspapers. In the first story, some women from better-off Dalit families in the village of Zanu near Ahmedabad 'started fetching water in metal pots', as opposed to the pots made of cheaper material which

[92] Gupta, '*"Fashioning" Swadeshi*', 82. [93] Ibid.

[94] Ramachandra Guha, 'Introduction', in Mulk Raj Anand, *Untouchable* (London: Penguin, 2014; first published 1935), xiv.

[95] On this point, see Arundhati Roy, 'The Doctor and the Saint', in B. R. Ambedkar, *Annihilation of Caste* (London: Verso, 2016), 17, 39.

they had previously used and were commonly used by other local Dalit householders. It then emerged that '[t]he Hindus looked upon the use of metal pots by Untouchables as an affront to their dignity'. Brimming with indignant rage, the Hindus of Zanu 'assaulted the Untouchable women for their impudence'. The second story concerned a Dalit man from Chakwara in Jaipur who decided to hold a dinner to celebrate his return from a pilgrimage. To make it a sumptuous meal, he served ghee as part of the dinner. Again, 'the Hindus [now] in their hundreds [and] armed with *lathis* [heavy sticks bound with iron] rushed to the scene, despoiled the food, and belaboured', that is, assaulted and abused, the party. The explanation given is that '[i]n righteous indignation [the Chakwara Hindus] avenged themselves for the wrong done to them by the Untouchables, who insulted them by treating ghee as an item of their food – which they ought to have known could not be theirs – consistently with the dignity of the Hindus'.[96]

At the beginning of this chapter, I quoted passages from Gandhi's writings that gave voice to his wish to awaken the masses to a sense of their dignity and power. In those passages, Gandhi appeals to Indians to discard their English apparel in order to keep their dignity as Indians, and looks forward to the day when India's relations with Britain will be redefined in a manner consistent with its people's self-respect and dignity. At times, Ambedkar spoke of dignity in something like that sense. Between 1947 and 1949, he served as Chairman of the Drafting Committee for the Indian Constitution, and in that capacity, he oversaw the insertion into the Constitution of language about the importance of assuring the 'dignity of the individual'.[97] His writings also brought sharply into focus the 'many indignities' heaped upon Dalit communities 'which are incompatible with the dignity' that belongs with all 'human life'.[98] By his account, the background conditions that made it important to assure the dignity of the individual certainly included the 'insult and indignity which [Dalits] have to bear as a result of

96 B. R. Ambedkar, *Annihilation of Caste* (London: Verso, 2016), 216–17.

97 *Constitution of India*, Preamble (referring to the promotion among all citizens of fraternity assuring, *inter alia*, the dignity of the individual).

98 *Selected Works of Dr B. R. Ambedkar*, 2996. References in this and subsequent footnotes to *Selected Works of Dr B. R. Ambedkar* are references to the digitised version, available at: https://judicialacademy.nic.in/sites/default/files/1458100182_selected%20work%20of%20Dr%20B%20Rambedkar.pdf.

the vicious social order'.[99] For the most part, however, Ambedkar spoke of dignity in a rather different sense – the sense exemplified by the events he retold from Zanu and Chakwara.

Luis Cabrera calls this the 'haughty face of dignity'.[100] The haughty face of dignity does not align itself with the universalist idea of dignity as an intrinsic attribute of all human beings and the related principle that everyone deserves equal concern and respect. To the contrary, it affirms social hierarchies, and is the ever-vigilant guardian of exclusive prerogatives, special privileges and asymmetrical entitlements to respect. As described by Cabrera, the haughty face of dignity entails a collective disposition to 'defensiveness, indignation and resentment against others as potential violators of rights'.[101] In the settings around which Ambedkar's work mostly revolved, Cabrera proposes that its characteristic form was a demand for 'deference from others accorded lower status within the Hindu caste system'.[102] Conceptually speaking, dignity was figured as a 'social property possessed by those of higher status in the Hindu caste hierarchy, who jealously guard it and respond with indignation and anger when they perceive that those of lower standing have not shown them due deference'.[103] And if dignity was a social property possessed by those with higher status in the caste hierarchy of Hindu society, then Cabrera further proposes that that status was 'dependent on the existence of an underclass … from which a retinue of subservients may be freely drawn, and against whom elites can measure their own ranking dignity'.[104]

Laying the basis for this analysis in *Annihilation of Caste* and other works, Ambedkar foregrounds the situation of Dalits as the primary underclass against which the ranking dignity of caste Hindus is measured. After all, '[w]hy will a Hindu not touch an untouchable?' 'Why will not a Hindu allow an untouchable to enter a temple or use the village well? Why will not a Hindu admit an untouchable to the inn? … why will not a Brahmin priest officiate at religious ceremonies performed by an untouchable? Why will not a barber serve an untouchable?' 'The answer to each one of these questions

[99] *Selected Works of Dr B. R. Ambedkar*, 2259.
[100] Luis Cabrera, 'Ambedkar on the Haughty Face of Dignity', *Politics and Religion* 14(1) (2020) 83.
[101] Ibid., 84. [102] Ibid. [103] Ibid., 85. [104] Ibid., 86.

is the same ... It is that it is below dignity to do so.'[105] A corresponding logic was used to justify the imposition on Dalits of particular duties. Thus, he continues, '[u]nder the Established Order, the work of lifting and removing dead cattle as well as doing the scavenger's work [of manually removing excrement from pits and buckets or other vessels used as toilets] is beneath the dignity of the Hindus. It must be done by the Untouchables.'[106] Requirements to attend in other ways to the needs of caste Hindus contributed still further to '[enabling the cultivation of] a feeling of pride and dignity befitting a master class which cannot be fostered and sustained unless there is beneath it a servile class to look down upon'.[107]

As Ambedkar told it, then, the sufferings of Dalit people could not be understood without reference to dignity, and to the exploitation and oppression that were justified in its name. Equally, a campaign for dignity was inadequate to halt those sufferings if, or insofar as, it failed to contest and transform the social arrangements that made such justification possible. Ambedkar believed that the nub of the problem was the Hindu system of caste. While caste persisted, dignity could not set things right – a point he reinforced with reference to another story, now drawn from his own personal experience of the complex and sometimes intentionally, but sometimes also unintentionally, harmful interplay of dignity, status and caste. In 1929, Ambedkar was appointed as chairman of a Committee tasked with investigating grievances of Dalits in the Bombay province. This work took him to the city of Chalisgaon, where he was invited to stay overnight with the local Dalit community. Upon arrival at the railway station, he was met by a contingent from the community. They lived a short distance away, across a river channelled under the train tracks through a culvert. One could walk there, or alternatively one could take one of the many horse carriages for hire at the station.

Ambedkar was not led to the Dalit neighbourhood on foot, but nor was he immediately taken to one of the available horse carriages. Instead, he was made to wait about an hour and eventually

[105] Vasant Moon (ed., 1st ed.), Hari Narke (ed., 2nd ed.), *Dr Babasaheb Ambedkar: Writings and Speeches, Vol. 2*, 492, available at: www.mea.gov.in/Images/attach/amb/Volume_02.pdf.

[106] *Selected Works of Dr B. R. Ambedkar*, 3991.

[107] Ibid., 4324.

shown to a carriage with an evidently inexperienced driver. As the carriage approached the end of the culvert, its horse turned the wrong way and bolted, causing the vehicle to topple and Ambedkar to be thrown out. Badly injured, he later learned what had happened. 'The delay at the railway station was due to the fact that the [carriage drivers] were not prepared to drive ... with a passenger who was an untouchable. It was beneath their dignity.' But the Dalit contingent who met him 'could not tolerate that I should walk to their quarters. It was not in keeping with their sense of my dignity.' A compromise was therefore reached, whereby the owner of a carriage would allow it to be used to convey Ambedkar, and one of the Dalit men (with no knowledge of carriage-driving) would drive it in the owner's place. Ambedkar comments that the Dalits of Chalisgaon believed this 'a happy solution. But they evidently forgot that the safety of a passenger was more important than the maintenance of his dignity. If they had thought of this they would have considered whether they could get a driver who could safely conduct me to my destination.'[108]

A Frayed History

It is perhaps an index of the significance of cotton cloth in South Asian history that the various processes associated with it have passed into the metaphorical language used in narratives of that history. Authors write of how the subcontinent's cotton manufacturing industry was 'reduced to tatters' during the nineteenth century.[109] They study the 'frayed history' of cotton in India,[110] and point to the early twentieth-century developments by which *khadi* became a symbol that would be 'woven into the fabric of Indian politics and culture for decades to come'.[111] The multiple meanings of *khadi* are said to have facilitated the process by which nationalists '[tailored] *swadeshi* to suit different political circumstances'.[112] And so it was, we read, that when Gandhi launched his *swadeshi* campaign at the beginning of the 1920s, this everyday item could at

108 Ibid., 4083–84.

109 Meena Menon and Uzramaa, *A Frayed History: The Journey of Cotton in India* (Delhi: Oxford University Press, 2017), 33.

110 Ibid. 111 Trivedi, *Clothing Gandhi's Nation*, 2. 112 Ibid., xx.

once be 'clothed in the rhetoric of traditional community and ... supersede traditional community boundaries'.[113]

For those participating in that campaign, what seems to have mattered most was the 'symbolic paradox [that] the consumption of millions of rupees worth of foreign [cloth had left] Indian men and women poor and naked'.[114] Metaphorically but also in many cases literally, Indians had been denuded by their Lancashire garments, and the proposition advanced by Gandhi was that only the use of domestically produced cloth which had been handwoven from hand-spun yarn could dispel their shame. We have seen that he identified *khadi* with the recovery of dignity at a number of different levels. To begin with, there was the dignity that was involved in simply assuming the capacity to define what is dignified in one's own way and by one's own lights. *Khadi* – the country cloth and the nationalist uniform – would stand for the rejection of colonial measures of value, propriety and taste and their supersession by new measures with roots in Indian tradition.

Secondly, there was the dignity that is a consequence of basic security and possession of the means for a decent life. With his 'undignified' variant of the nationalist uniform, Gandhi would communicate to the world that much of South Asia had been deprived of such means under British administration, or at the least reduced to a precarious existence of dreadful vulnerability. Stripped down to a *khadi* loincloth, he would expose the indignity behind the dignified facade of British India, and would gesture towards a different future in which the means for a decent life were assured to all. At a third level, Gandhi laid consistent emphasis in his writings and speeches on the dignity that comes from self-government and self-sufficiency or, at any rate, economic independence. The wearing of *khadi* would signal Indians' non-violent resistance to colonial rule and their determination to regain control of their own affairs and emancipate themselves from exploitation and domination by the British.

Finally, it is evident from Gandhi's published works that he identified *khadi* with recuperation of the dignity which he considered to be a function of productive labour. The launch of a nationwide programme of spinning would put an end to under-

[113] Ibid., 43. [114] Bayly, 'The Origins of Swadeshi (Home Industry)', 285, 312.

employment, and provide greatly enhanced opportunities for coming to know the 'dignity of work'. As Gandhi conceived it, then, dignity was collective and individual, symbolic and material, an everyday practice and a political aspiration. What kind of practice? What kind of aspiration? Alongside his conception, we have seen that Ambedkar evoked a quite different notion of dignity. Informed by the distinctive experience of India's Dalit populations, the haughty face of dignity that emerges in Ambedkar's roughly contemporaneous writings has as its most typical attitude *indignation* – specifically, the indignation of those with higher social status towards those with lower social status who are believed to have transgressed social boundaries and thereby caused them affront.

Ambedkar directs attention to the status dignity that is embedded in social structures, and that will remain after the termination of colonial rule unless and until those structures are transformed. He points out that Dalits and other subordinated groups will still be made to know their place and keep to their station. Caste Hindus and other relatively privileged groups will still be disposed to stand on their dignity, and to respond with aggressive indignation when their social subordinates are perceived to have slighted them. For those social subordinates, dignity will still eclipse considerations of safety, security and well-being. In an essay about *Annihilation of Caste*, Arundhati Roy observes that Ambedkar recognised that '"the people" was not a homogeneous category'. 'He knew that, regardless of what Gandhi said, it would inevitably be the majority community that decided what form *swaraj* would take.'[115] So now, she urges, let the diverse population of today's India, and especially its majority community, listen to Ambedkar; let them appreciate his insight and also his undisguised anger, which, she further suggests, 'gives us all a little shelter, a little dignity'.[116]

[115] Roy, 'The Doctor and the Saint', 45. [116] Ibid., 48.

5

Dignity and Indignity in the South African Toilet Wars

Sanitation is Dignity

What does dignity mean in the twenty-first century? For many people today, an everyday experience that raises the issue of dignity literally every day is going to the toilet. As the slogan used in campaigns for improved access to toilets has it, 'Sanitation is dignity'.[1] One organisation attached that title to a project in which cut-out images of people crouching as if to use a toilet were set up in public places, next to signs that read 'Where would you hide? 2,600,000,000 people toiletless'.[2] To be sure, sanitation is also health, hygiene, personal safety, and much else besides. Yet even the most cursory glance at relevant materials will reveal that dignity looms large in the matter of toilet access.

There exist struggles around sanitation in all countries of the world. In this chapter we look at a country where those struggles have been exceptionally fraught, or at any rate exceptionally conspicuous in recent decades: South Africa. An upper-middle-income country in World Bank terms, South Africa combines rich-world living standards with conditions that involve serious development deficits. It is consistently ranked as one of the world's most unequal societies. This is widely recognised in official circles within the

[1] See, for example, https://thewaterchannel.tv/videos/water-is-life-sanitation-is-dignity/.

[2] Touring exhibition in 2008–9 by German Toilet Organization; see https://germantoilet.org/en/policy/campaigns-sanitation-is-dignity/. The same organisation puts the number of people without safe sanitation at 4.5 billion today; see https://germantoilet.org/en/facts-and-figures/.

country. For example, a recent report by the national statistical service on inequality trends takes as its starting-point the 'extremely high' and 'remarkably persistent' character of South African inequality. 'Despite many efforts by government to reduce inequality since our democratic transition in 1994', the report comments, 'progress has been limited'.[3]

Public infrastructure is a domain in which inequality remains particularly stark, and in perhaps no dimension more so than in sanitation. The question of how South Africa's history of racial segregation bears on its current sanitary realities will be central to our enquiry in the pages to follow. For now, it suffices to note that access to waterborne sanitation was historically a benefit created for, and enjoyed by, the country's white minority and a limited number of others. Infrastructural investment prioritised white neighbourhoods of cities and towns and some large, white-owned farms. For black South Africans, going to the toilet generally meant the so-called 'black bucket system' – buckets with seats provided to communities for use as (notoriously malodorous and unsanitary) dry toilets – or open defecation in fields or bushes.

The post-apartheid period has seen very considerable improvements in the sphere of sanitation. As just mentioned, however, this period has also seen the perpetuation of large disparities in the distribution of sanitation services. Thus, one learns from the statistical service's general household survey that, in 2021, 64 percent of South African households had access to a flush toilet, whether private or public, and whether connected to a public sewerage system or to a septic tank.[4] Members of the remaining households used a range of facilities, of which pit latrines with or without ventilation pipes were the most common, or they had no facility at all. In just under one percent of cases, corresponding to 151,000 households, the bucket system continued to be used. (The title of an article in the *Cape Times* – 'Bucket toilets still deny poor's dignity' – signals a recurrent theme in media coverage of that state of affairs.[5]) A further 112,000

[3] *Inequality Trends in South Africa* (Pretoria: Statistics South Africa, 2019), 2.

[4] *General Household Survey 2021* (Pretoria: Statistics South Africa, 2022), 36 (table 10.2). I have rounded percentages up or down to the nearest whole percentage.

[5] Odwa Mkentane, 'Bucket Toilets Still Deny Poor's Dignity', *Cape Times*, 23 July 2022.

households had no sanitation facility and hence practised open defecation.[6]

The survey breaks down sanitation facilities (or the lack thereof) by population group of the household head. It emerges that pit latrines with or without ventilation pipes, along with chemical toilets, the bucket system and open defecation were entirely confined to households headed by a person classified as black African or coloured. No households headed by a person classified as white did not have access to a flush toilet. Of households headed by a person classified as black African, 47 percent had access to a flush toilet.[7] The survey also breaks down sanitation facilities by type of dwelling. Here the data show that pit latrines with or without ventilation pipes, chemical toilets and the bucket system were overwhelmingly a feature of informal dwellings, by which was meant 'shacks' situated in backyards or other kinds of housing in 'squatter' settlements.[8] With regard to the distribution of housing types, the survey shows that 12 percent of South African households occupy informal dwellings,[9] and that substantial concentrations of such dwellings are located on the peripheries of the country's two largest cities: Johannesburg and Cape Town.[10]

Our discussion in this chapter will take us to both those cities and their peri-urban informal settlements and apartheid-built townships. It will also take us to a third city, Durban, where municipal planners have gained a reputation in recent years for innovation in the delivery of sanitation services. We will follow efforts by poor communities to secure better sanitation through resort to a variety of tactics, including – but not limited to – legal proceedings against public authorities. Such litigation has relied on a raft of legislative enactments and standard-setting policies that have been adopted in the years since 1994 concerning water infrastructure and access to improved sanitation facilities.[11] The litigation has also relied on the South African Constitution of 1996, with its celebrated protection of

[6] *General Household Survey 2021: Addendum Tables* (Pretoria: Statistics South Africa, 2022), 59 (addendum table 12.2).

[7] Ibid., 59 (addendum table 12.2).

[8] Ibid., 61 (addendum table 12.3).

[9] Ibid., 29 (table 8.1).

[10] Ibid., 30 (table 8.2). Around 17 percent of the inhabitants of both those cities live in informal dwellings.

[11] See Jackie Dugard, *The Right to Sanitation in South Africa* (Johannesburg: Foundation for Human Rights, 2016), esp. 5–8.

socio-economic rights and its celebrated provisions concerning human dignity.

Among the socio-economic rights protected in the South African Constitution are rights relating to water and housing. Section 27(1) provides that '[e]veryone has the right to have access to ... sufficient ... water'. Section 26(1) provides that '[e]veryone has the right to have access to adequate housing'. According to section 1 of the Constitution, equality is among the foundational values of the state, and section 9(2) specifies that equality 'includes the full and equal enjoyment' of these and other rights. Another of the foundational values proclaimed in section 1 is human dignity. In section 7(1), it is said that the Constitution's Bill of Rights affirms that value. Section 10 then declares that '[e]veryone has inherent dignity, and the right to have their dignity respected and protected'. Together, sections 1, 7(1) and 10 of the Constitution have been understood to bring with them a constitutional set-up in which dignity is both a foundational value to be promoted and a justiciable and enforceable right.[12]

In a speech to the United Nations in 1985, Bishop (later Archbishop) Desmond Tutu memorably described how, for black people, apartheid meant that '[y]our dignity is not just rubbed in the dust. It is trodden underfoot and spat on.'[13] Ten years later, in an early judgment of the South African Constitutional Court, and using language frequently quoted in subsequent cases and legal commentary, Justice O'Regan wrote that the recognition and protection of dignity is the 'touchstone of [the country's] new political order'.[14] Indeed, dignity occupied a prominent place in South Africa's transitional justice discourse. It was, for example, part of

[12] See also Constitution of the Republic of South Africa, sections 37(5) (on the non-derogability of the right guaranteed in section 10) and 39(1)(a) (on the obligation to interpret this part of the Constitution in a manner which promotes the values that underlie an open and democratic society based on, *inter alia*, human dignity). On the character of dignity as 'a value fundamental to our Constitution ... [and] a justiciable and enforceable right', see *Dawood and Another v. Minister of Home Affairs and Others; Shalabi and Another v. Minister of Home Affairs and Others; Thomas and Another v. Minister of Home Affairs and Others* [2000] ZACC 8; 2000 (3) SA 936 (CC), para. 35.

[13] Quoted in 'Transitional Justice in South Africa', 12 May 2020, available at: www.facinghistory.org/resource-library/transitional-justice-south-africa.

[14] *S v. Makwanyane and Another* [1995] ZACC 3; 1995 (3) SA 391 (CC) (O'Regan, J., concurring), para. 329.

the mandate of the Truth and Reconciliation Commission, chaired by Tutu, to restore the 'human and civil dignity' of the victims of gross violations of human rights under apartheid 'by granting them an opportunity to relate their own accounts' of what happened to them.[15]

The question of whether, how, and to what extent this process did in fact, and could, restore dignity to the victims of gross violations of human rights under apartheid – not to mention the victims of apartheid more generally – is, of course, a matter of ongoing debate. Nadine Gordimer seems to have anticipated something of that debate, or rather, something of the difficulty underlying it, in her novel *July's People*.[16] Published in 1981, the novel is set in a future South Africa. It imagines a violent end to apartheid. As civil war rages, a white couple, Bamford and Maureen Smales, and their children flee Johannesburg with their black servant whom they call July, travelling with him to his village and living there under his protection. The couple are liberal people who believe they have treated their servant with dignity.[17]

Pertinently to our current topic, we learn that one aspect of this concerns sanitation. In the Smales family house, July had his own bathroom with a 'bath, white china lavatory, everything'.[18] Over the course of the novel, a series of confrontations occur between Maureen and July which eventually compel Maureen to realise that, from July's perspective, 'to be dignified for *her*' meant nothing; 'his measure as a man was taken elsewhere'.[19] Regarding the lavatory, the point is presumably that sanitation cannot be dignity in conditions of servitude. But if access to a flush toilet could not signify dignity to Mwawate (for we are told that that is his birth name) so long as it depended on his being July, the Smales family's servant, what view will such a man take once – as in actual post-apartheid South Africa – he becomes a constitutionally equal citizen?

[15] Promotion of National Unity and Reconciliation Act 34 of 1995 (South Africa), section 3(1)(c).

[16] Nadine Gordimer, *July's People* (London: Bloomsbury, 2005).

[17] Ibid., 87 ('If I offended you, if I hurt your dignity, if what I thought was my friendliness, the feeling I had for you...') and 119 ('the special consideration she had shown for his dignity as a man').

[18] Ibid., 26. [19] Ibid., 186 (emphasis in original).

Metrologies of Dignity

Bringing about improvements to sanitation facilities is an important challenge, but in beginning now to go into this dimension of recent South African history a little more deeply, we need to register that sometimes the challenge has been simply to preserve existing levels of access to improved sanitation. That circumstance was brought sharply into focus by the case of *Mazibuko and Others v. City of Johannesburg and Others,* initiated in 2006.[20] The applicants – Lindiwe Mazibuko, Grace Munyai, Jennifer Makoatsane, Sophia Malekutu and Vusimuzi Paki – were residents of Phiri, a township in Soweto established in the early years of apartheid and still with an almost entirely black population, and their claim related to certain changes that had been implemented affecting the supply of water to their homes. The respondents were the City of Johannesburg, within the local governance of which Soweto was incorporated in 2002, and two other entities with responsibility for water supply to the area.

Until 2004, the system of water supply in Soweto was that residents received an unlimited amount of water, for which they were charged a flat rate. The flat rate was calculated on the basis of deemed consumption. It seems that this rate was too low to recover the cost of actual consumption and of losses due to leakage and wastage across the various Soweto townships, including Phiri. On top of that, credit control was lax, householders routinely remained in arrears with their payments, and a substantial programme of infrastructural upgrading and repair was needed to stem the leakages. In keeping with global trends, the water authorities decided to move to a more commercially functional system. Residents were presented with two options. Either they could have their in-house water disconnected and thenceforth get their water from an outside standpipe (or from a well, a reservoir, or whatever other external source they could find),[21] or they could maintain their in-house water connection and have a prepayment meter installed.

[20] *Mazibuko and Others v. City of Johannesburg and Others* [2009] ZACC 28; 2010 (4) SA 1 (CC).

[21] When the first applicant's in-house water was disconnected, she fetched water from a reservoir three kilometres from her home. At a certain point, the reservoir was closed.

Apparently, some residents initially took the first – disconnection – option. However, the hardships involved in having to fetch water from an external source led almost all eventually to accept the installation of prepayment meters. Under the pre-existing system of water metering which was used in wealthier and predominantly white parts of Johannesburg, water was provided on credit – that is, bills were sent out for water already supplied – and households were given notice and an opportunity to make representations before supply was cut off. In contrast, the new prepayment metering system delivered a fixed amount of so-called 'free basic water' and, when that ran out, the supply of water was automatically cut off until the next month unless additional water credits were purchased. The free basic water allowance was 6,000 litres per household per month. This was reckoned as 25 litres per person per day, based on a household size of eight. In reality, however, the number of people sharing a water connection was often considerably more than eight. Large households, multiple households (i.e. a main house and a number of informal shacks on a single site) and households with a fluctuating membership that at times expanded greatly were common in Phiri.[22]

At any rate, like many of those affected, the applicants could not survive on 6,000 litres per month. And like many of those affected too, they did not have the money to purchase any or sufficient additional water credits, which were charged according to a relatively steep-rising tariff. As a result, their water supply regularly stopped before the end of the month, and they then had to wait days or, quite commonly, weeks for reconnection. Faced with this situation and in order to put an end to it, the applicants challenged the constitutionality and regulatory legality both of the prepayment metering system and of the amount fixed as the free basic water allowance. They sought a declaration that they and others in Phiri on whose behalf they brought this class action were entitled to 12,000 litres of water per household per month, an amount that corresponded to 50 litres of water per person per

[22] Among the applicants, the number of people sharing the water connection ranged from twenty, in the case of the first applicant, to three in the case of the fourth applicant. See *Mazibuko and Others v. City of Johannesburg and Others* [2009] ZACC 28; 2010 (4) SA 1 (CC), para. 4.

day when calculated on the same eight person-household basis as the 6,000-litre allowance which the water authorities had set.

At first instance, Justice Tsoka upheld the applicants' challenge and made the declaration they sought.[23] As well as finding the system of prepayment meters illegal on administrative law grounds, he ruled that the prepayment meters contravened the equality guarantee in the Constitution. *Inter alia*, he considered it 'inexplicable why some residents of the City are entitled to water on credit', while others, who do not live in 'rich and white areas', are denied that.[24] He also ruled that the arrangements put in place in Phiri were inconsistent with the applicants' constitutional right to have their dignity respected and protected. By his assessment, 50 litres of water per person per day calculated for a household size of eight was indeed the amount necessary for them to maintain a dignified existence. On appeal by the respondents, the Supreme Court of Appeal agreed that 25 litres per person per day was too little. However, having regard to conflicting expert evidence, it reduced the amount fixed by Justice Tsoka to 42 litres per person per day (or 10,000 litres per household per month). The Supreme Court of Appeal also gave the water authorities two years to attempt to legalise the use of prepayment meters.[25]

The applicants then took their case to the Constitutional Court, which dismissed their appeal and set aside any increase in their water entitlement beyond the original 6,000 litres per household per month.[26] I quoted earlier section 27(1) of the South African Constitution on the right to sufficient water. Along similar lines to the International Covenant on Economic, Social and Cultural Rights, section 27(2) provides that it is the correlative obligation of the state to 'take reasonable … measures, within its available resources, to achieve the progressive realisation' of that right. Writing for the Constitutional Court, Justice O'Regan emphasised this aspect and summarised its implications in the following terms. 'If government takes no steps to realise the [right to sufficient

[23] *Mazibuko and Others v. City of Johannesburg and Others* [2008] ZAGPHC 491; [2008] 4 All SA 471 (W).

[24] Ibid., para. 151.

[25] *Mazibuko and Others v. City of Johannesburg and Others* [2009] ZASCA 20; 2009 (3) SA 592 (SCA).

[26] *Mazibuko and Others v. City of Johannesburg and Others* [2009] ZACC 28; 2010 (4) SA 1 (CC).

water], the courts will require government to take steps. If government's adopted measures are unreasonable, the courts will similarly require that they be reviewed so as to meet the constitutional standard of reasonableness.'[27] As she glossed this, it was not for the court to quantify the content of the obligation imposed on the state. Rather, it was for the governing authorities to explain and justify the choices they had made as reasonable measures to achieve the progressive realisation of the right to sufficient water within available resources.[28]

To Justice O'Regan and the other members of the Constitutional Court, the respondents had done this satisfactorily. The prepayment metering system was not unreasonable, and nor was the water authorities' decision regarding the free basic water allowance unreasonable. Justice O'Regan noted that 'the obligation in relation to the right of access to sufficient water will vary depending upon circumstance'. For example, 'what constitutes sufficient water depends on the manner in which water is supplied and the purpose for which it is used'. She went on: 'Even where the manner in which and the purpose for which it is supplied are clear [and relatively uniform] – as in this case where we know that in Phiri piped water is generally provided to brick houses with water-borne sanitation – the expert evidence on the record provides numerous different answers to the question of what constitutes "sufficient water", and courts are ill-placed to make these assessments for both institutional and democratic reasons'.[29] Justice Tsoka and the Supreme Court of Appeal had given inadequate weight to that latter consideration, and to article 27(2) of the Constitution itself. Let us pause at this point to take brief stock of the divergent expert evidence to which Justice O'Regan refers.

The experts on which each side relied more or less agreed on the amount of water required per person per day for drinking, bathing, laundry, house cleaning and meal preparation. Where they differed was on the amount needed for sanitation. As can be gleaned from the passage in Justice O'Regan's judgment I just quoted, Phiri was connected to mains sewerage. The five applicants were among those South Africans who had access to a flush toilet. According to the expert evidence adduced on their behalf, the basic

[27] Ibid., para. 67. [28] Ibid., para. 71. [29] Ibid., para. 62.

requirement for waterborne sanitation starts at 20 litres per person per day, but where houses are connected to inefficient sewerage systems, as is commonly the case in South African townships, that rises to more than 75 litres.[30] According to the evidence adduced on behalf of the respondents, the appropriate figure is instead 15 litres, calculated as 1.5 toilet flushes per person per day. Explaining this, the water authorities' expert, who was also their civil engineering consultant, said that it 'is in fact only essential to flush after defecation, which takes place once for a healthy adult . . . [F]lushing a toilet after urination has no health benefit and is probably done for aesthetic reasons more than anything else.' It followed that an allowance of 1.5 flushes – the amount for sanitation which could be accommodated within a free basic water allowance of 25 litres per person day or 6,000 litres per household per month – was 'entirely reasonable'.[31]

Those statements appeared in a section of the consultant's report headed: 'Quantifying the amount of water needed for health (and human dignity)'.[32] How many times is it reasonable, necessary and dignified to flush the toilet each day? For the judge at first instance, 'to expect the applicants to . . . [limit] the number of toilet flushes [they make] . . . is to deny them the right . . . to lead a dignified lifestyle'.[33] In reaching this conclusion, he pointed to the country's history of inequality and indignity which he said was still too fresh in peoples' minds to ignore.[34] And just as he pointed to history, so too Justice Tsoka highlighted the significance of geography. I mentioned earlier his ruling that the prepayment metering system contravened the Constitution's equality guarantee. Specifically, what he said was that the system 'discriminates between the residents of the City on the basis of geography', and that the situation was one where 'geography . . . [revealed] the true basis of

[30] See Affidavit of Peter Henry Gleick, para. 22, available at: http://apf.org.za/spip.php?article160.

[31] Affidavit of Ian Palmer, partly quoted in Antina von Schnitzler, *Democracy's Infrastructure: Techno-Politics and Protest after Apartheid* (Princeton, NJ: Princeton University Press, 2016), 187; also partly quoted in Affidavit of Teboho Mosikili, Application for Leave to Appeal, 88 (para. 217).

[32] Affidavit of Ian Palmer, quoted in von Schnitzler, *Democracy's Infrastructure,* 186.

[33] *Mazibuko and Others v. City of Johannesburg and Others* [2008] ZAGPHC 491; [2008] 4 All SA 471 (W), para. 179.

[34] Ibid., para. 166.

discrimination as colour'.[35] The Constitutional Court gave short shift to this aspect of the case, fairly quickly dismissing the allegations of inequality. Justice O'Regan observed for the Court that the prepayment metering system was not used in all historically black areas of the city. Moreover, the residents of historically white areas were as restricted as those in Phiri, in that they were compelled to use conventional (credit) meters and could not opt to have prepayment water meters installed in their homes.

Likewise, the Constitutional Court did not dwell on the dignity guarantee. Yet if, as Justice O'Regan writes, it was not for the court to quantify the amount of water sufficient to enable the applicants to lead a dignified life – if, as she observes, courts are ill-placed to make such assessments, and the only relevant issue for judicial determination is whether or not the governing authorities have acted reasonably – from the applicants' perspective, Phiri residents had a constitutional right to water and a constitutional right to dignity, and the result of the Constitutional Court's decision was that 6,000 litres of water per household per month, or 1.5 toilet flushes per person per day, were what those rights entitled them to. For them, the Court's reasonableness standard could not elide the 'metrologies of dignity'[36] which, in Antina von Schnitzler's helpful formulation, were inevitably involved. Von Schnitzler is an anthropologist interested in legal processes and how they relate to lived experience. In a series of interviews with the applicants in this case after the proceedings were over, she posed the question to Jennifer Makoatsane, the third applicant: '[s]o, if you were given 50 litres per person per day, would that be fine?' The answer that came back was: '[it is] not for them to tell us'.[37]

Makoatsane's 'them' is presumably a capacious reference to all those with power over water supply – courts (even where they profess themselves not to be the right bodies to 'tell' how much water is needed for a dignified life), along with other authorities of various kinds and those consulted by, or influential on, them. As von Schnitzler hears the response, Makoatsane is not objecting to calculation *per se.* Rather, and here it is material to mention that part of the applicants' grievance was that the people of Phiri were not consulted before the new prepayment system was introduced,

[35] Ibid., para. 155. [36] von Schnitzler, *Democracy's Infrastructure,* 184.
[37] Ibid., 190.

she is objecting to 'who did these calculations and how'.[38] Human dignity is declared by philosophers and constitutions and treaties to be inherent and primordial, the fundament upon which the modern state is founded. As we have seen, it is a foundational value of the South African Constitution, and, as we saw in Chapter 2, Kant teaches that it is elevated above any price, and has absolute worth in the sense that it is incapable of being brought under any common standard of measurement.[39] But to this 35-year-old unemployed woman,[40] nothing could be clearer than that dignity was evaluated, measured out and dispensed in these juridical and administrative procedures. Nothing could be clearer than that, far from being foundational, dignity was an outcome of these determinations by judges, policy-makers, officials, managers and consultants through which authoritative knowledge regarding it was produced. Yet, in her words, 'they don't know'.[41]

Spectacles of Indignity

In a moment we will move from Johannesburg to Cape Town, but just before leaving the *Mazibuko* case, I want to touch on an episode that occurred shortly before the case was heard by the Supreme Court of Appeal. On 12 February 2009, a group of women staged a march through downtown Johannesburg in support of the five residents' legal challenge (Figure 5.1). According to a statement by the organiser of the demonstration, 'Women without water and sanitation are as good as dead and have no dignity. With the prepaid meters our ability to access water will be denied and inability to access water denies human beings the right to life and more with women the right to dignity.'[42] There were banners with messages like 'Sanitation = Water is Dignity for Women' and 'Stop the War on Women's Bodies', and it is reported that some of the

[38] Ibid., 191 (emphasis omitted). [39] On this, see Chapter 2.
[40] Affidavit of Jennifer Makoatsane, para. 1, available at: https://apf.org.za/spip.php?article159.
[41] von Schnitzler, *Democracy's Infrastructure*, 190.
[42] See Dieketseng Maleke and Zandile Mbabela, 'Women Protest Water Meters', *The Times* (South Africa), 12 February 2009, quoted in von Schnitzler, *Democracy's Infrastructure*, 190. See also Louise McAuliffe, 'Bloody Underwear Protest in Johannesburg – To Demand Free Water', *The Sowetan*, 12 February 2009, available at: abahlali.org/node/4796.

Figure 5.1 *Women for Water March: March Front*, 2009. Photograph. Anti-Privatisation Forum.

women wore underwear stained with blood or red dye on top of their clothes. Interviewed by a journalist, one demonstrator said: 'We are marching because we are dirty.'[43]

In his judgment for the High Court, Justice Tsoka remarked that 'South Africa is a patriarchal society. Many domestic chores are performed by women. Many households in poor black areas are headed by women.' He then noted evidence given by the first applicant to the effect that, before committing to the new system of prepayment meters, she had travelled three kilometres to fetch water on behalf of her household. In this context, he held that the prepayment metering system violated the constitutional guarantee of equality not only for the reasons to which I have already referred, but also because the meters 'discriminate against women unfairly because of their sex'.[44] Von Schnitzler describes how, at a far more

[43] See Maleke and Mbabela, 'Women Protest Water Meters', quoted in von Schnitzler, *Democracy's Infrastructure*, 189.

[44] *Mazibuko and Others v. City of Johannesburg and Others* [2008] ZAGPHC 491; [2008] 4 All SA 471 (W), para. 159.

general level, the legal proceedings required the applicants to present to the court the 'exposed body and its needs'.[45] Making their case entailed setting out the (partly gendered) realities of their indigence, vulnerability and indeed shame – testifying, for example, to the particular problems caused by the prepayment meters and the 6,000-litre allowance when residents menstruated, in that, to quote from the record of evidence, '[d]uring this time ... I would feel very embarrassed should a male person ... use an unflushed toilet behind me'.[46]

The demonstration was evidently an attempt to dramatise and politicise that embarrassment. As von Schnitzler comments, '[w]-hile the formal legal submission implicitly defined "indignity" as the subjection to the urgency and shame of bodily needs', in the march, 'activists mobilised this notion outside the courtroom'. Repeating 'modes of subordination' for the sake of publicising and subverting them, they 'performed' gender-based indignity in a way that resignified shame.[47] In other reflections on the protest, Karen Zivi puts this more strongly still.[48] These demonstrators 'turned notions of female impropriety against the state', she writes. 'The women refused to be shamed, and instead shamed the state'[49] for the class structure and associated inequalities of race and gender of which, to them, the prepayment metering system was an emblem and material component. Activism of something like this kind has played a much-discussed role in disputes with the Cape Town municipal authorities over sanitation arrangements there. Let us turn to that set of issues now, which surfaced at around the same time as the events in Johannesburg I have recounted, as well as in subsequent years.

The township of Khayelitsha was established late in the apartheid era on the sandy, low-lying Cape Flats to the south-east of central Cape Town. Growing rapidly, it encompassed by the 2000s a

45 von Schnitzler, *Democracy's Infrastructure,* 182.
46 Affidavit of Jennifer Makoatsane, para. 18, available at: https://apf.org.za/spip.php?article159.
47 von Schnitzler, *Democracy's Infrastructure,* 190.
48 See Karen Zivi, 'Hiding in Public or Going with the Flow: Human Rights, Human Dignity, and the Movement for Menstrual Equity', *Human Rights Quarterly* 42(1) (2020) 119, 138–40.
49 Ibid., 140.

number of informal settlements.[50] In 2004, a project was launched to upgrade some of these settlements and, as part of the project, to provide waterborne sanitation ahead of new housing. Initially, the plan was to build communal toilets, one for every five households, but the City accepted the community's contention that this would be unsatisfactory. Under a revised plan, private toilets – one for each household – would be provided. However, no structures would be built around the toilets. That is to say, only the plumbing and fixtures would be installed, and it would be left to individual residents to construct the necessary enclosures for them. The installation of unenclosed toilets took place in 2009. By early 2010, most of the 1,316 toilets had been enclosed by residents, but in the Makhaza section of Khayelitsha, around fifty toilets remained unenclosed.[51] Photographs of open toilets circulated widely in the media, along with stories of users having to cover themselves with blankets.

As elsewhere in the world, attacks on women and girls are a concomitant of inadequate sanitation in South Africa, and one evening, Makhaza resident Ntombentsha Beja was stabbed while she was on her way to use a communal toilet ten minutes from her home. Aged seventy-four at the time, Beja was among those whose 'private' toilet remained unenclosed. In June 2010, the South African Human Rights Commission issued a report in which it denounced the unenclosed toilets as a violation of the residents' rights, including in particular their right under section 10 of the Constitution to have their dignity respected and protected.[52] For her part, Beja, along with two others, brought proceedings against the City of Cape Town and other relevant officials and governmental agencies in the Western Cape High Court, asking the Court to declare, similarly, that the respondents had violated their constitutional rights and to order the respondents to enclose all the toilets that formed part of the sanitation project. Delivering

[50] See Stanley Brunn and Matthew Wilson, 'Cape Town's Million Plus Black Township of Khayelitsha: Terra Incognitae and the Geographies and Cartographies of Silence', *Habitat International* 39 (2013) 284.

[51] See *Makhaza Open Toilet Finding* (*African National Congress Youth League and Others v. City of Cape Town*), South African Human Rights Commission Report, 11 June 2010, available at: www.sahrc.org.za/home/21/files/Makhaza%20Finding%202010.pdf.

[52] Ibid.

judgment for the Court, Justice Erasmus upheld the applicants' claims and made the declaration and order they sought.[53]

His judgment reports '[observing] firsthand the living conditions of the affected community, ... [and] in particular the aspects relating to the toilets'.[54] As originally installed, the toilets were 'completely open and in full view of every person in the community, and mostly situated close to the road'.[55] Even where enclosures had subsequently been erected, those enclosures consisted of whatever mixed materials residents without money could find, and were 'unsatisfactory to satisfy dignity and privacy'. He gave the example of being shown a toilet that was partly screened, but had 'no door' and an 'opening [that] faced a public thoroughfare'. He expressed particular concern at the situation of an elderly and wheelchair-bound resident whose toilet enclosure was constructed out of pieces of wood that made wheelchair access almost impossible and lacked a roof.[56] In outlining these aspects of life in Makhaza, Justice Erasmus remarked that it was 'disturbing to note from correspondence between the consulting engineers and the municipal managers' that the unenclosed toilets were jokingly referred to as '[loos] with a view'. This terminology 'is reprehensible', he said, 'and fails to afford any regard to the dignity of poor people, compelled to use these toilets in unfortunate circumstances'.[57]

Overall, the judge opined that the municipal authorities had 'lost sight of the needs of the poorest of the poor and their human dignity'.[58] In a study of the *Beja* case and related developments, Steven Robins comments that, prior to this point, 'the shocking sanitation conditions in [South African] informal settlements seldom made it into the mainstream media or national political discourse'.[59] Thanks to the 'spectacular image of the open toilet', that public silence was broken, and sanitation came to be framed as

[53] *Beja and Others v. Premier of the Western Cape and Others* [2011] ZAWCHC 97; [2011] 3 All SA 401 (WCC).

[54] Ibid., para. 29. [55] Ibid., para. 19. [56] Ibid., para. 29.

[57] Ibid., para. 19. For an ironic account of the 'loos with a view', see David Smith, 'Why is South Africa Still Providing "Apartheid Toilets"?', *The Guardian*, 17 May 2011.

[58] *Beja and Others v. Premier of the Western Cape and Others* [2011] ZAWCHC 97; [2011] 3 All SA 401, para. 144.

[59] Steven Robins, 'The 2011 Toilet Wars in South Africa: Justice and Transition between the Exceptional and the Everyday after Apartheid', *Development and Change* 45(3) (2014) 479, 480.

a matter of broad public interest, and hence a 'concern for politicians, activists, journalists, citizens' – and, as we have seen, human rights commissioners and judges.[60] Or rather, for the sanitation deficits of course had a context, 'this spectacle of the open toilet came to stand in for the indignities and injustices of daily life under apartheid as well as the limits of transformation after apartheid'.[61] With clear implications for post-apartheid policy, the unenclosed toilets of Khayelitsha challenged dominant narratives about 'transitional justice', and increased the 'visibility of everyday realities of structural poverty' that could 'only be addressed by long-term state interventions at a systemic level'.[62]

That said, Robins also comments that Justice Erasmus's language in the *Beja* case was 'easily assimilated into an official public script that re-enacted the commitment of the caring, post-revolutionary state'.[63] The judgment opened with reference to the idea that South Africa's Constitution 'has as its primary objective the protection and the restoration of human dignity', and emphasised that the corollary of this was that '[w]e have a duty, more particularly public representatives and government [have a duty,] to promote human dignity'.[64] Constitutionally mandated to see to the dignity and equal worth of all South Africans, the state could not tolerate open toilets, just as it could have no truck with contemptuous engineers and managers disposed to make light of the sufferings of the poor. With regard to the immediate issues of sanitation faced by Ntombentsha Beja and her fellow residents, it seems to have been a result of the judgment, and at any rate of the larger open toilet scandal, to put an end to the installation by city authorities of unenclosed flush toilets. As would soon become clear, however, Cape Town's 'toilet wars' were only just beginning.

A further major episode erupted in 2013. This related to another scheme of sanitation in Khayelitsha informal settlements, involving the provision of portable toilets. Presented as a temporary measure, portable toilets had been placed in some parts of the area for many years. Toilets of that sort have detachable waste tanks which need

[60] Ibid. [61] Ibid. [62] Ibid., 480–81. [63] Ibid., 489.

[64] *Beja and Others v. Premier of the Western Cape and Others* [2011] ZAWCHC 97; [2011] 3 All SA 401, para. 1.

frequent emptying, but there were problems with the municipal arrangements for collecting the waste tanks, and the portable toilets were commonly in an atrocious state. At best, they suffused residents' dwellings with the smell of human waste. Efforts to avoid having to go into them included the use of makeshift pits, plastic bags, or toilets belonging to relatives or friends some distance away. To draw attention to this situation, a campaign of direct action was initiated that saw the contents of portable toilets deposited in a number of public places.[65] Faeces was thrown onto the steps of the provincial parliament, onto the entrance of a government building, onto officials' passing cars, onto a busy motorway, and – the target that seems to have garnered the most publicity – onto the main terminal building of Cape Town International Airport. City centre demonstrations were also held at which protesters came with portable toilets and sat on them, and wore or waved around cardboard cutouts of toilet seats.

As in the Johannesburg women's march, there thus unfolded on Cape Town's streets an ironic performance of indignity. These protesters staged a parody of abjection that again resignified shame and threw it – now literally in the form of excrement hurled from portable toilets – back at the state. Writing about the history of the portable toilet, Nadine Botha traces its passage 'from camping accessory to protest totem'.[66] She explains that the first patent for a portable toilet was filed by the Thetford Corporation of Ann Arbor, Michigan in 1969. We learn from her that Thetford portable toilets, along with another brand, are those used in the informal settlements of Khayelitsha, though apparently there is no mention in the company's publicity material of bulk sales to the City of Cape Town. The latest models of Thetford's portable toilet receive glowing reviews on Amazon from recreational vehicle users, truck drivers, boat owners and campers. As Botha observes, however, occasional use of well-maintained portable toilets by people with access to a conventional toilet in their regular lives is one thing. Daily use of poorly maintained portable toilets over many years by

[65] Much discussion of these events highlights a link with relevant electoral cycles. That aspect need not concern us here.

[66] Nadine Botha, 'The Portable Flush Toilet: From Camping Accessory to Protest Totem', *Design and Culture* 10(1) (2018) 17.

large households whose only other sanitation options are as bad or worse is quite another.[67]

Botha proposes that '[w]hat makes the [portable toilet] such a potent totem is that … it is "actual poverty" … not just a signifier. Its vulgarity ridicules state power', puncturing official pretensions to dignity, decency and the pursuit of social justice for all.[68] As she tells it, the portable toilet 'facilitates the ongoing production of dispensable lives, on which basis the Cape Colony was founded, and it reveals the maintenance of beliefs and behaviors used to validate this production'.[69] Pointing to the 'simple urgency … of too many South Africans living too close to their own waste', Shannon Jackson and Steven Robins also remark on the sense in which Khayelitsha portable toilets belong with a pattern of social exclusion that renders residents of informal settlements themselves a kind of waste.[70] Like Botha, they connect this to Cape Town's longer history of racial and spatial ordering which, from early colonial times, conflated the original inhabitants with contaminating waste and expelled them outside the city limits. Jackson and Robins write of a 'potent semiotics of waste', with excrement now functioning as a 'weapon of political reversal'.[71] Through the actions of these toilet warriors, the undignified sights and smells of the periphery were being brought to, flung at, released in, and – crucially – made belongings of the privileged centre.[72]

The Long Walk

Why were prepayment water meters installed in Phiri? Why were toilets provided in Makhaza without walls? Budgetary considerations were clearly important, but I want to mention now another factor, highlighted in a statement by a leading Cape Town official of the time. She said, 'We have come to the conclusion that the best way to instil a sense of ownership and an ethos of respecting property is for each family to contribute to the construction and maintenance of their own toilet.' Residents of Makhaza and adjacent informal settlements were being left to build their own

[67] Ibid., 20–21. [68] Ibid., 28. [69] Ibid., 19.
[70] Shannon Jackson and Steven Robins, 'Making Sense of the Politics of Sanitation in Cape Town', *Social Dynamics* 44(1) (2018) 69, 71.
[71] Ibid., 71, 84. [72] Ibid., 83.

enclosures at least in part because this encouraged 'self-reliance and initiative'.[73] In reflections on the toilet controversies, Brendon Barnes provides insight into the significance of familiar themes along those lines for infrastructural improvement in South Africa.[74] According to Barnes, the 'post-apartheid state has promoted a version of active citizenship that ... acknowledges rights but emphasizes agency, choice, volition, responsibility and participation'. Communities are expected to 'help build facilities' and at the least to 'adopt technologies such as prepaid water meters and [portable toilets] until the state can figure out long term solutions'. Within this discourse, he explains, 'poor South Africans have a right to be unhappy about the slow progress of South Africa's development, but they should express their discontent responsibly', through voting and other recognised political channels.[75]

Barnes describes state-sponsored campaigns that also seek to mould behaviour in other ways. In connection with the installation of prepayment water meters, citizens were advised on how to use water responsibly (including how many times to flush the toilet). They were also exhorted to regard payment for water as an act of responsible citizenship, by means of such slogans as 'your right to services equals your right to pay' and 'I've paid for my services, have you?'.[76] From this perspective, prepayment water meters, toilets without enclosures, and portable toilets are not just (deficient) modes of sanitation. They are 'moral pedagogical devices'[77] that provide instruction in what it is to be a good citizen. I indicated at the beginning of this chapter that Durban would be part of my story, and I want now to refer to a final set of toilet-related measures which have provided similar instruction for the racialised poor of that city and surrounds, but which differ in that they are an outcome of efforts in South Africa and elsewhere to 'innovate' the state's way out of the problem of inadequate sanitation. Here, as we will see, the accent is on technological solutions – new objects, better-designed devices for dealing with human waste, to replace the bad, old, undignified ones.

[73] Helen Zille, quoted in Scott Baldauf, 'On Eve of World Cup, South Africa's "Toilet Wars" Reveal Volatile Politics', *Christian Science Monitor*, 10 June 2010.

[74] Brendon Barnes, 'Politics and Activism in the Water and Sanitation Wars in South Africa', *Journal of Social and Political Psychology* 6(2) (2018) 543.

[75] Ibid., 545–46. [76] Ibid., 546. [77] Ibid.

During the 2000s and 2010s, the Durban water authorities rolled out two types of dry toilets for use in peri-urban areas not connected to its sewerage system: Ventilated Improved Pit ('VIP') toilets and Urine Diversion ('UD') toilets. VIP toilets were originally invented in the 1970s by a research laboratory in what was then Rhodesia, now Zimbabwe. These are designed to reduce odours and inhibit the breeding of flies – unavoidable issues with the standard form of pit latrine – through the addition of a vertical ventilation pipe. The ventilation pipe enables air to circulate in the latrine, and directs flies and other insects towards the exterior light, where they are trapped by a wire mesh covering. UD toilets are a much newer and more sophisticated technology involving sealed units which divert urine into a separate compartment so that faeces can dry out more quickly and be more readily disposed of. In keeping with the ethos of responsibilisation just mentioned, UD toilets are self-maintained toilets. Once provided with them, householders must dig holes and dispose of the residue of faecal matter at suitable intervals themselves. In August 2010, a workshop was held to discuss the introduction of UD toilets in Durban, and Barbara Penner was among those attending.

Penner recalls that '[a]t first glance, the UD toilets appeared to me a relatively straightforward solution to the problem of providing basic sanitation to water-stressed regions' such as Durban.[78] After all, the 'developed world's waterborne model of sanitation, with its reliance on "big system" infrastructure', needs rethinking, and not only for reasons of cost. Water scarcity is only getting worse due to climate change. But the Durban scheme had encountered considerable community resistance. For while the 'UD toilet is unquestionably an "improved" form of sanitation if compared to a bucket, pit latrine or [portable toilet]', it did not look so good to residents when set against the plumbed-in flush toilet. Indeed, the UD toilet's self-maintained technology 'contrasts sharply with that in full service areas where householders do not maintain pipes beyond their property line and are able to "flush and forget" their waste'. The key

[78] Barbara Penner, 'Flush with Inequality: Sanitation in South Africa', *Places*, November 2010, available at: https://placesjournal.org/article/flush-with-inequality-sanitation-in-south-africa/ (also the source of the remaining quotations in this paragraph). An architectural scholar, Penner has written extensively on toilets; see especially Barbara Penner, *Bathroom* (London: Reaktion, 2014).

point was that residents needed only to 'look at the country's still predominantly white privileged class – whose members ... are not expected to use UD toilets – for proof that the distribution of sanitation options largely follows existing race and class lines'. In the end, Penner proposes that a 'central reason why improvement projects stumble is ... asymmetrical provision and resource allocation'. 'If the effort to achieve social justice and to conserve resources is to be credible', she writes, 'the behavior, habits and expectations of full-service users must be reformed alongside those on the bottom rung (who, let us not forget, consume the least)'.

Some years after Penner's seminar, Noshipo Mkhize and colleagues conducted a study of attitudes to UD toilets by their users in Durban. Among Mkhize and colleagues' findings was that all of those surveyed 'aspired to have a flush toilet, which is associated with being a first class citizen'.[79] Peter Redfield and Steven Robins have an illuminating take on the gap here between popular and official thinking.[80] In their analysis, two quite distinct conceptions of first-class citizenship or, in this book's terms, dignified life can be discerned in this context, corresponding to two quite distinct technopolitical 'imaginaries'. Starting on the official side, there is a 'humanitarian design imaginary'. I have been speaking about UD toilets, but in fact this is one of many attempts in recent decades to develop new forms of dry toilet, especially for low- and middle-income countries where infrastructure is scant, and significant proportions of the population lack adequate sanitation. Underpinning these attempts is the claim that the flush toilet, however originally progressive and still valuable, fails to meet global needs. In 2011, the Bill and Melinda Gates Foundation launched a 'Reinvent the Toilet Challenge', and since then, a series of 'reinvented toilet' fairs have been held in various parts of the world.[81]

[79] Noshipo Mkhize et al., 'Urine Diversion Dry Toilets in eThekwini Municipality, South Africa: Acceptance, Use and Maintenance through Users' Eyes', *Journal of Water, Sanitation and Hygiene for Development* 7(1) (2017) 111, 114.

[80] Peter Redfield and Steven Robins, 'An Index of Waste: Humanitarian Design, "Dignified Living" and the Politics of Infrastructure in Cape Town', *Anthropology Southern Africa* 39(2) (2016) 145.

[81] See www.gatesfoundation.org/what-we-do/global-growth-and-opportunity/water-sanitation-and-hygiene/reinvent-the-toilet-challenge-and-expo. On this, see Redfield and Robins, 'An Index of Waste', 147–49.

If you visit the website of a design consultancy called Bridge Factory, you will see pictures and a description of a toilet that won first prize in another humanitarian industrial design competition relating to sanitation.[82] No prizes, however, for guessing the name of that toilet: 'Dignity'. The Dignity toilet is an attractive lime-green and white moulded plastic object reminiscent of a piece of modernist furniture, and is said to provide 'sealed sanitary storage for solid waste for three people for approximately seven days'.[83] After that period, the toilet is removed from its 'dock' and taken to a 'predetermined, communal area', where its contents are 'manually augered' – bored down – into the soil for decomposition. Bridge Factory's promotional material bills the Dignity toilet as a 'product that inspires pride in its owners, not a disposable commodity'. It is this way of approaching things that constitutes what Redfield and Robins term the humanitarian design imaginary. In their words, '[f]or the designers, dignity is a question of technology and the aesthetics of individual experience'.[84] Humanitarian designers and their utilities-sector customers conjure 'dignified living' through innovative 'sanitation solutions' that combine clever engineering with careful attention to design (and marketing).

To this, Redfield and Robins counterpose a quite different 'social justice imaginary'. Figuring dignity as instead a political issue and problem of social justice, the social justice imaginary is reflected in the events I have mostly been narrating in this chapter and in the findings of Mkhize and colleagues about attitudes to UD toilets in Durban. Central to its way of approaching things is a belief that the question of dignified living cannot be addressed without reference to history and its legacies in the present. Whereas the humanitarian design imaginary largely 'floats free of any specific legacy of the past' (except the invention of the water closet itself),[85] the social

[82] See www.bridgefactory.com/#/the-dignity-toilet/. On this, see Redfield and Robins, 'An Index of Waste', 152–53. (The name of the design consultancy associated with the Dignity toilet appears to have changed a number of times.)

[83] It is worth noting in this context that, in the *Mazibuko* case, the judge at first instance made a finding of fact that the average household size in Phiri was around sixteen. At a time when many families in the area had been ravaged by AIDS, the judge highlighted the prevalence of households in which children had been left without parents and were being brought up by grandmothers and aunts. See *Mazibuko and Others v. City of Johannesburg and Others* [2008] ZAGPHC 491; [2008] 4 All SA 471 (W), para. 166.

[84] Redfield and Robins, 'An Index of Waste', 153.

[85] Ibid., 151.

justice imaginary invokes an intimate history of racial and gender injustice with notable geographical dimensions. To be sure, the intimacy of the toilet and what goes on there also has a history and a geography, not to mention, for some theorists, a psychology.[86] The humanitarian design imaginary and the social justice imaginary co-exist in a world shaped by those developments. Where the social justice imaginary departs is in holding that dignity in the sphere of sanitation is not just a technological challenge (however much it may also be that) and an associated promotional strategy; it is a problem of structural inequality.

In her work on portable toilets, Botha suggests that the passage from camping accessory to protest totem happened precisely because, in the relevant context, portable toilets became problems that could not 'be solved by replacing' existing objects with other objects.[87] Khayelitsha's portable toilets were not simple '[designs] to be improved', and nor was its crisis of sanitation merely a 'technical equation of users, faeces, grid, and budget'.[88] At stake was an 'historical narrative about human beings, dignity, spatial justice, and inclusion'.[89] 'The toilet wars in Cape Town are about far more than sanitation', she writes, 'and ... sanitation is not just toilets'.[90] Social Justice Coalition, to the activities of which Botha refers in her essay, is a Cape Town-based non-governmental organisation active in the area of sanitation. On 21 March 2010, the organisation staged a protest they called the 'Long Walk to Human Dignity'.[91] The protest involved SJC members forming a long, snaking queue for a public toilet in the wealthy Cape Town district of Sea Point. One reads on the organisation's website that '[i]n this area – as in other affluent suburbs – public toilets are cleaned and maintained regularly by a dedicated caretaker, well lit, and monitored frequently by security personnel. This is in stark contrast to [the] public toilets [in Khayelitsha], which are unsafe, never cleaned or maintained, nor provided with the luxuries of toilet paper or a simple toilet seat.'

The 'Long Walk to Human Dignity' alludes, of course, to Nelson Mandela's autobiography, *Long Walk to Freedom*. In a much-quoted

[86] The classic study of this is Dominique Laporte (Rodolphe el-Khoury, trans.), *A History of Shit* (Cambridge, MA: MIT Press, 2002).
[87] Botha, 'The Portable Flush Toilet', 28. [88] Ibid., 19, 26. [89] Ibid., 26
[90] Ibid., 25. [91] See https://sjc.org.za/posts/the-long-walk-to-human-dignity.

passage of that book, Mandela writes of how prison and the authorities conspired to rob him of his dignity, and of how that paradoxically assured that he would survive, inasmuch as 'any man or institution that tries to rob me of my dignity will lose because I will not part with it at any price or under any pressure'.[92] It's a noble and appealing sentiment, but the Long Walk to Human Dignity refocuses on indignity and its persistence after, and notwithstanding, liberation. At the level of ordinary life, the Long Walk to Human Dignity reminds us of the indignity of being deprived of access to a clean and safe toilet, along with the indignity of being provided with a toilet that preserves your status as a second-class citizen, the indignity of being precluded, when you have a flush toilet, from using the flush with the frequency you deem necessary, and the indignity of knowing that such is the social-systemic order under which you live that privileged South Africans, spared these experiences, rob you of your dignity each and every day.[93]

And Whites Must See It

In the same transitional decade as *Long Walk to Freedom* came out, J. M. Coetzee's novel *Disgrace* appeared.[94] It tells the story of David Lurie, a lecturer in English literature at a university in Cape Town, and his adult daughter Lucy, who lives on a farm in the nearby Eastern Cape. After many vicissitudes, David and Lucy have a discussion about Lucy's future. Something terrible has happened to her, and she has decided that she needs to make a new start, and that, in doing so, there is a particular course of action she must follow which involves humiliation and self-abnegation, and seems completely at odds with her interests and welfare. When David expresses dismay, this is how Lucy responds:

> Yes, I agree it is humiliating. But perhaps that is a good point to start from again. Perhaps that is what I must learn to accept. To start at ground level.

92 Nelson Mandela, *Long Walk to Freedom* (New York: Hachette, 2013), 391.

93 For similar observations as part of a response to the Constitutional Court's judgment in the *Mazibuko* case, see Barnes, 'Politics and Activism in the Water and Sanitation Wars in South Africa', 550.

94 J. M. Coetzee, *Disgrace* (London: Vintage, 2000), first published in 1999.

With nothing … No cards, no weapons, no property, no rights, no dignity.[95]

Disgrace is often read as an allegory of post-apartheid South Africa and a critique of the Truth and Reconciliation process that was ongoing at the time it was written. Lucy is a white South African, and here Coetzee is having her express the belief that dignity, at least as she has known and enjoyed it, must be renounced, as part of the same political and social order that brought South Africa 'cards', 'weapons', 'property' and 'rights'. We might understand that catalogue to imply the intersection of white supremacy (symbolised by the identity 'cards' of the apartheid era), violent subjugation ('weapons'), economic exploitation ('property') and legally protected privilege ('rights'). A fantastically complex novel, *Disgrace* does not, I think, purport to resolve the unsettling issues it raises. Regarding dignity, one thing it does clearly signal, however, is that confined to the realm of abstract metaphysics the issues are not.

We have seen in this chapter how dignity and indignity have played a part in disputes over inequality and sanitation in post-apartheid South Africa. Starting with Gordimer's July, of whom Maureen finally learns that being 'dignified for her' meant nothing, we have seen how dignity has been variously fought for, measured out, sent up, turned down, thrown back, and finally, in Coetzee's novel, given away. It has been defended as a constitutional right, and in the process, exposed to view as a product of the decisions of courts, policy-makers, officials and managers. It is what Tutu and other black South Africans had trampled underfoot and spat on during apartheid times, and what Mandela would not part with while he was in prison at any price. It is the touchstone of South Africa's post-apartheid legal order and the right to 1.5 toilet flushes per day. It is the name of a reinvented toilet which does not allow you to flush and forget, but yet is not a disposable commodity.

There is just one further element I wish to add to the mix that relates to the larger struggle within which these matters find their place. It is well known that the Rhodes Must Fall campaign emerged in early 2015 in connection with a longstanding demand to have a bronze statue of the mining magnate and leading colonial governor and ideologue, Cecil Rhodes, removed from the campus of the

[95] Ibid., 205.

University of Cape Town. Erected in 1934, the statue stood on a high plinth at the foot of the steps leading up to the university's convocation hall where ceremonial occasions are held, and it depicted Rhodes seated and with a contemplative air. The university authorities eventually hired a crane to take it away on 9 April 2015. For its part, Rhodes Must Fall went on to catalyse and energise a project of decolonial activism in higher education, cultural heritage and everything else, both in South Africa and around the world. What may be less well-known is how this great movement began.

On 12 March 2015, one Chumani Maxwele, a 30-year-old fourth-year political science student, stood beneath the statue of Rhodes and, with all his force, flung up at it the contents of a portable toilet which he had carried to the campus in a minibus from his home in Khayelitsha.[96] Addressing the assembled crowd, he is reported to have declared: 'There is no [black] collective history here – where are our heroes and ancestors?'[97] It was a powerful point about practices of memorialisation and how they may be suffused with the lingering stench of empire. But in a later interview, Maxwele explained that there was also something else he wanted to communicate. He said that he threw faeces at the statue to highlight 'our shame'. 'We want white people to know how we live', he told the interviewer. 'We live in poo. I am from a very poor family; we are using portaloos [portable toilets] ... In order for me to bring evidence, I have to give Cecil John Rhodes a poo shower and whites will have to see it.'[98]

[96] See Eve Fairbanks, 'The Birth of Rhodes Must Fall', *The Guardian,* 18 November 2015.

[97] Aly Verbaan, 'UCT Student in Poo Protest', *Cape Times,* 10 March 2015.

[98] Lin Sampson, 'Poo-Pooing at UCT', *The Times* (South Africa), 13 March 2015, available at: www.timeslive.co.za/news/south-africa/2015-03-13-poo-pooing-at-uct/#.

6

Conclusion: Dignity and Its Outsiders

Many Things

Our counter-history of dignity has alighted on diverse issues, times and places, and the moment has now arrived to note down something of what has emerged. Thinking back to the discussion in Chapter 1, we might start by logging the heterogeneity of the concept of dignity itself, by which I mean that it names many things. An adequate response to the question 'what does one speak about when one speaks about dignity?' needs to mention that dignity is an idea, but also an experience. It is a personal quality or attribute, but also a practice and performance. Dignity is a way of being with yourself and a manner of engagement with others, a mode of action and an approach to interaction. It is a right, as well as a common responsibility. It can be heard at demonstrations and read on banners and in protest literature, where it is a rallying cry. At the same time, it is a brand name for certain kinds of consumer products and services in the market. You will recall that I once saw it on the registration plate of a car.[1]

In the US state of South Dakota there is a sculpture called 'Dignity' (Figure 6.1). Located on a bluff above the Missouri River near Chamberlain, and standing more than fifteen metres tall, it depicts a Native American woman in Plains-style dress holding behind her with outstretched arms a huge star quilt. Descriptions

[1] See Chapter 1.

Figure 6.1 Dale Lamphere, *Dignity: Of Earth & Sky*, 2016.

of the work explain that, among people of the Lakota (Sioux) and a number of other Northern Plains Nations, the star quilt is a symbol of honour, generosity and respect. Regarding the sculpture's overall significance, its designer, Dale Lamphere, has said that 'Dignity represents the courage, perseverance and wisdom of the Lakota and Dakota culture in South Dakota'.[2] Long before his commission, American cinema presented its audiences with another memorable dignity of a very different kind. Near the beginning of the 1952 musical comedy, *Singin' in the Rain*, the silent-movie star who

[2] Quoted at www.travelsouthdakota.com/trip-ideas/story/dignity-earth-sky.

is one of the film's main protagonists, Don Lockwood, tells of how dignity is, and always has been, his personal motto: 'I've had one motto that I've always lived by – *dignity, always dignity*.'[3] Just as Don makes that claim, however, a series of flashbacks falsifies it by revealing that his past is, in fact, rather disreputable. Far from rising dignifiedly to stardom, he has worked his way up by first performing in smoky saloons, on vaudeville stages, and at cheap, boisterous variety shows.

If dignity bespeaks honour and fortitude, *Singin' in the Rain* invites us to consider that it can also bespeak humbug and cant. In celebrating Native American courage, perseverance and wisdom, South Dakota's Dignity also (and whether or not intentionally) exposes the hollowness of an 'official' dignity against which First Nations must continue to struggle for restitution and rights. One needs always to look beneath the surface when it comes to dignity, applying a particularly robust hermeneutic of suspicion to the dignity claimed by elites. There will be more to say about that point later, but let us stay with the question of what the referent is in a discourse of dignity, and turn now to the matter of defining dignity, which is, after all, another, very familiar way of dealing with that question. Alongside dictionary definitions, definitions of dignity abound in juridical texts, scholarly literature and writing about dignity aimed at a general readership. These definitions typically identify dignity with worthiness – the quality of being worthy of respect, honour or esteem – and self-command – an aspect, manner or style that is calm, composed, serious and seemly. In further clarifications, dignity is set against concepts that relate to it negatively, including humiliation, abjection, shame, ignominy, vulgarity, disgrace and disrepute.

Attention is also called to the distinctiveness of dignity with respect to other terms in the same conceptual constellation. For Avishai Margalit, for example, '[d]ignity is similar to pride', but '[p]ride is the expression of self-esteem', and self-esteem comes from personal achievement. In contrast, dignity is the expression of 'self-respect', which is the 'attitude persons have to the fact of their being human'. More precisely, dignity is the 'external aspect of self-respect', understood (internally) as the 'respect persons feel

[3] *Singin in the Rain*, dir. Stanley Donen and Gene Kelly, Metro-Goldwyn-Mayer, 1952, with Gene Kelly in the role of Don Lockwood.

towards themselves as human beings'.[4] Honour is a key concept in Margalit's work, and in analysing it, he proposes another rendering of dignity as 'the honor that everyone deserves in equal measure'. That said, he then specifies that '[f]rom the viewpoint of those conferring such honor we speak of respect for humans, while from the viewpoint of those honored we speak of dignity'.[5] Donna Hicks puts forward an account of dignity in which the distinction between dignity and respect assumes fundamental significance. For her, '[d]ignity is different from respect', inasmuch as '[d]ignity is a birthright',[6] whereas '[r]espect must be earned'. 'If I say I respect someone, it is because he or she has done something extraordinary ... to deserve my admiration'. 'Dignity is something we all deserve, no matter what we do'; 'it is our inherent value and worth'.[7]

Margalit's characterisations of self-esteem and self-respect are linked to a distinction between esteem as 'a basis for ranking people' in the light of their achievements, and respect as 'a ground for treating people equally'. (As he explains, '[a] variety of moral theories tell us that we ought to respect people purely on the basis of their humanity, but no moral theory tells us that we ought to esteem people simply because they are human'.[8]) So it seems that Hicks's 'respect' resembles Margalit's 'esteem', and Margalit's 'respect' is like Hicks's 'dignity', viewed from the perspective of those recognising and honouring it in others. As for Margalit's 'dignity', it overlaps with Hicks's, yet also departs in picking out the perspective of the person whose dignity is at issue – that is to say, the element of self-respect in his sense. Similarities and divergences of this sort can be found across the literature on dignity as a whole, and clearly they testify to a level of conceptual slippage that may cause difficulties. As will be equally clear to readers of this book, however, I do not join the ranks of those trying to fix that. I have no new and better definition of dignity to offer, nor any tried and tested one to recommend.

[4] Avishai Margalit (Naomi Goldblum, trans.), *The Decent Society* (Cambridge, MA: Harvard University Press, 1996), 51–52.

[5] Ibid., 43. [6] Donna Hicks, *Dignity* (New Haven: Yale University Press, 2011), 4.

[7] Donna Hicks, *Leading with Dignity* (New Haven: Yale University Press, 2018), 2 (emphasis omitted).

[8] Margalit, *The Decent Society*, 44.

Andrew Sayer advises that 'if you want to know the meaning of a word [such as dignity], don't ask for a definition, but examine the different ways and situations in which it, and cognate terms, are used', not always consistently.[9] Regarding those usages, Sayer observes that dignity takes on particular pertinence where it is at risk. Vulnerability has a central role here, and it is unsurprising that, as we have seen, dignity is a major topic in the spheres of health care, social care and workplace relations.[10] Sayer also observes that efforts to improve practice in such spheres 'tend to provide a complex and contextualized view of dignity – one that emphasizes relations between people and their material circumstances, while the philosophical literature mostly [emphasises] autonomy, and particularly … the capacity for reason'.[11] This is not to say that autonomy is absent from the practical views; it is just to say that they range further. Notable too is the vernacular significance of dignity as at once 'something quite ordinary' and a kind of 'base-line' or outer limit to life and indeed death in a decent society to which appeal is made at moments of crisis.[12] 'At least I got out with my dignity intact', we hear. Or, 'My mother must be allowed to die with dignity'. Or again, 'Bread, dignity, freedom!'[13]

Attempts to get to grips with dignity often revolve around its negation. In meditations on the subject, Jay Bernstein takes as his guide the memoir of Austrian Holocaust survivor Jean Améry, *At the Mind's Limits: Contemplations by a Survivor on Auschwitz and Its Realities.*[14] With Améry's help, Bernstein describes in terrible detail the passage at the Nazi death camps from acts of humiliation, through devastation and mortification, to genocidal killing and the transformation of human corpses into valueless garbage thrown into ditches. It was, he writes, the 'exorbitance of

[9] Andrew Sayer, *Why Things Matter to People* (Cambridge: Cambridge University Press, 2011), 192.

[10] See Chapter 1. [11] Sayer, *Why Things Matter to People*, 191. [12] Ibid., 189.

[13] On keeping dignity intact and dying with dignity, see Sayer, *Why Things Matter to People*, 189. On 'bread, dignity, freedom!', see Ece Temelkuran, 'From Tahrir to Trump: Nationalism has Hijacked the Hope of the People', *The Guardian*, 14 February 2019.

[14] Jay Bernstein, *Torture and Dignity* (Chicago, IL: Chicago University Press, 2015), chap. 6. Jean Améry (Sidney Rosenfeld and Stella Rosenfeld, trans.), *At the Mind's Limits: Contemplations by a Survivor on Auschwitz and Its Realities* (Bloomington, IN: Indiana University Press, 1980).

Nazi practice [to turn] the legislative denial of dignity into the practical destruction of dignity – ending with mass, anonymous death'.[15] Bernstein is one of many authors for whom the Holocaust has served as a reference point for understanding dignity, and while his analysis is fantastically subtle, the same can scarcely be said about that reference point. To be sure, illumination in the 'glare of absolute contrast'[16] is revealing and necessary, but as Colin Bird suggests, 'to wield any sharp critical edge, dignitarian humanism must take us beyond' well-documented atrocities like the Holocaust, and become associated also with 'more surprising' enquiries[17] – or at any rate, enquiries that may involve surprises for some. The question then becomes: what is the sharp critical edge that dignity might wield, and how can it be – how has it been – put to work?

A Worldly Perspective

At the beginning of this book, I foreshadowed a study of dignity and its worldliness. In everyday parlance, the word 'worldly' is mostly used to convey the idea of being 'worldly-wise', that is to say, knowledgeable about, and experienced in, the ways of the world. In a more specialised usage, it refers to the domain of the secular or temporal ('this-worldly'), in contradistinction to the domain of the spiritual. I use it here to signal an interest in dignity as a phenomenon in and of the world. One aspect of that has to do with the physicality and especially corporeality of dignity. Sayer remarks that the modalities by which 'dignity is maintained or threatened and communicated via the body, often wordlessly' are often passed over in philosophical accounts, which explicate dignity in terms of 'reason, as the "highest" of our powers, as opposed to the "lowly" qualities of the body'.[18]

15 Bernstein, *Torture and Dignity*, 278 (emphasis omitted). On the transformation of human corpses into garbage, see esp. 278–81.

16 I borrow this phrase from Alan Ryan. See Alan Ryan, 'The Politics of Dignity', *New York Review of Books*, 11 July 1996.

17 Colin Bird, *Human Dignity and Political Criticism* (Cambridge: Cambridge University Press, 2021), 219.

18 Sayer, *Why Things Matter to People*, 191. Jay Bernstein is among the exceptions, though it is notable that his account of the connection between dignity and embodiment still remains largely abstract, revolving as it does around an effort

Deeply rooted in familiar themes and patterns of European thought, such an approach has generated important ideas, but it provides limited purchase on a concept that registers in daily life as 'comportment, eye contact and bodily control'.[19] We touched in an earlier chapter on the 'dance of dignity'[20] – a phrase that points to the gestures, actions and moves that can be seen to signify dignity.

Quite clearly, however, bodies do not float free of the conditions in which they exist, and to speak again with Sayer, some people 'will find it easier to maintain their dignity than others'.[21] In part, that may have to do with differentiated capacities and needs. For example, the inability to control particular bodily functions, or a need for care that involves unaccustomed exposure of the body, may pose threats to dignity not faced by those who can (currently) control such functions, and do not (currently) require such care. Yet vulnerabilities of this sort and the various forms of 'dignity work' undertaken to mitigate them are hardly independent variables. Rather, they are mediated by, and cannot be understood without reference to, social inequalities. As Sayer writes, the problems of unequal dignity are not primarily the product of disrespect within 'ephemeral, interpersonal social relations, but of social structures that make people's lives objectively unequal within their society'.[22] Going beyond the physical and embodied worldliness of dignity, there is, then, the fundamental worldliness that comes from enmeshment with prevailing dynamics, processes and structures of privilege and power. A worldly perspective, as I use the term, is one which takes that enmeshment into account. It is a perspective which prioritises engagement with realities over abstract investigation, considering dignity not just as a concept with a history, but as a concept in history, that is to

to defend the claim that 'human dignity inheres in the capacity of the individual to be self-presenting' and hence to establish 'self-conscious agency'. (Bernstein contends that 'the individual' establishes this by '[regulating] in socially recognizable ways the relation between the autonomous body and the body that is forever beyond final control'.) See Bernstein, *Torture and Dignity*, 297–99.

19 Sayer, *Why Things Matter to People*, 191–92.

20 Ibid., 192. See Chapter 1 above.

21 Sayer, *Why Things Matter to People*, 208.

22 Ibid., 215.

say, an element in the flux and friction[23] of existence under historically specific conditions.

Anyone who has read Kazuo Ishiguro's *The Remains of the Day* will remember that dignity is a central and very explicit issue in the novel. Like *July's People*, to which I made brief mention in Chapter 1, *The Remains of the Day* explores the concept in relation to domestic service.[24] Stevens, the story's narrator, embarks on a journey in the mid 1950s, during which he reflects on his life as a butler at an English stately home, Darlington Hall. His reflections lead him, early on, to the general question 'what is a great butler?'. Stevens's answer is that 'the factor which distinguishes [great butlers] from those butlers who are merely extremely competent is most closely captured by [the] word "dignity"'. He immediately acknowledges that 'this merely begs the further question: of what is "dignity" comprised?'.[25] Stevens answers that question by relating a series of anecdotes he heard from his father, a butler before him. In one anecdote, Stevens Senior valets temporarily for a retired general who pays a visit to his employer. Some years earlier, this retired general had been responsible for an incident in South Africa during the Anglo-Boer war in which Stevens's brother had been killed. Stevens describes the incident as 'a most un-British attack on civilian Boer settlements', and tells us that, on top of that, overwhelming evidence had emerged of 'several floutings of elementary military precautions, so that the men who had died ... had died quite needlessly'.[26]

Stevens explains that his father's feelings towards the visitor 'were, naturally, those of utmost loathing', but 'so well did my father hide his feelings, so professionally did he carry out his duties' that, at the end of the visit, the retired general 'complimented [Stevens Senior's employer] on the excellence of his butler and ... left an unusually large tip in appreciation'.[27] The conclusion proposed is that 'emotional restraint' is the core of

[23] On the idea of dignity as friction, see Vincent Lloyd, *Black Dignity: The Struggle against Domination* (New Haven, NJ: Yale University Press, 2022), 2. On Lloyd's argument in this book, see below.

[24] See David Medalie, '"What Dignity is There in That?" The Crisis of Dignity in Selected Late Twentieth-Century Novels', *Journal of Literary Studies* 20(1/2) (2004) 48, 51.

[25] Kazuo Ishiguro, *The Remains of the Day* (London: Faber and Faber, 1989), 33.

[26] Ibid., 40. [27] Ibid., 41–42.

dignity. A butler who possesses dignity wears his professionalism 'as a decent gentleman will wear his suit': 'he will not let ruffians or circumstance tear it off him in the public gaze'; only when he is alone will he ever discard it.[28] However, Stevens's confidence in this notion of dignity is unsettled when he encounters on his journey a man named Mr Harry Smith. Stevens falls into conversation with Harry Smith and some others about a member of the local gentry who has behaved badly. The question is posed, how can you tell a true gentleman from a false one? Stevens again offers the answer that dignity is the decisive criterion, but Harry Smith sees things differently. '[W]ith all respect for what you say, sir ... [d]ignity isn't just something gentlemen have. Dignity's something every man and woman in this country can strive for and get ... That's what we fought Hitler for, after all ... We won the right to be free citizens. And it's one of the privileges of being born English that no matter who you are, no matter if you're rich or poor, you're born free and you're born so that you can express your opinion freely ... That's what dignity's really about.'[29]

Stevens is resistant to Harry Smith's democratic worldview. 'Up to a point, no doubt, there is some truth in what he says', but it is 'far too idealistic, far too theoretical'. How can ordinary people like the two of them be expected to have opinions on 'all manner of things'? How can it be supposed that they can contribute meaningfully to the 'great debates of the nation'?[30] Clearly such debates must be left to their social betters. But then, it has transpired that Stevens's most relevant 'social better' – the man whom he served at Darlington Hall for most of his working life, Lord Darlington – was a Nazi sympathiser. During the 1920s and 1930s, with Stevens in unfailingly loyal attendance, Lord Darlington held at his home gatherings to rally support for appeasement with Hitler. Looking back, Stevens still maintains at the end of the novel that 'Lord Darlington wasn't a bad man'. The point for him is that Lord Darlington 'chose a certain path in life, it proved to be a misguided one, but there, he chose it'. In contrast, 'I cannot even claim that. You see, I trusted.' Stevens tells of how, all the years he had served Lord Darlington, he had trusted that he was 'doing something worthwhile'. 'I can't even

[28] Ibid., 43. [29] Ibid., 185–86. [30] Ibid., 194.

say I made my own mistakes. Really – one has to ask oneself – what dignity is there in that?'[31]

Stevens's Victorian-era code of honour, bound to the values of deference, repression and self-effacement, has deceived him, and his faith in it plainly cannot survive. In one of the novel's final episodes, he is asked by another man he meets on his journey what he takes dignity to be about, and can now only venture a hesitant and facile reply: 'It's a rather hard thing to explain in a few words . . . But I suspect it comes down to not removing one's clothing in public.'[32] Yet if Stevens becomes uncertain about an archaic conception of dignity invested in status, *The Remains of the Day* prompts the thought that Harry Smith's modern, egalitarian conception of dignity as intrinsic human worth – the idea that commands our faith today – also needs questioning. For, as David Medalie writes, what we learn from the novel is that the notion of dignity 'as a concept adrift from (or transcending) the defining or limiting categories of human society simply does not exist'.[33] Appealing though Harry's universalist vision assuredly is, his way of conceptualising dignity may itself deceive its adherents insofar as it elides unequal power relations, and obscures the material bases of inequality and unfreedom. At the least, to be told that dignity is something which everyone can strive for and get – or, in more philosophical language, that equal concern and respect are things to which everyone is entitled – is of limited help when the real issue is the unequal distribution of those social goods. The real issues are why some people – and always the *same* people – *don't* get the dignity that is theirs and *aren't* treated with equal concern and respect, and what it would take to change that situation.

Allow me to refer to one further passage from *The Remains of the Day*, in which we learn of a second anecdote used by Stevens to illustrate the meaning of dignity as the attribute that distinguishes a great butler from a merely extremely competent one. Again the story is said to have been related to Stevens by his father, but in this case, it does not actually involve Stevens Senior A butler is travelling with his employer in India, and finds a tiger under the table in the dining room. After discreetly alerting his

[31] Ibid., 243 (emphasis omitted). [32] Ibid., 210.
[33] Medalie, '"What Dignity is There in That?"', 50.

employer, the butler kills the tiger, and then reports back that '[d]inner will be served at the usual time and I am pleased to say that there will be no discernible traces left of the recent occurrence by that time'.[34] Stevens proposes that the calmness and restraint displayed here are distinctively English qualities which, according to him, can also be discerned in the natural environment of England. 'It is the very lack of obvious drama or spectacle that sets the beauty of our land apart', we read. 'What is pertinent is the calmness of that beauty, its sense of restraint.' Stevens contrasts this with 'the sorts of sights offered in such places as Africa and America [which], though undoubtedly very exciting, would, I am sure, strike the objective viewer as inferior on account of their unseemly demonstrativeness'.[35] Like the anecdote about Stevens's father valeting for the man responsible for his son's death in South Africa, this story of a butler who finds a tiger under a dining table in India and these statements about the landscapes of 'such places as Africa and America' reach beyond the novel's immediate setting in southern England, to situate dignity within the wider context of the British Empire.

I have suggested that a worldly perspective on dignity is, first of all, one that attends to the physical and especially corporeal aspects of dignity. Secondly, and more generally, I have associated worldliness with a perspective that foregrounds the realities of dignity, that is to say, its character as an historical artefact and a site of political struggle. Ishiguro brings into focus here a third, related dimension of this worldliness. Enquiry informed by a worldly perspective does not have regard only to the milieux of European thought around which histories of dignity mostly revolve. Rather, it is worldly in the simple sense that it includes within its purview the world as a whole, taking into consideration the highly consequential role in the concept's development of colonialism and anti-colonialism. For Stevens, England is the privileged site of dignity, and as Susie O'Brien reads the text, that is in part because 'England's ability to confer order on [the] more unruly parts of the world [that is, the parts of the world characterised by unseemly, if exciting demonstrativeness] was strongly predicated on the dignity

[34] Ishiguro, *The Remains of the Day*, 36. [35] Ibid., 28–29 (emphasis omitted).

of its serving classes'.[36] In the story of the tiger under the dining table in India, the summary killing of the animal may hint at the repressive violence which is a concomitant of that system of dignified restraint – as may the anecdote about the man who commanded British troops during the Anglo-Boer War in South Africa, with its allusion to atrocities committed against Boer civilians.

Defined by Inequalities

India and South Africa, along with Australia, have likewise featured in our explorations of dignity in the preceding chapters of this book. Chapter 3 looked at dignity in relation to a series of photographs taken in colonial Australia of Trucanini, a Tasmanian Aboriginal woman of the Nuenonne people. These photographs were informed by the colonialist ideology of the 'doomed race', according to which Tasmanian Aboriginal people were a 'doomed race' that would soon cease to exist. The most famous of the pictures was taken as part of an effort systematically to document the people's physical traits, represented as a 'missing link' with earlier evolutionary stages. Such photography involved for Trucanini multiple, immensely grievous forms of indignity, on some of which we touched. At the same time, viewers have remarked on the dignity she appeared to retain. We noted the co-production necessarily involved in portrait photography and the ineradicable element of self-representation with regard to the sitter. We also noted the dignity conferred on these pictures insofar as they have been reappropriated by recent generations of Tasmanian Aboriginal people, who have imbued them with fresh meanings that challenge messages they have still been seen to carry, long after the retreat of empire.

Chapter 4 considered dignity in the movement for Indian independence when, during the 1920s and 1930s, Gandhi promoted the making and wearing of homespun cotton cloth or *khadi* as an instrument and a symbol of non-cooperation, self-reliance and dignity. The subcontinent had been the world leader

[36] Susie O'Brien, 'Serving a New World Order: Postcolonial Politics in Kazuo Ishiguro's *The Remains of the Day*', *Modern Fiction Studies* 42(4) (1996) 787, 790.

in the manufacture of cotton textiles throughout most of history. Under British rule, that situation changed to the point where there was almost complete dependence on imports, and Gandhi now appealed to Indians to 'realise their dignity' by discarding their foreign, mostly English-made, cloth and renewing their home textile industry. At a certain moment, he began himself to dress in a mere loincloth made of *khadi*, using his 'undignified' near-nakedness to expose the shame of India's impoverishment by the 'dignified' British. Yet if Gandhi questioned British assumptions about what constituted dignity and indignity in this context, and by whom they were respectively exemplified, we recalled that Ambedkar in turn questioned Gandhian assumptions about how dignity could be achieved. Given the negative role of dignity in the lives of Dalits as that which caste Hindus upheld ('stood upon') as the justification for oppressing and exploiting them, Ambedkar argued that dignity could not be achieved for all Indians without social transformation, including the dismantling of the Hindu system of caste.

Chapter 5 examined dignity in the so-called 'toilet wars' waged at various urban locations in twenty-first-century South Africa. We observed that sanitation bears on an important aspect of what many people today understand by dignity. Indeed, as a campaigning slogan has it, 'sanitation is dignity'. South Africa is a country in which there exist large disparities in the distribution of sanitation services, with black South Africans considerably less well served than white South Africans. We followed the efforts of poor black communities to secure or defend access to sanitation through litigation and public protest. The South African Constitution declares that 'everyone has inherent dignity, and the right to have their dignity respected and protected', and we saw how the issue arose in one Constitutional Court case of how many times a person must be able to flush the toilet each day in order to maintain a healthy and dignified existence. We also saw how, in protests linked to that case and to other developments relating to sanitation, community members staged ironic performances of abjection that returned the indignity of poor sanitation to the state. Finally, we took note of the gap between sanitation policy that is oriented towards technological solutions and sanitation policy that engages with access to sanitation as a political problem and a matter of social justice.

I don't suppose much needs to be said to make known the ways in which these mini-studies of dignity instantiate and illustrate the worldly perspective I have sketched. The human body is an explicit part of the subject matter of each of the three chapters. So too each of them sidesteps abstraction in favour of an approach that sets dignity within the stream of politics and of history. In doing so, each of the chapters investigates dignity at a site that permits consideration of the significance for the concept of the colonial encounter and/or the latter's ongoing realities in post-colonial societies. Against the prevalent preoccupation in discussions of dignity with the twists and turns of intellectual life in Europe (or, depending on the time frame, Europe and the United States), these chapters move east and south to see how dignity has been produced, shaped and contested elsewhere. The story is, of course, quite different in each case, but there are cross-cutting strands. Photography was a central issue in Chapter 3, but Chapter 4 also called to mind some iconic photographs of Gandhi, while media coverage, including images, underpinned our discussion of the toilet wars in Chapter 5. Clothing accounted for much of what chiefly concerned us in Chapter 4, but when it came to Chapter 3 to the photographs taken of Trucanini on her own and in groups, there could be no ignoring how she and her companions were dressed.

Let us pause briefly over sanitation, which served as the focus of Chapter 5, but also received glancing attention in Chapter 4, inasmuch as the allocation to Dalits of the work of cleaning toilets was registered there as an aspect of the caste system. In a paper about sanitation in India, Assa Doron and Ira Raja observe that this is often said to be an 'unpopular subject that people prefer to avoid'.[37] They quote a speech by the UN Secretary-General in which he suggests that '[p]erhaps that is why the sanitation crisis [in many countries] has not been met with the kind of response we need' – a state of affairs that 'must change'. But, ask the authors, 'is it really the unpleasantness of the subject that has led to its neglect?'[38] They also evoke initiatives such as the 'toilet festivals' held in Indian cities to exhibit and applaud public toilets built by and for the poor.

[37] Assa Doron and Ira Raja, 'The Cultural Politics of Shit: Class, Gender and Public Space in India', *Postcolonial Studies* 18(2) (2015) 189, 190.
[38] Ibid.

Arjun Appardurai advanced the argument in an earlier paper that these festivals provided an occasion for transforming the 'humiliation and victimization' of having no access to a toilet into 'exercises of technical initiative and self-dignification'.[39] But again Doron and Raja are unconvinced. Is it really technical initiative that will fix the problem? 'In the absence of effective public sanitation', they write, the rich are unaffected, and the 'poor make do, but the ways in which they make do are ... defined by inequalities among themselves'.[40]

Picking up that thread, I want now to turn to more theoretical matters. Theoretical matters? Have I not insisted on a perspective that foregrounds the realities of dignity? It bears emphasis that directing attention to empirical realities is not the same as anti-theoretical empiricism or, to borrow a phrase from Jean Comaroff and John Comaroff, 'born-again realism'.[41] In their work on 'theory from the south', Comaroff and Comaroff comment that '[f]or the global south, the refusal of theory has long been an unaffordable luxury'.[42] But this theory that is necessary (also to deprivileged populations in the global north) is not a 'flight into pure abstraction'. Instead, it is 'grounded theory', and Comaroff and Comaroff explain that, by that, they intend 'the historically contextualized ... effort to account for the production of social and cultural "facts" in the world by recourse to an imaginative counterpoint between ... the concrete and the concept; also, in a different register, between the epic and the everyday, [and] the meaningful and the material'.[43] Our enquiries into dignity have taken us from the epic events of Tasmania's Black War and its aftermath to the everyday conditions of life in post-apartheid South Africa, and the meaningful symbolism deployed in the movement for Indian independence. It remains to connect the concrete and material with the concept.

39 Arjun Appardurai, 'Deep Democracy: Urban Governmentality and the Horizon of Politics', *Environment & Urbanization* 13(2) (2001) 23, 37.
40 Doron and Raja, 'The Cultural Politics of Shit', 197.
41 Jean Comaroff and John Comaroff, *Theory from the South* (London: Taylor & Francis, 2018), 47.
42 Ibid., 48. My attention was called to this passage in this context by Norman Ajari (Matthew Smith, trans.), *Dignity or Death: Ethics and Politics of Race* (Cambridge: Polity Press, 2023), 44.
43 Comaroff and Comaroff, *Theory from the South*, 48.

A recurrent claim or presupposition in discussions of dignity is the distinction between two kinds of dignity corresponding to two forms of worthiness. In Chapter 2, I dubbed these 'intrinsic dignity', understood as the worthiness that belongs to every human being simply by virtue of their being human, and 'status dignity', understood as the worthiness that comes from holding high office or occupying some other particular status or role.[44] I noted that scholars writing about the history of the concept of dignity have associated status dignity with the 'old' dignity signified by the Latin term *dignitas*, and intrinsic dignity with the 'new' dignity – the universal human dignity – proclaimed in the constitutions and human rights instruments of the present day. On the question of what happened to status dignity, I made reference to the prominent argument put forward by Jeremy Waldron that intrinsic dignity was formed through 'an upwards equalization of rank', so that everyone now has the dignity and rank formerly reserved only for a few.[45] 'Every man a Brahmin', Waldron added to reinforce the point.[46] Yet immediately we see the flaw here. For there to exist Brahmins, not everyone (not even every male person) can be one. For there to exist equality, there can be no Brahmins. That is what we learn from Ambedkar. So long as caste (or other category of entrenched social stratification) persists, status dignity persists with it. Universal human dignity depends not on the upwards equalisation of rank, but on the abolition of rank, and on the social structural transformation needed to achieve that.

Along somewhat similar lines to Waldron, Jürgen Habermas has advanced the contention, to which I also made reference, that the modern concept of human dignity arose out of a 'generalisation' or 'coalescence' of status dignities.[47] To speak of intrinsic, human dignity might be to suggest that dignity is a natural endowment or property determined by nothing other than arrival in the world, but Habermas wants us to see that it requires anchoring in a recognition-conferring status. What sets

[44] See Chapter 2.
[45] Jeremy Waldron, *Dignity, Rank and Rights* (Oxford: Oxford University Press, 2012), 33–34; see further Chapter 2.
[46] Waldron, *Dignity, Rank and Rights*, 34.
[47] Jürgen Habermas, 'The Concept of Human Dignity and the Realistic Utopia of Human Rights', *Metaphilosophy* 41(4) (2010) 464; see further Chapter 2.

human dignity apart from status dignity, so his argument goes, is that the appropriate status is no longer some particular office or role. Rather, there is one and the same status for everyone, namely, 'democratic citizenship'.[48] To see the flaw there, it is enough to recall the paper I cited in Chapter 5 by Noshipo Mkhize and colleagues, where they presented the results of a survey which followed up on an initiative by the Durban city authorities to improve sanitation in poor black communities by providing households with a type of dry toilet known as a UD toilet.[49] Among the researchers' findings was that all of the UD toilet users would have preferred a plumbed-in flush toilet, 'which is associated with being a first-class citizen'.[50] If such a phrase can be used and understood, it is because democratic citizenship is not one and the same status for everyone. In this case, and despite the political equality of the post-apartheid period, access to the facilities perceived as the basis for sanitary dignity still remained a component of white South Africans' privilege.

Digging Dignity Out

The distinction between intrinsic dignity and status dignity brings with it an historical narrative that has as one – and perhaps the most celebrated – of its protagonists the eighteenth-century Prussian philosopher, Immanuel Kant. I recalled in Chapter 2 that the key text of Kant's on which reliance is placed is the *Groundwork of the Metaphysics of Morals*, where Kant laid out the idea that in the moral domain 'everything has either a price or a dignity'. 'What has a price can be replaced with something else', he explains, 'whereas what is elevated above any price, and allows of no equivalent, has a dignity'.[51] For contemporary scholars, the

[48] Habermas, 'The Concept of Human Dignity and the Realistic Utopia of Human Rights', 475.

[49] See further Chapter 5.

[50] Noshipo Mkhize et al., 'Urine Diversion Dry Toilets in eThekwini Municipality, South Africa: Acceptance, Use and Maintenance through Users' Eyes', *Journal of Water, Sanitation and Hygiene for Development* 7(1) (2017) 111, 114; see Chapter 5.

[51] Immanuel Kant (Mary Gregor and Jens Timmerman, trans. and ed.), *Groundwork of the Metaphysics of Morals* (Cambridge: Cambridge University Press, rev. ed. 2012), 46 (emphasis omitted).

modern conception of human dignity builds on the intellectual foundations of that notion of dignity as incomparable, incalculable, inestimable worth, worth beyond measure. To be sure, not everyone goes along with this line of thought. Some argue for an interpretation of the *Groundwork* and other relevant Kantian texts which casts his understanding of dignity in a different light.[52] But what of the assumption that the modern conception of human dignity is itself to be identified with a kind of worth which is incomparable, incalculable and inestimable? When the issue arises in a court case of how many times a person must be able to flush the toilet each day in order to maintain a healthy and dignified existence,[53] one might well wonder whether those are the right epithets to use, and whether, instead, we should be talking about the 'metrologies of dignity'[54] applied in constitutional and human rights law.

Kant subsumed his work on dignity under the category of 'moral science', and in turn, he allocated moral science to the 'rational part' of ethics. I retold in Chapter 2 the story of how he had long taught courses on anthropology and geography, and allocated those disciplines to the 'empirical part' of ethics, from which he said the rational part needed to be kept separate. Kant's thinking about anthropology and geography is documented in a range of surviving texts. Among these is *Of the Different Races of Human Beings*, in which he elaborates a theory to account for what he takes to be the division of humanity into four races distinguished from one another by skin colour and ranked in order of 'perfectibility', with the white race at the top. The theory puts on a 'scientific' footing the racism and white supremacism that also surface in his other 'empirical' writings. Kant's work on anthropology and geography is not nearly as well-known today as his work on moral philosophy. Some scholars dismiss its significance, representing it as unserious and, at any rate, marginal to Kant's scholarship as a whole,[55] but the question of what Kant's

[52] See, for example, Oliver Sensen, *Kant on Human Dignity* (Berlin and Boston: de Gruyter, 2011).

[53] See Chapter 5.

[54] Antina von Schnitzler, *Democracy's Infrastructure: Techno-Politics and Protest after Apartheid* (Princeton, NJ: Princeton University Press, 2016), 184.

[55] See, for example, Katrin Flikshuh and Lea Ypi (eds.), *Kant and Colonialism* (Oxford: Oxford University Press, 2014).

raciology has to do with his metaphysics is not easily evaded. As other scholars have demonstrated, '[r]acial science was not some marginal concern at the corners of European philosophy, it was an integral component of its intellectual framework'.[56] Importantly too, Kant's racial theorising was not simply 'the contamination of scientific findings with customary prejudice'; it was the 'transformation' of customary prejudice into scientific knowledge, with 'philosophical sanction'.[57]

Supported by racial science, a discourse of dignity figured in the ideology used to justify colonial domination and exploitation. In *Culture and Imperialism*, Edward Said highlights the statement made in 1910 by French colonial administrator Jules Harmand that '[o]ur dignity ... underlies our right to direct the rest of humanity'.[58] Conversely, Eleni Coundouriotis points to the trope in anti-colonial literature that portrays dignity as a 'marker of the arrogance of colonial power, a way in which the official presence of empire asserts its superiority over the native'.[59] Coundouriotis gives an example from the novel by Chinua Achebe, *Things Fall Apart*, first published in 1958. Set in south-eastern Nigeria at the outset of British colonisation, the novel contains near the end a scene in which it is reported that a colonial messenger has been killed in an act of resistance to British rule, and the man responsible has hanged himself from a tree. The dead man's comrades ask the area's senior colonial official ('District Commissioner') to help them by having the body taken down. They are not able to do this themselves, they explain, as suicide is considered an abomination in their tradition, so only strangers may touch the corpse. The District Commissioner orders a subordinate to do what is asked, and Achebe has him reflect that '[i]n the many years in which he had toiled to bring civilization to different parts of Africa he had learnt a number of things. One of them was that a District Commissioner must never attend to such undignified details as cutting down a

[56] Kehinde Andrews, *The New Age of Empire: How Racism and Colonialism Still Rule the World* (London: Penguin Books, 2021), 10.

[57] Wulf Hund, '"It Must Come from Europe": The Racisms of Immanuel Kant', in Wulf Hund et al. (eds.), *Racisms Made in Germany* (Racism Analysis Series B: Yearbook, vol. 2) (Berlin and Vienna: LIT Verlag, 2011), 69, 78.

[58] Edward Said, *Culture and Imperialism* (London: Vintage Books, 1994), 17.

[59] Eleni Coundouriotis, 'The Dignity of the "Unfittest": Victims' Stories in South Africa', *Human Rights Quarterly* 28(4) (2006) 842, 844–45.

dead man from the tree. Such attention would give the natives a poor opinion of him.'[60]

If colonial authority depended on claiming dignity, it also depended on defining dignity – a power that casts in intriguing light the figure of the 'noble savage', on which we touched in connection with representations of Trucanini in Chapter 3. Men and women depicted in that register were evidently acknowledged to possess their own form of dignity different from that of the colonisers. Yet, as we saw, the context for such images was a pervasive 'extinction discourse' and 'doomed race theory'.[61] Repackaging the violent destruction and dispossession of First Nations as natural extinction or disappearance due to incapacity for adaptation to changing conditions, artists, photographers and scholars set about documenting Indigenous life before it fell victim to the onward march of human progress. To be a noble savage was to be a 'vanishing savage', and inasmuch as these representations were often tinged with sadness or regret, we noted the connection with the narrative mode of proleptic elegy, in which colonial writers prospectively mourned the loss of what they took themselves to supersede. Of course, a noble savage was also still a 'savage', and in studying the various photographs of Trucanini, we observed something of the effects of the civilising mission to which Achebe alludes. It was perhaps most of all in the elaborately staged group photographs by Henry Frith that we could discern the perspective of colonists committed to a project of 'rescuing' Aboriginal people by Europeanising them.[62]

Shane Chalmers has explored these ideas with reference to another visual representation from colonial Australia, a painting by Samuel Thomas Gill made in Sydney in 1860 and entitled *Native Dignity* (Figure 6.2).[63] The work depicts an Aboriginal man and woman taking a walk along a city street. What is most striking about the image is the couple's clothing: they wear European clothes, but not in the normal way. On the upper part of their bodies are the smart, if in parts tattered, garments one would expect to see in this context, while on the lower part are only undergarments. The man carries a swagger stick and the woman a parasol, and they wear hats

[60] Chinua Achebe, *Things Fall Apart* (London: Penguin, Books, 2001), 151.
[61] See further Chapter 3. [62] See further Chapter 3.
[63] Shane Chalmers, 'Native Dignity', *Griffith Law Review* 29(2) (2020) 175.

Figure 6.2 S. T. Gill, *Native Dignity*, 1866. Lithograph.

but no shoes. Chalmers cites settler writings of the period which indicate that great weight was attached to dress as an agent of civilisation. Clothing the body in the European style would 'moralise' the natives. Put more bluntly, it would 'humanise' them,[64] and defiance of this assimilatory practice was apparently made a punishable offence in some places. On the other hand, Chalmers also cites reports which bear witness to much mockery and defiance on the part of Aboriginal people, and much anxiety about being ridiculed and undermined on the part of the colonists. With these points in mind, it is not difficult to see in Gill's painting an effort to mobilise 'the power of humiliation' by taking down the 'uppity pretensions'[65] of mimic men and women, while at the same time

[64] Ibid., 182. [65] Ibid., 186.

reinforcing the imperative of a civilising mission in which clothing played a central role.

Yet Chalmers shows that there is more – another layer of meaning signposted by the artwork's title. For, as he explains, the phrase 'native dignity' carried a telling ambiguity. It was at once the dignity of the native – the Aboriginal person – and the native or inborn dignity – in the terminology I have used, the intrinsic dignity – said to be possessed by all human beings purely by virtue of being human. In the circumstances of Australian settler-colonialism, Chalmers writes of how an aporia opened up in that second idea of native dignity as a universal quality of all human beings. '[T]o possess the native dignity [meaning here the intrinsic dignity] that Europeans naturally possessed', Aboriginal people had to become assimilated to Europeans (and to dress accordingly). Naked, or clothed in their own manner, they possessed only 'the native dignity of the savage'.[66] In the half-half state in which the painting depicted them, they exhibited native dignity of neither sort; they were natives without dignity. And so *Native Dignity* put before its viewers a conception of dignity that alternatively 'arrested [the] dynamism' of Aboriginal peoples by tying them to an image of the noble savage condemned to stasis and ultimate die out, or 'dynamited their existence as peoples' by forcing them to assimilate and attempt to transform themselves into an image of the dignified human identified with European Man.[67] Though definitionally independent of status, intrinsic dignity was thus revealed to depend on a particular status, or at least on accepting to assume the trappings of that status.[68]

I have dwelled a little on how racial science informed a discourse of dignity that was, and is, used to justify the domination and exploitation of non-European peoples. The other side of this story concerns the use of a discourse of dignity in aid of emancipatory activism. Taking the example of Gandhi's campaign for homespun cloth as a symbol of, and means to, Indian self-reliance and self-rule, we investigated that dimension in Chapter 4. We saw that talk of dignity suffused his writings and speeches, and that its subject was at once collective and individual. At stake, he believed, was the dignity of the colonised

[66] Ibid., 190. [67] Ibid. [68] Ibid.

peoples of British India and each individual belonging to those peoples. Gandhi's engagement with dignity included the repudiation of imperial conceptions of dignity, a stance made famous when he attended a reception at Buckingham Palace in attire which paid no heed to those conceptions and was unquestionably undignified if judged by reference to them. This practice of 'owning' or performing indignity for the sake of challenging what passes for dignity also came into view, albeit rather differently, in our enquiry into the South African toilet wars in Chapter 5. To draw attention to the situation of poor, black women living without sufficient water for use in flush toilets, demonstrators in Johannesburg marched with red-blotted underwear over their clothes. To bring home to privileged people what it is to have no option but to use malodorous and often filthy portable toilets, protesters in Cape Town threw faeces onto cars and public buildings. If these actions counted as undignified, then spectators were invited to consider that the real indignity, the real shame, was the denial of adequate sanitation that occasioned them.[69]

One may reasonably guess that emancipatory discourses of dignity are as consistent and as varied, as enduring and as protean, as the oppression they challenge. In Chapter 1, I mentioned a study by Vincent Lloyd in which he elucidates dignity as a concept to which those engaged in Black struggle have long made appeal.[70] Focusing mostly on the United States, Lloyd traces a history of Black dignity discourse that encompasses texts by Frederick Douglass, Ida Wells, Langston Hughes, Malcolm X, Martin Luther King Jr, Audre Lorde, Eldridge Cleaver, James Cone, Huey Newton, Angela Davis and bell hooks, among others. As he reads it, 'African American writing ... uses the language of dignity ... in the way it is used in the ambient culture', but also in another way. That other usage, to which he applies the label 'Black dignity', 'both admires and mocks the pretenses of American dignity to universality', and affirms instead an idea of dignity as the 'struggle against domination'.[71] With Black dignity, dignity becomes a relative quality, rather than an absolute one. 'The more struggle, the more dignity; the less struggle, the less dignity' – whereby 'struggle' is simply meant 'someone ... not

[69] On these events, see further Chapter 5. [70] Lloyd, *Black Dignity*.
[71] Vincent Lloyd, 'Black Dignity', *Crosscurrents* (March 2018) 73, 87–88.

[playing] her part'. That is to say, struggle 'does not have to look like a political protest ... it can also look like song, dance, jokes, sermons, or silence'. Whatever is involved, a crucial point, for Lloyd, is that dignity is located in the domain of practice. Black 'dignity names ... activity',[72] whether organised or spontaneous, large-scale or small-scale, conventionally political or occurring within the routines of ordinary life.

Part of Lloyd's impetus for this work comes from the Black Lives Matter movement. He writes of how activists in the movement have drawn on, and contributed to, the tradition of Black dignity. Certainly, dignity is not the only concept to which they refer, but he proposes that it has special significance insofar as it shapes 'all the concepts' that form the 'new moral vocabulary emerging around Black Lives Matter'.[73] At the same time, it is itself reshaped, or, in his words, '[cleaved] ... from its false copies' – among them, respectability. Whereas respectability is often regarded as interchangeable with dignity, Lloyd highlights that these activists, or some of them, have decried respectability as the fulfilment of 'white fantasies [about] how "good" Black people look and act'. Turning into a general principle the kinds of dissident practice I illustrated in the preceding paragraph, they have insisted that '[r]espectability is the illusion of dignity'.[74] This way of thinking about dignity and deploying it as an element within 'the conceptual arsenal of an engaged politics' also informs, and is analysed in, another recent study of racial injustice and Black dignity, by Norman Ajari.[75] Ajari's reference-points are not identical to Lloyd's, but one shared reference-point is the Black liberation theologian, James Cone. In particular, Ajari commends the following statement in Cone's book from 1972, *The Spirituals and the Blues*:

> [Slave] [r]esistance made dignity more than just a word to be analyzed philosophically. Dignity was a reality that could only be dug out the shit of [a] white environment ... [in which] [w]hite people achieved what they called dignity by their enslavement of black Africans.[76]

[72] Lloyd, *Black Dignity*, 8–9. [73] Ibid., 34. [74] Ibid., 5.
[75] Ajari, *Dignity or Death*, 7.
[76] James Cone, *The Spirituals and the Blues* (Maryknoll, NY: Orbis Books, 1991, first published 1972), 27–28 (emphasis omitted). Quoted in Ajari, *Dignity or Death*, 7.

Just by Being Themselves

I too am struck by that statement, which brings together many of the ideas, approaches, issues, dynamics and even substances that have preoccupied us in this book. *In the first place,* there is the observation that dignity is not just a word, but also a reality. The concept which I have used in that connection is 'worldliness'. I have suggested that a worldly perspective is needed to capture the embodied, enacted and relational character of dignity, along with its social effects and the politics of its distribution. Lloyd also evokes the concept of worldliness inasmuch as he encourages activism that '[sees] dignity as it appears in this world – not in some pure form imagined in a world redeemed'.[77] With similar import, Ajari questions the vision of the 'human person' which has informed philosophical understandings of dignity on the ground that it 'neglects social relations and the lived experience of the individual'. 'To consider dignity as an abstract property detached from experience and context and set apart from the violence and dangers that plague existence' is to '[rob] the notion of dignity of its historicity', he declares.[78] A worldly perspective restores that historicity, eschewing the representation of human dignity as timeless and unvarying.

The history into which Cone re-inserts dignity is obviously that of the American South and its antebellum slave economy. He tells of how, in that time and place, white people achieved what they called dignity through their enslavement of Black Africans. Indeed, they not only chalked up their profits, but also 'measured their importance by the number of Africans they enslaved'.[79] *Secondly,* then, Cone's statement invokes scrutiny of the nexus between ideas about dignity on the one hand, and arrangements for the production of wealth and the social structures and ideological processes that support those arrangements on the other. We have encountered the haughty face of dignity – the face that expresses entitlement to subjugate and exploit – in various contexts in this book. Some would invite us to see in it the superannuated face of status dignity, but our investigations have led us to a different assessment. Chalmers encapsulates a core

[77] Lloyd, 'Black Dignity', *Crosscurrents,* 84. [78] Ajari, *Dignity or Death,* 30, 34, 35.
[79] Cone, *The Spirituals and the Blues,* 28.

aspect in his writing about the painting *Native Dignity*. As he interprets it, the work made manifest an 'unsettling truth – that "native dignity" [i.e. in this context, human dignity], that revolutionary human-based concept, was actually a retrograde status-based one'. Chalmers continues: '[f]or Europeans, native dignity was supposed to be a radical, egalitarian, emancipatory concept, set against a long tradition of thinking about dignity as a matter of [elevated] rank... And yet for Aboriginal people, it was exactly that: a matter of rank'.[80]

In like manner, this disjuncture has repeatedly appeared before us. Dignity is said to be something everyone has purely by virtue of being human – a universal human dignity that stands in contrast with the status-based notions which preceded it (and which coexist with it to the limited extent that there still remains talk of the special dignity of certain institutions and offices). From the vantage point of unprivileged people, however, such a contrast can be difficult to discern. For them, human dignity often looks a lot like status dignity, and those who pretend otherwise turn away from a reality in which dignity forms part of the advantage systematically accruing to groups accorded higher status within prevailing social hierarchies. The backdrop to that reality is colonial capitalism and the deep imprint it has left on ideas about dignity. Colonial capitalism has not been a standard constituent of histories of dignity, but it needs to be brought into account insofar as imperial expansion and class struggle have enduringly and consequentially marked the concept. Not the least – and this is a *third* point highlighted in Cone's statement, and one which has been central to our story – they have put on it a racial mark, the stamp of white supremacy. In Ajari's crisp formulation, 'Black people regularly contradicted human dignity just by being themselves'.[81]

That dignity formed part of the gift of civilisation to savage peoples meant that the latter were not only to be taught what dignity was. They were also to be taught how abjection should be construed and, in particular, why it should be identified with their own ways. At the same time, colonial ideology leaned on pre-colonial forms of social distinction and the practices of dignification

[80] Chalmers, 'Native Dignity', 190. [81] Ajari, *Dignity or Death*, 32.

and abjectification linked to them. Significant in Cone's statement, *fourthly*, is an invitation to consider dignity from the perspective of those pushed outside it. Rather than treating indignity only as a problem to be remedied, we have seen that it provides vital diagnostic information. People who are demeaned have important truths to reveal about dignity and its relation to the structures and processes that make up the organisation of the world. Recognising this is not a matter of romanticising abjection or celebrating resilience;[82] it is simply a matter of looking in the places where it is necessary to look in order to gain an adequate understanding of dignity. Again, such an approach has not generally been adopted in writing on the subject, which has tended instead to work with an idea of indignity as flawed, lapsed or compromised dignity, awaiting correction. But what if 'indignity logically precedes the conceptualization of dignity'?[83]

As much as dignity is bound up with power, it is also bound up with resistance. Attention to the resistant side of dignity, where we witness dignity being asserted in the face of its denial and/or with a view to subverting the socio-political dispensation that rationalises denial, is a *fifth* component of Cone's statement. After the passage I have quoted, he asks: '[W]hat were the slaves to do? How could they assert their dignity, their humanity, and self-worth?' He then proceeds to explain that '[t]hey chose a life style defined by their group. The respected slave was the one who successfully challenged the rules of white society.'[84] In their work on Black dignity, Lloyd and Ajari echo that approach, associating dignity with the struggle against domination – albeit without making success a criterion. Jana Costas, whose study of cleaning work at a mall in present-day Berlin you will recall from Chapter 1, shows how, at the level of what she terms the daily 'dramas of dignity', successes indeed come mixed with failures.[85] The cleaners she got to know – a diverse group, tied together by a shared history of social marginality (unemployment,

[82] I take this thought from the work, in a different context, of Lila Abu Lughod. See esp. Lila Abu Lughod, 'The Romance of Resistance: Tracing Transformations of Power through Bedouin Women', *American Ethnologist* 17 (1) (1990) 41, 41–42.

[83] Ajari, *Dignity or Death*, 39.

[84] Cone, *The Spirituals and the Blues*, 28.

[85] Jana Costas, *Dramas of Dignity: Cleaners in the Corporate Underworld of Berlin* (Cambridge: Cambridge University Press, 2022).

immigration, homelessness, etc.) and now engaged in low-wage, low-status work[86] – were able to confront disvaluation and disrespect to some degree. But when they talked back to managers, customers and others at the mall, they risked losing a job they needed, and that risk was intensified by the surveillance they experienced, which could only be partially evaded.

Among the infinite array of ways in which dignity, humanity and self-worth may be asserted by those denied them is the conspicuous and even spectacular 'owning' of indignity. We have seen how members of subordinated groups may embrace indignity in order to lay it bare and compel the authorities to take notice. At least in part, that may be a matter of illuminating the undignified character or consequences of what passes for dignity. So the message may be 'our indignity is your indignity'. But it may also be a matter of signalling the refusal by those concerned to be dignified by the things that are supposed to confer dignity on them.[87] So the message may equally be 'your dignity is not our dignity'. Either way, the display or performance of indignity belongs with an effort to promote a more inclusory economy of dignity and the conditions consistent with it. This brings me to a *sixth* and final respect in which Cone's statement anticipates our themes. In writing of how dignity was a reality that could only be dug out of the shit of the white environment, he brings undignified excrement into the conversation and makes it a metonym for racial (and, by extension, other) injustice. The connection between human waste and the modern history of imperialist exploitation is further clarified by Alison Moore, from whom one learns that the world's first flushing public toilet was installed at the Great Exhibition which took place in London in 1851,[88] alongside the exotic tokens of Britain's colonial prosperity.[89]

[86] Ibid., 7.

[87] I take this thought from the work, in a different context, of Sara Ahmed. See Sara Ahmed, *The Promise of Happiness* (Durham, NC: Duke University Press, 2010).

[88] Also known as the Crystal Palace Exhibition, after the structure erected for it in London's Hyde Park (later relocated to south London and destroyed by fire in 1936).

[89] Alison Moore, 'Colonial Visions of "Third World" Toilets: A Nineteenth-Century Discourse That Haunts Contemporary Tourism', in Olga Gershenson and Barbara Penner (eds.), *Ladies and Gents: Public Toilets and Gender* (Philadelphia, PA: Temple University Press, 2009), 105, 110.

Awkward Questions

Pervaded as much discussion of it is by a 'warm uplifting atmosphere',[90] dignity all too easily passes under the radar of critical scrutiny. No one is against it, even if some have worried about its role in bioethics and other spheres, given the particular (religious-conservative) agenda it has been used to promote there.[91] In recent years, a body of critical literature on dignity has begun to take shape, led by the scholarship explicating Black dignity. This book is offered as a contribution to that literature. Reaching the book's final pages, I find apposite the following words of Lloyd's, in which he addresses his readers directly: 'You interrupt. *But what am I to do?* ... [Y]ou demand to know my political platform. You would prefer a numbered, prioritized list. But really you would be equally pleased to be told that the demands cannot be enumerated, the problem so grave only silent witness will suffice.' He goes on: 'Moralizing and policymaking offer pleasures to both speaker and listener', but it is necessary to 'see the world rightly' in order to 'respond rightly', and '[s]eeing the world rightly, clouded as it is by systems of domination', is already a huge task.[92]

Like Lloyd, I tender no numbered, prioritised list, and make no call to bear silent, solemn witness. Unlike Lloyd, who is clear that 'dignity means struggle against domination',[93] I do not even advance a claim about the true, authentic dignity that is to be recovered from false dignity. What I have wanted to provide are elements that might count towards the effort to see the world rightly when it comes to dignity. For me, that puts the accent less on what dignity means than on how dignity works – the functions it performs, the ends it serves, and the interests it furthers. I have not approached the enquiry with any assumption that dignity has worked, and now works, in ways that are beneficial to, or valued by, everyone. There can be little doubt that such an assumption would be unfounded. It is always relevant to ask whose dignity is at issue. In commentary on *The Remains of the Day* and *July's People*, David Medalie writes of how the two novels lift dignity 'down from [its] moral pedestal', presenting it 'neither as an uncomplicated

[90] Alan Ryan, 'The Politics of Dignity'.
[91] See further Chapter 1 (touching on relevant writing by Ruth Macklin, Steven Pinker and others).
[92] Lloyd, *Black Dignity*, 33–34.
[93] Ibid., 8 (emphasis omitted).

virtue nor as an absolute good'. 'Instead, it becomes a problem, a crisis and a site of contestation, implicated in and inseparable from awkward questions of power, race and class.'[94]

If those works, along with *Disgrace* and *Things Fall Apart* (about which the same things could be said), have featured in our story,[95] it is because that is the perspective I have likewise sought to adopt. In doing so, I have proceeded from the premise that the awkward questions of power, race and class in which dignity is implicated, and from which it is inseparable, are best investigated in specific historical settings, rather than abstractly. Examining them in that manner brings out the complexity of a concept that is at once ethical and political, oppositional and hegemonic, fragile and imprescriptible, ambient and inherent, and normative and declarative. Dignity is what everyone wants. But then, as Steffen Jensen remarks in a study of violence and survival in a South African township, it is also 'what no one wants because it is actualized in situations of [oppression and offence]'.[96] It is 'what powerless people have left when all else fails', 'what the poor person wraps around him- or herself as the last residue of a supposedly ontological self', and at the same time, what authority 'hands down to the poor and the marginalized' at the moment of their humiliation ('a woman … utterly humiliated by a welfare worker … might still preserve her dignity while she stoically leaves the government offices').[97] To learn about such realities is to be reminded that 'the exploration of dignity [needs] to be conducted within the context of an inequitable distribution of power'.[98]

At the end of the eighteenth century, Friedrich Schiller elaborated an ethical-aesthetic scheme, in which dignity was said to signify tranquillity in suffering. According to him, 'dignity … holds nature's expressions back, and even in the fear of death and the most bitter suffering …, imparts serenity to a person's features'.[99] Schiller's Romantic idea – which took as its exemplar of dignity the depiction in a Hellenistic sculpture of Laocoön

[94] Medalie, '"What Dignity is There in That?"', 51. [95] See also Chapter 1.
[96] Steffen Jensen, *Gangs, Politics and Dignity in Cape Town* (Oxford: James Currey, 2008), 11.
[97] Ibid., 9, 10, 196. [98] Medalie, '"What Dignity is There in That?"', 51.
[99] Friedrich Schiller (Jane Curran, trans.), 'On Grace and Dignity', in Jane Curran and Christophe Fricker (eds.), *Schiller's "On Grace and Dignity" in Its Cultural Context* (Rochester, NY: Camden House/Boydell and Brewer, 2005), 123, 164.

remaining composed while being strangled to death by sea serpents – still retains considerable influence today. That is presumably why, in 2010, it made sense for Stéphane Hessel to put out a pamphlet entitled *Indignez-vous!*, translated into English as *Time for Outrage!*.[100] Hessel's bestselling text speaks to a range of anxieties, but for us what is noteworthy is his sense of dignity as a tranquilliser to be renounced. A further concern has to do not with the inherited orientation to tranquillity, but with the inherited emphasis on suffering. Lynn Festa touches on this in an essay about the early history of humanitarianism, in which she considers how, in that connection, the 'parameters of the human' were delineated.[101] Festa shows that the delineation of the parameters of the human was informed by literary works which 'selectively [excited] feelings' about 'moving examples of suffering', and recognised people as subjects of humanity 'exclusively based on the fact of that suffering'. 'As a result', what was 'granted [was] only a diluted form of humanity grounded in pain and victimhood, a humanity ... only as enduring (or as fleeting) as the recognition of the metropolitan subject who [bestowed] it'.[102]

I have entitled this book *Trucanini's Stare* to prompt reflection on human dignity and its subject. The reference is to a particular photograph taken by Charles Woolley for the Tasmanian stand at the Intercolonial Exhibition – a spin-off of the Great Exhibition of 1851 – convened in Melbourne in 1866.[103] If viewers have commented on the 'pathos and dignity' of Trucanini's gaze in this portrait,[104] it is easy to see why. Woolley turned her into a biological specimen of a dying race, and there she is, composed and unflinching, a seeming model of fortitude with 'nature's expressions' held firmly back. A hundred and twenty-seven years after Woolley took his picture, the Indigenous Australian artist Clinton Naina made a painting which reproduced the colonial photograph in miniature form and splattered it with ink.[105] In Naina's work, the dignity of Woolley's sitter eludes determination, perhaps like the concept

[100] Stéphane Hessel (Damion Searls with Alba Arrikha, trans.), *Time for Outrage!* (London: Quartet Books, 2011).
[101] Lynn Festa, 'Humanity without Feathers', *Humanity* 1(1) (2010) 3.
[102] Ibid., 4. See also, on this, the work of Wendy Brown, *States of Injury: Power and Freedom in Late Modernity* (Princeton, NJ: Princeton University Press, 1995).
[103] See Figure 3.1. [104] See Chapter 1. [105] See Figure 3.9.

itself. Looking at this painting, one can scarcely make out Trucanini's face. One cannot judge whether she is suffering, or tranquil, or neither of those things. Her emotions are inaccessible, her pain and victimhood unknown, the grounds of her humanity not up for bestowal or dilution. There is only an iconic 'stare'[106] and the trace of a woman who once lived.

[106] See Chapter 1.

Index

Index

Index

For EU product safety concerns, contact us at Calle de José Abascal, 56–1°,
28003 Madrid, Spain or eugpsr@cambridge.org.

www.ingramcontent.com/pod-product-compliance
Lightning Source LLC
LaVergne TN
LVHW010336220926
848484LV00004BB/913

* 9 7 8 1 0 0 9 5 4 3 2 3 1 *